Welcome to Nikon

The Complete Manual

Photography is one of the world's favourite pastimes and Nikon is leading the way with its technology. They remain one of the biggest contenders and within this bookazine we discover why. Discover the essential kit, how to clean your camera and the best lenses to use. We will also take you through the best way to compose your shots, using the flash. The How to section will assist you with all different types of shots and the best way to achieve them. Finally, get to grips with Nikon's editing and sharing software. Enjoy the book.

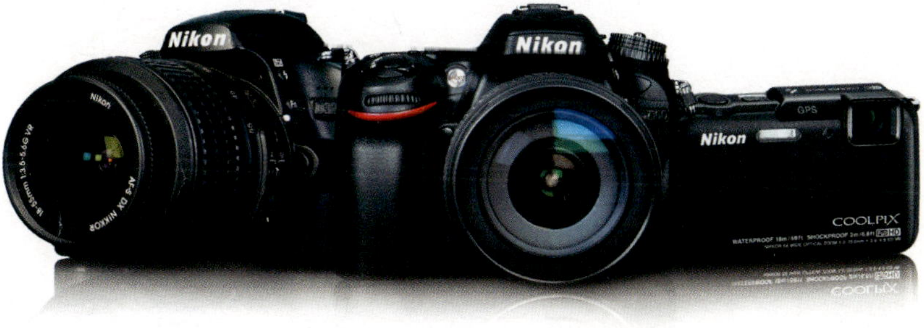

Nikon
The Complete Manual

Imagine Publishing Ltd
Richmond House
33 Richmond Hill
Bournemouth
Dorset BH2 6EZ
☎ +44 (0) 1202 586200
Website: www.imagine-publishing.co.uk
Twitter: @Books_Imagine
Facebook: www.facebook.com/ImagineBookazines

Publishing Director
Aaron Asadi

Head of Design
Ross Andrews

Production Editor
Jen Neal

Senior Art Editor
Greg Whitaker

Art Editor
Ali Innes

Photographer
James Sheppard

Printed by
William Gibbons, 26 Planetary Road, Willenhall, West Midlands, WV13 3XT

Distributed in the UK, Eire & the Rest of the World by
Marketforce, Blue Fin Building, 110 Southwark Street, London, SE1 0SU
Tel 0203 148 3300, www.marketforce.co.uk

Distributed in Australia by
Network Services (a division of Bauer Media Group), Level 21 Civic Tower, 66-68 Goulburn Street, Sydney, New South Wales 2000, Australia, Tel +61 2 8667 5288

ISBN 978 1910 155 394

Part of the Digital Photographer bookazine series

IMAGINE PUBLISHING

Contents

What you can find inside the bookazine

Introducing Nikon

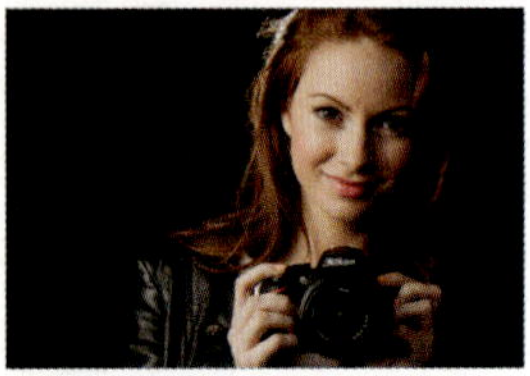

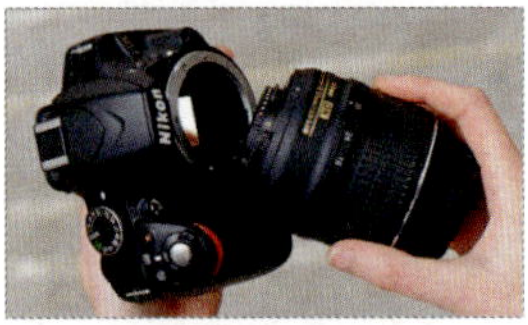

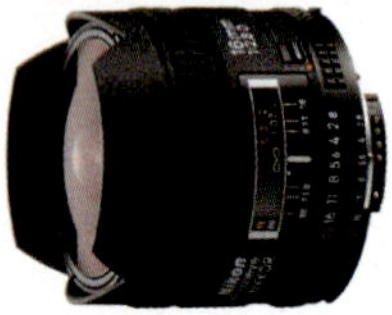

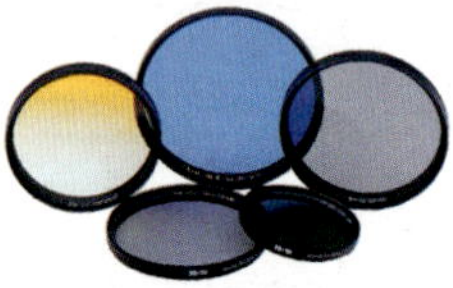

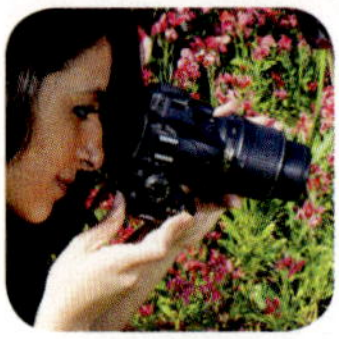

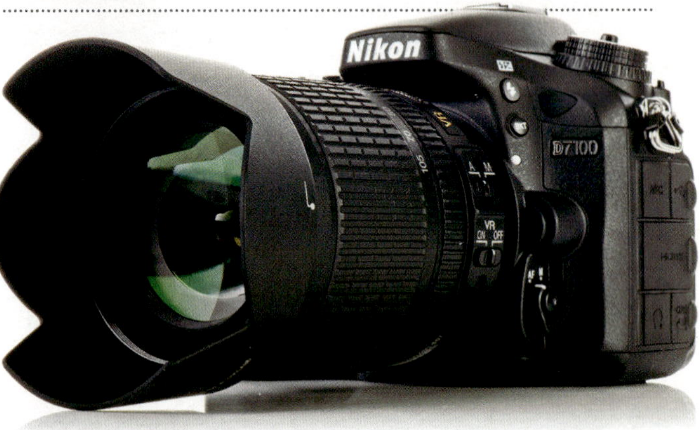

Using your Nikon

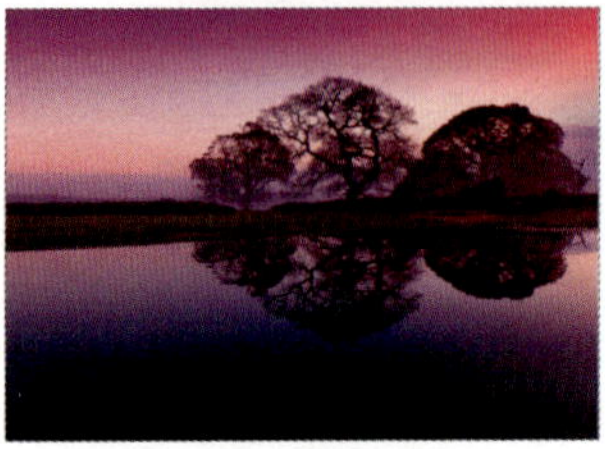

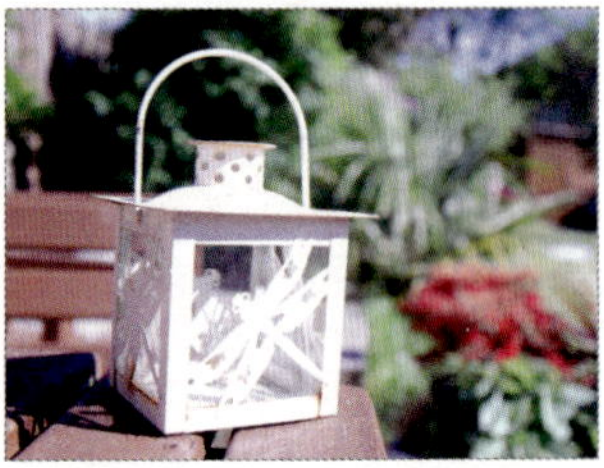

For all Nikon Cameras

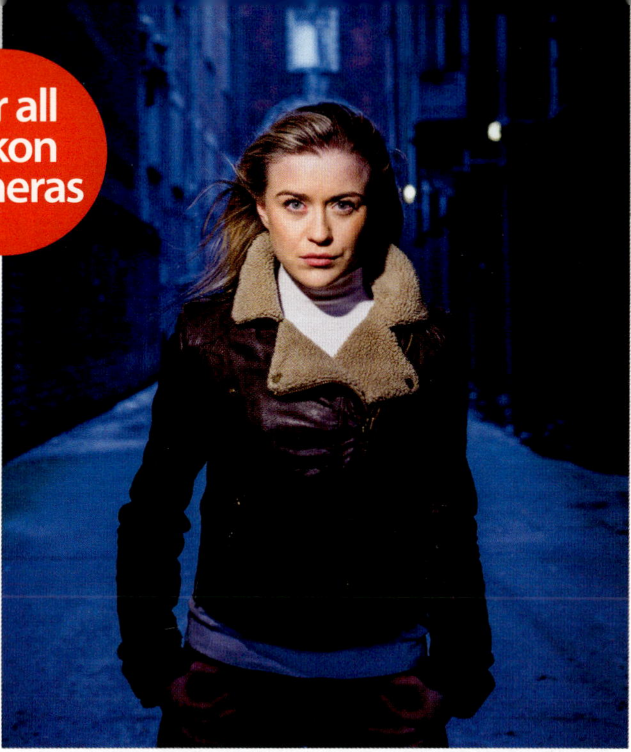

How to

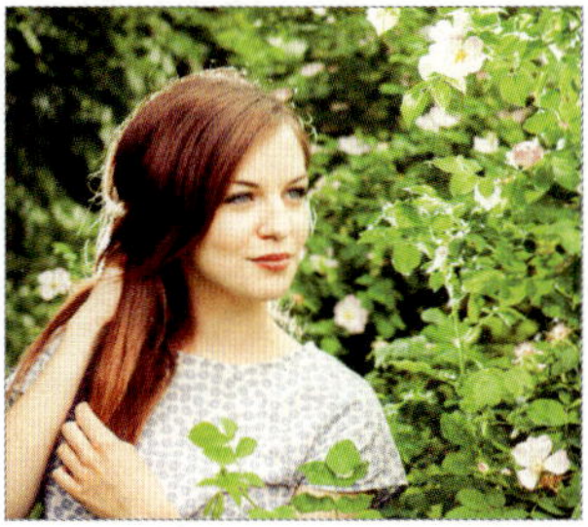

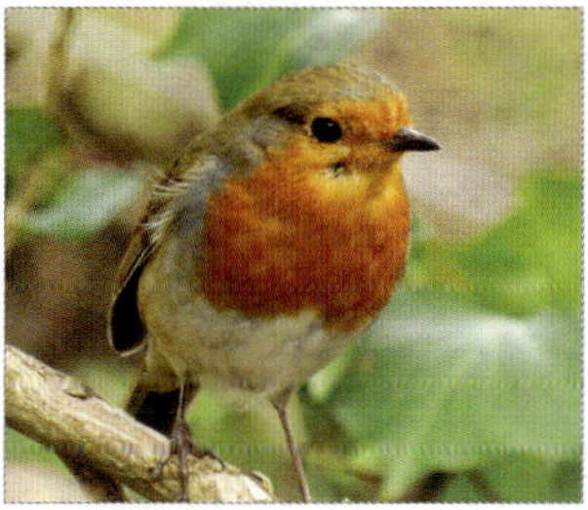

After the shot

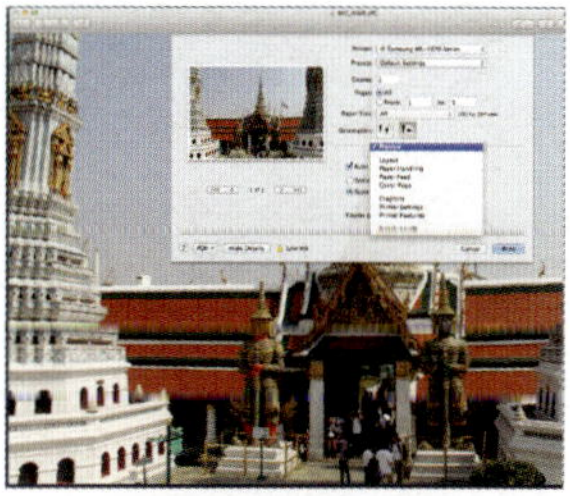

Introducing Nikon

Meet the Nikon family of cameras; with something to suit every photographer

Nikon was first established back in 1917 and quickly became one of the world's leading camera manufacturers. The company has a rich history in both film and digital camera markets and now has an extensive line-up of cameras to suit all skill levels and budgets. From the successful range of COOLPIX compacts and superzooms, to the feature-packed Digital SLR cameras, there is something for everyone in the Nikon family. There is also plenty of opportunity to expand your kit with the ever-growing range of NIKKOR lenses compatible with both the DSLR and Nikon 1 compact system cameras, plus all the other accessories such as speedlights, camera straps and bags to go along with it.

However, let's start with the digital camera line-up and discover the very latest Nikon kit that's on offer. Whether you're after a simple snapper or a serious shooter, you'll find the perfect model in this guide.

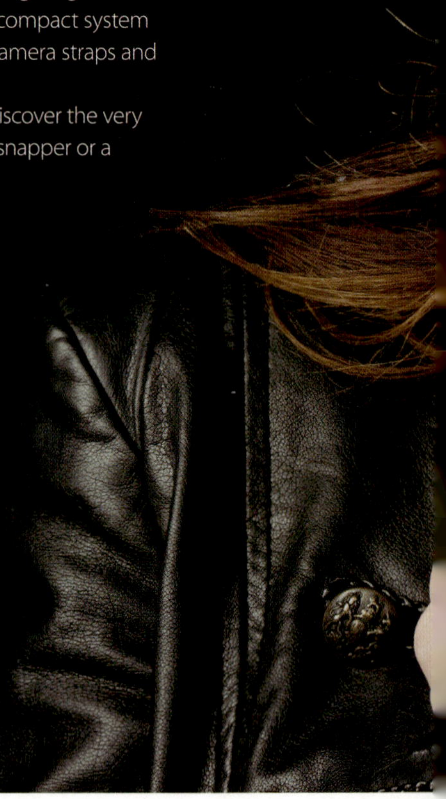

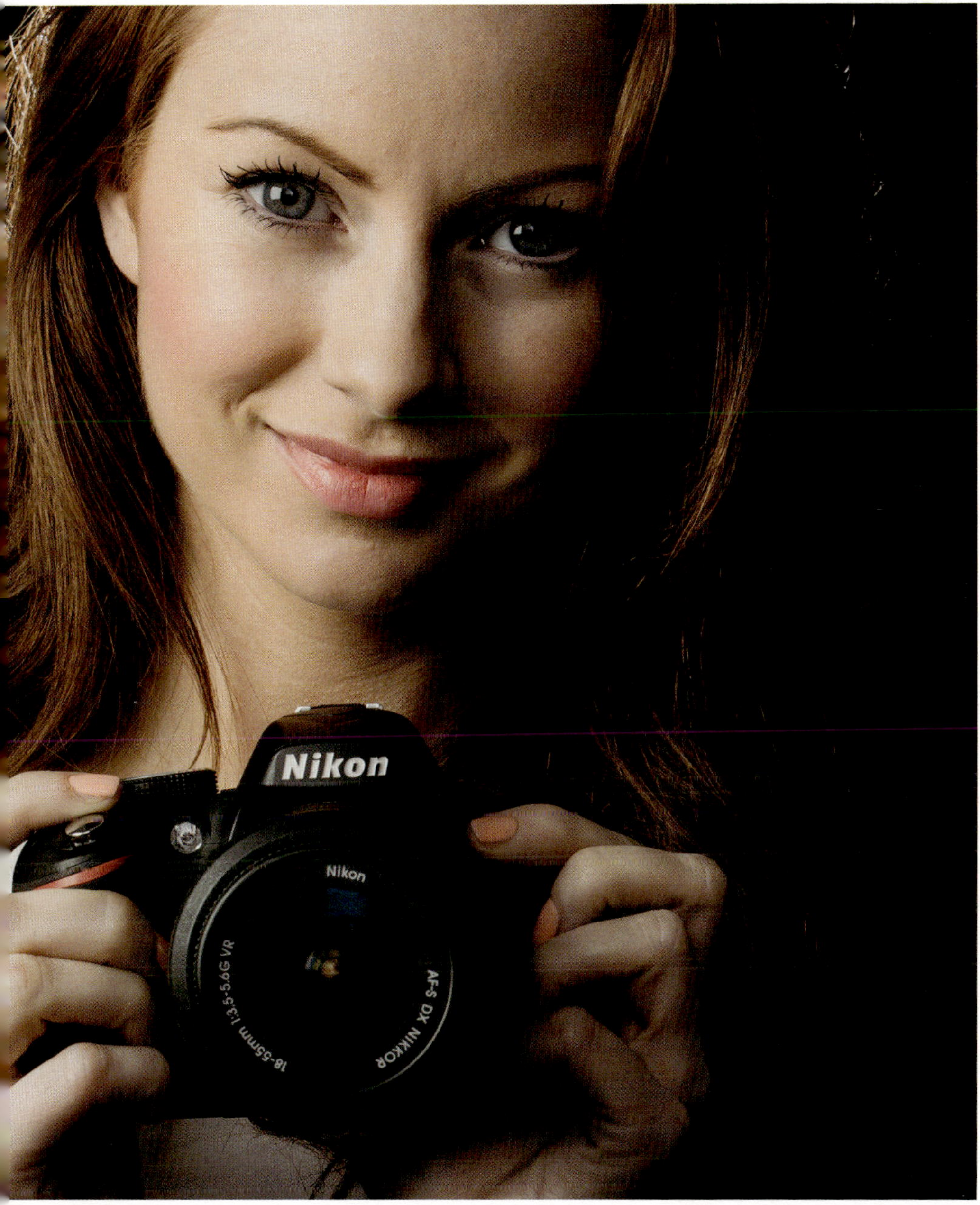
Nikon
Nikon
18-55mm 1:3.5-5.6G VR
AF-S DX NIKKOR

DSLR

Gives creative control and professional-quality images for beginners and advanced photographers

Digital Single-Lens Reflex cameras (DSLRs) are typically the biggest and most expensive digital cameras available, but they also offer the most functionality. The bulkier size is caused by the mirror system inside that bounces the image recorded by the lens up to an optical viewfinder so that you can see exactly what you're photographing. DSLRs also have larger sensors for taking high-quality photos, but some are larger than others. Nikon's FX-format cameras contain full-frame sensors, which are approximately the same size as the 35mm used in film cameras. They are designed to offer superior image quality with better sensitivity in low-light situations, but also cause the camera to be much bigger and more expensive. Alternatively, Nikon's DX-format cameras contain slightly smaller sensors and so tend to be cheaper and more compact. Nikon also produces both DX and FX compatible lenses for use with its range of DSLRs.

"DSLRs are the biggest and most expensive digital cameras available, but they offer the most functionality"

Optical viewfinder
The optical viewfinder on top shows you exactly what the lens sees, for a true representation of the scene you're photographing

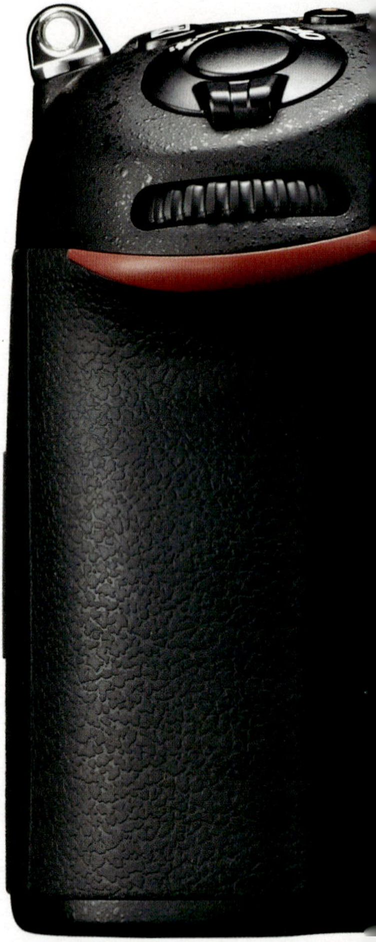

Mirror system
When you take a photo, the mirror inside the camera moves out of the way so the sensor can record the light travelling through the lens to produce a photograph

Extra accessories
Most DSLRs feature a hot shoe on top that you can attach accessories to, such as an external speedlight that is more powerful than the default pop-up flash

Manual controls
All DSLRs feature manual modes that let you take full control over your exposure settings for more creative possibilities

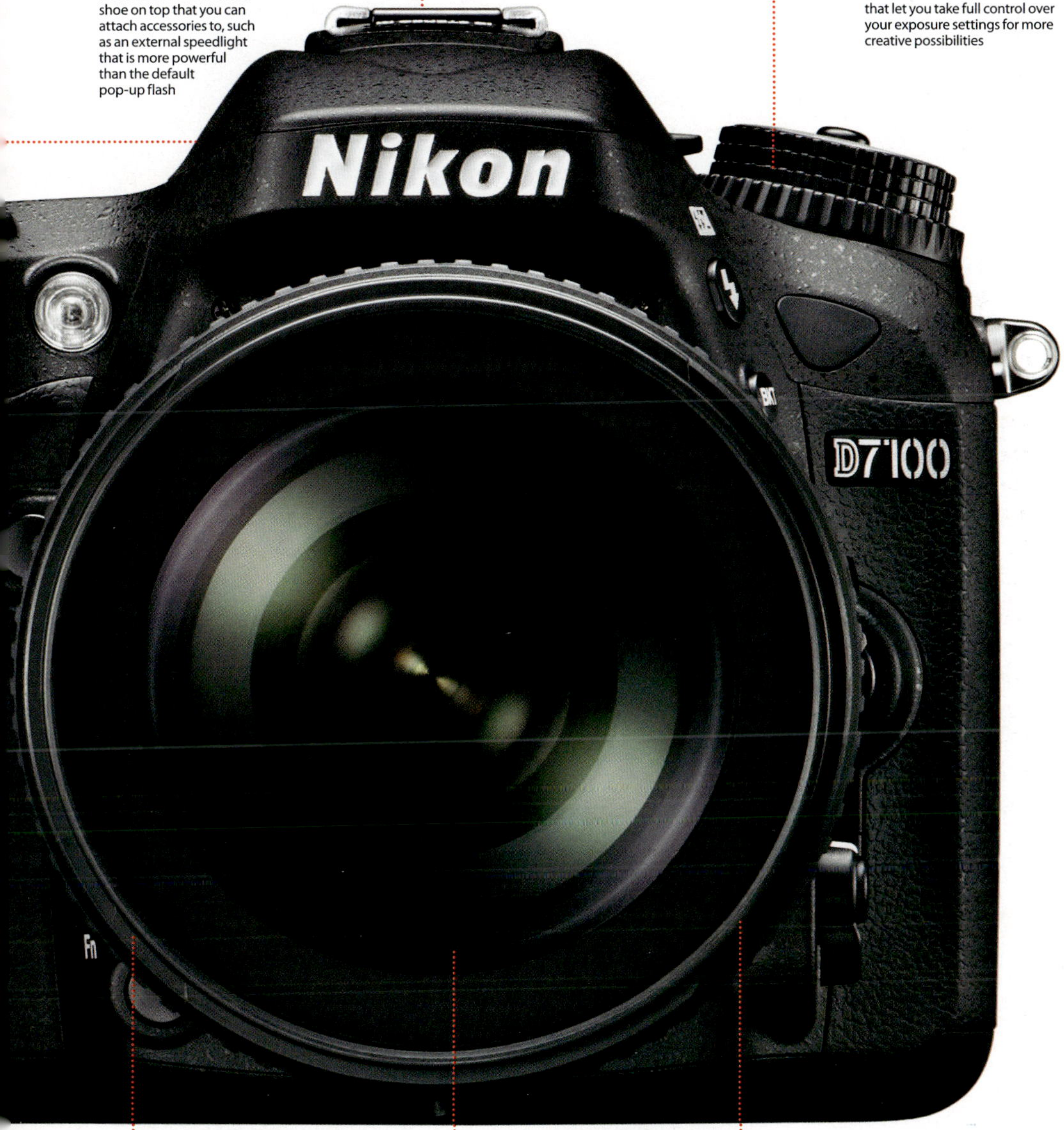

Kit lens
DSLRs usually come with a supplied kit lens that typically has an 18-55mm focal range, or you can buy the camera body only

Lens system
You will need to buy lenses that are compatible with your camera's lens mount, so make sure you check before you buy

Technical data

Price	£399.99 (body only)/$649.95 (with 18-55mm lens)
Megapixels (effective)	24.2
Max resolution (pixels)	6000 x 4000
Sensor information	23.5 x 15.6 mm DX-format CMOS sensor
Lens data	By lens
Zoom	By lens
Focus/macro	By lens
Shutter speed	1/4000sec – 30sec
ISO sensitivity	100-12800
Exposure modes	Auto, P, S, A, M
Metering options	M, CW, S
Flash modes	Auto, RE, SS, Fon, Foff, RC
Weight	410g (body only)
Dimensions (mm)	124 x 98 x 75.5
Batteries	Li-ion
Storage	SD/SDHC/SDXC
LCD	3" 921k-dot TFT
Viewfinder:	OVF

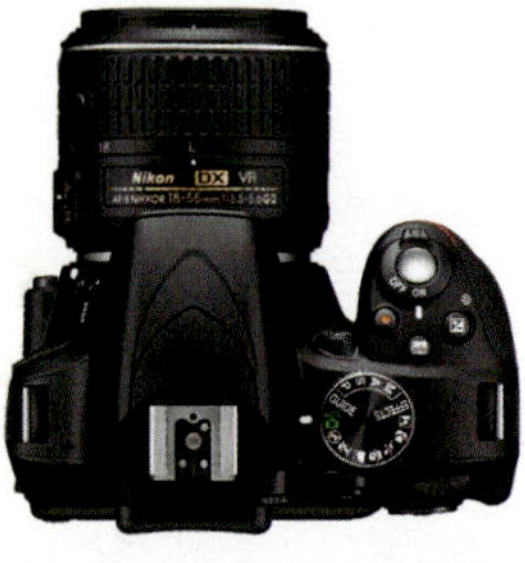

▲The Nikon D3300 has a feature-packed mode dial that includes lots of useful scene modes and a beginner-friendly guide mode

Summary

The Nikon D3300 is a great first DSLR for beginners looking to develop their photography skills and take high-quality photos.

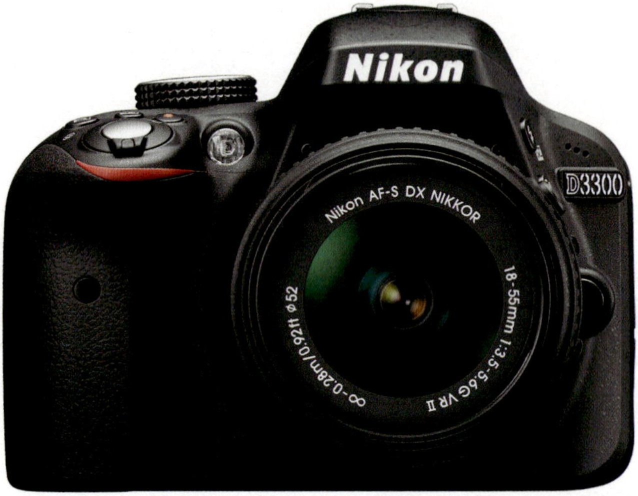

Nikon D3300

The D3300 is Nikon's entry-level DSLR, offering advanced functionality in a relatively cheap and compact body. It features full manual controls and a large 24.2 megapixel sensor for producing professional-quality images, yet is still very easy to use. The built-in Guide Mode offers step-by-step advice for getting to grips with the camera as well as simple instructions and sample images to help you shoot great photos and full HD videos. Operating the camera is also easy, as pressing the 'i' button gives you instant access to commonly used settings so you don't need to scroll through the menus every time the scene or lighting changes.

For framing photos, the 3-inch LCD monitor gives a clear, wide view of what you're shooting, or you can use the optical viewfinder. Keeping up with the action is easy thanks to the fast 11-point autofocus system that can lock onto moving subjects, and the continuous shooting mode can capture up to 5 images per second.

To give your shots a final creative touch, you can apply one of 13 different filter effects before you shoot and instantly transform the scene before you. Then, once you've taken your photos, you can share them wirelessly via your smart device using Nikon's optional WU-1a adapter (see page 134).

Nikon D5300

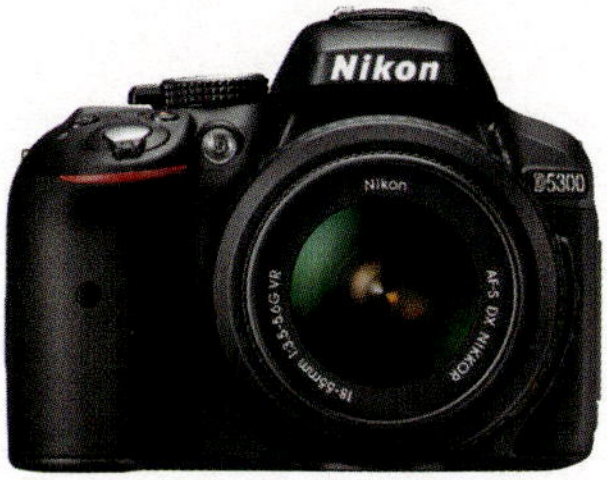

The D5300 sits in the middle of Nikon's DSLR range with a big sensor and large ISO range for taking bright shots in low-light conditions. The large vari-angle LCD monitor helps you frame shots from awkward angles and you can record plenty of detail in even difficult lighting conditions thanks to Nikon's built-in Active D-Lighting and HDR modes. Wi-Fi connectivity is also built into the camera allowing you to share images from your smart device and the built-in GPS automatically geotags your shots with location data, too.

Summary

A feature-packed DSLR for photography enthusiasts who want plenty of control.

Technical data

Price	£629.99/$799.95 (body only)
Megapixels (effective)	24.2
Max resolution (pixels)	6000 x 4000
Sensor information	23.5 x 15.6 mm DX-format CMOS sensor
Lens data	By lens
Zoom	By lens
Focus/macro	By lens
Shutter speed	1/4000sec – 30sec
ISO sensitivity	100-25600
Exposure modes	Auto, P, A, S, M
Metering options	M, CW, S
Flash modes	Auto, RE, SS, Fon, Foff, RC
Weight	480g (body only)
Dimensions (mm)	125 x 98 x 76
Batteries	Li-ion
Storage	SD/SDHC/SDXC
LCD	3.2" 1037k-dot vari-angle TFT
Viewfinder:	OVF

Nikon D610

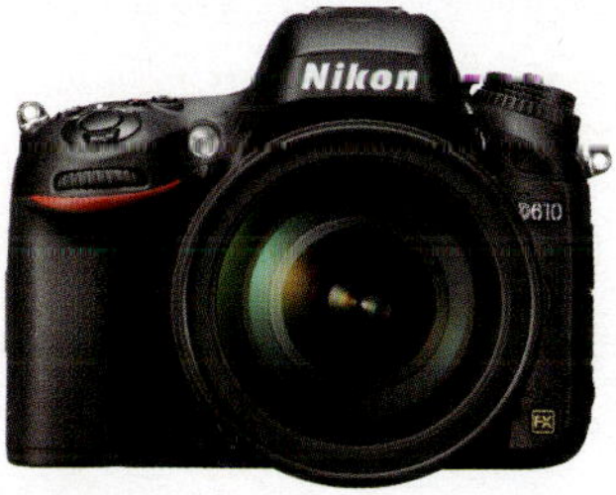

Featuring an FX format full-frame sensor, the D610 is one of Nikon's high-end DSLRs aimed at professional photographers. It can record an extremely wide angle of view with an incredible amount of detail, even at high ISO values. The quiet release burst mode can shoot up to 6 frames per second for fantastic action and wildlife shots, and there is a built-in time-lapse function for shooting slow changing scenes. The camera body is weather sealed for added durability and it features twin SD card slots for more storage flexibility.

Summary

With advanced features and a full-frame sensor, the D610 can produce truly professional-quality images.

Technical data

Price	£1799.99/$1999.95 (body only)
Megapixels (effective)	24.3
Max resolution (pixels)	6016 x 4016
Sensor information	35.9 x 24.0 mm FX format CMOS sensor
Lens data	By lens
Zoom	By lens
Focus/macro	By lens
Shutter speed	1/4000sec – 30sec
ISO sensitivity	100-25600
Exposure modes	Auto, P, S, A, M
Metering options	M, CW, S, A
Flash modes	Auto, RE, SS, Fon, Foff, RC
Weight	760g (body only)
Dimensions (mm)	141 x 113 x 82
Batteries	Li-ion
Storage	SD/SDHC/SDXC
LCD	3.2" 921k-dot TFT
Viewfinder:	OVF

CSC

Enjoy manual modes and lens flexibility in a more portable and easy-to-use camera

Compact system cameras (CSCs) are the newest breed of camera, introduced as a more portable solution to bulky interchangeable lens cameras. Like DSLRs, they feature manual controls and a relatively large sensor, but they do not contain a mirror system, hence why they are sometimes known as mirrorless cameras. Instead, the light travels straight down the lens to the image sensor, so there is no option to have an optical viewfinder; just an electrical one that displays a digital representation of the scene. Most CSCs feature smaller cropped sensors because they are so compact in size.

Because this type of camera is quite new, there are not as many lens options available as there are for DSLRs. However, as their popularity grows, so does the lens line-up, and the Nikon 1 range of CSCs already has a wide range of 1 NIKKOR lenses to choose from.

"Like DSLRs, CSCs feature manual controls and a large sensor, but they do not contain a mirror system"

Shooting modes
With both automatic and manual modes, there should be something to suit photographers of all abilities, making this type of camera perfect for beginners and pros alike

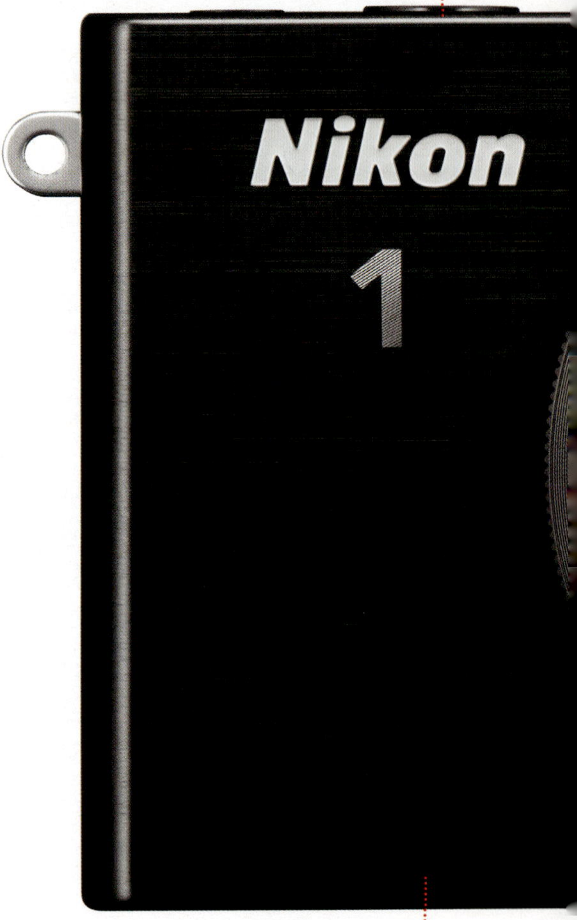

Compact design
CSCs are so named for their compact design, but they usually feature just as many functions as a larger DSLR camera

Framing options
Some CSCs have electronic viewfinders for framing shots, but some simply have LCD screens for composing and reviewing images

Sensor size
The size of the image sensor differs from model to model, with some a similar size to that of a compact camera and others much larger

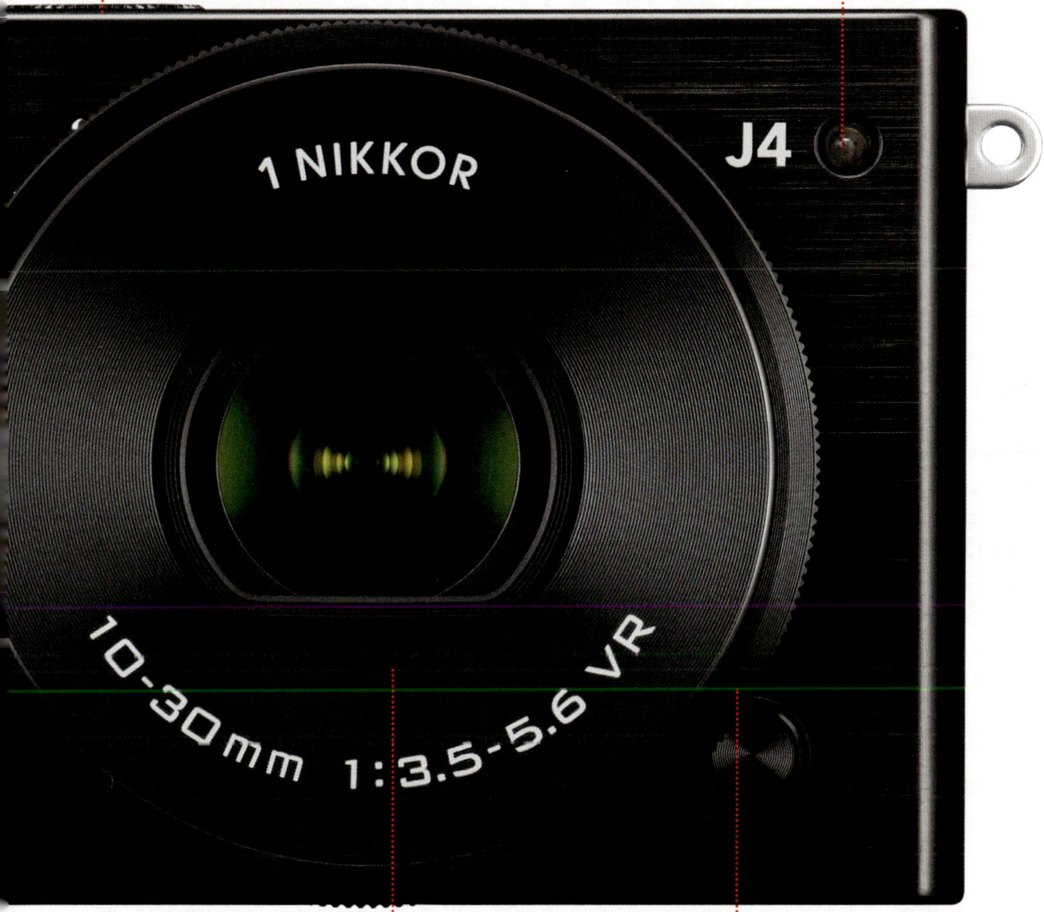

Kit expansion
With a choice of lenses available, you can expand your kit to suit your shooting style and increase your camera's creative potential

Interchangeable lenses
Compatible lenses for CSCs also tend to be quite compact to suit the cameras they are attached to without adding too much bulk

Technical data

Price	£379.99/$449.95 (with 11-27.5mm lens)
Megapixels (effective)	14.2
Max resolution (pixels)	4592 x 3072
Sensor information	13.1 mm x 8.8 mm CX-format CMOS sensor
Lens data	By lens
Zoom	By lens
Focus/macro	By lens
Shutter speed	1/16000sec – 30sec
ISO sensitivity	200-12800
Exposure modes	Auto, P, S, A, M
Metering options	M, CW, S
Flash modes	Auto, RE, SS, Fon, Foff, RC
Weight	190g (body only)
Dimensions (mm)	101 x 60.8 x 29.4
Batteries	Li-ion
Storage	microSD/microSDHC/microSDXC
LCD	3" 460k-dot TFT
Viewfinder:	n/a

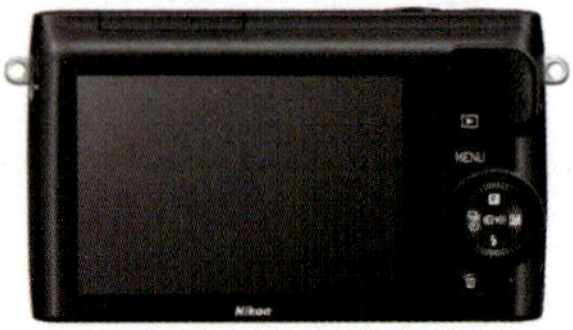

▲The Nikon 1 S2's compact body has basic buttons for the main controls but features many more functions within the menus

Summary

The Nikon 1 S2 is a portable camera with creative features, fast operation and an expandable lens system.

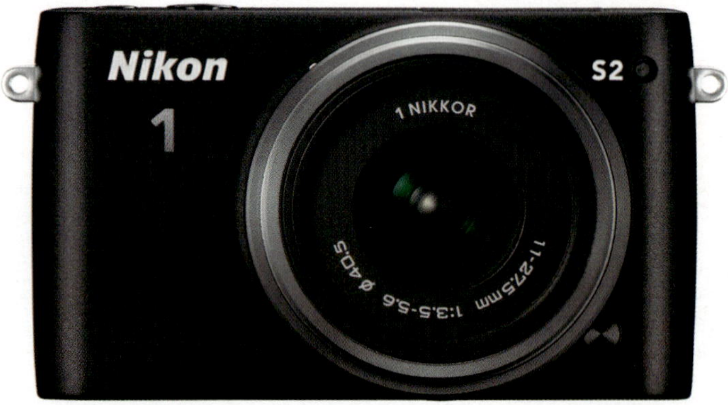

Nikon 1 S2

The Nikon 1 S2 packs a lot into a small and stylish camera body, with a large 14.2 megapixel sensor for shooting high-quality images. It is also incredibly quick, as you can record up to 20 frames per second with continuous autofocus and 60 frames per second with the focus fixed on the first frame. Getting the perfect shot is made easy with the Active Selection function, which enables you to take up to 10 high-resolution shots in just one second and choose the best one to keep. You can even record still images whilst shooting Full HD movies by simply pressing the shutter button, or let Auto Image Caption automatically take a shot when it thinks the conditions are best. There are lots of creative movie modes to choose from too, including Fast Motion for speeding things up and Jump Cut for creating stop-motion animation. Motion Snapshot mode will even create a living image by capturing a slow-motion video that ends with a high-resolution photo and lets you add background music or ambient sounds to the clip.

Taking regular photos is made easy with Live Image Control that lets you make quick adjustments to freeze motion, blur backgrounds and tweak lighting before you shoot. There are also plenty of creative filters on hand to give your shots a unique twist, including miniature and toy camera effects.

The Nikon 1 S2 is available in a range of bright colours to suit your style, including lipstick red and sunshine yellow.

Nikon 1 V3

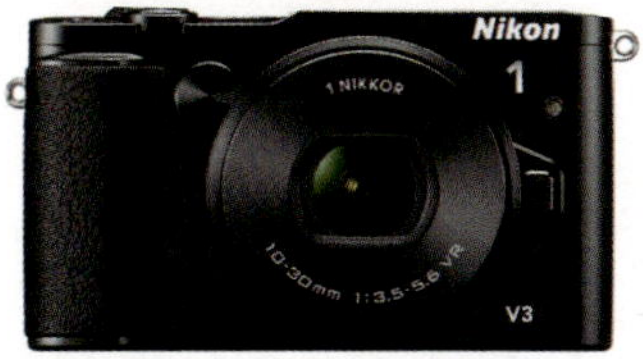

The Nikon 1 V3 packs lots of functionality into its small body, such as fast shooting speeds of up to 60 frames per second as well as lots of creative movie and still image modes to help you get the perfect shot. The tilting screen is a real help when it comes to framing shots at unusual angles and the V3 features touch control for quickly adjusting your settings with just a few taps. Built-in Wi-Fi means that you can you share images instantly or shoot remotely using your smartphone. An optional electronic viewfinder and grip are also available for increased functionality and ergonomics.

Summary

An advanced CSC that handles like a DSLR and shoots high-quality images at impressive speeds.

Technical data

Price	£799.99 (with 10-30mm lens)/$1199.95 (with 10-30mm, EVF & grip)
Megapixels (effective)	18.4
Max resolution (pixels)	5232 x 3488
Sensor information	13.2 x 8.8 mm CX-format CMOS sensor
Lens data	By lens
Zoom	By lens
Focus/macro	By lens
Shutter speed	1/16000sec – 30sec
ISO sensitivity	200-12800
Exposure modes	Auto, P, A, S, M
Metering options	M, CW, S
Flash modes	Auto, RE, SS, Fon, Foff, RC
Weight	324g
Dimensions (mm)	110.9 x 65 x 33.2
Batteries	Li-ion
Storage	microSD/microSDHC/microSDXC
LCD	3" 1037k-dot vari-angle TFT
Viewfinder:	n/a

Nikon 1 AW1

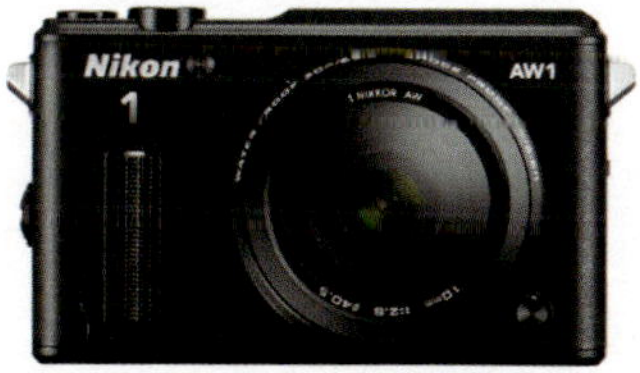

The Nikon 1 AW1 is a waterproof, shockproof, freezeproof and dustproof CSC for shooting in any environment. Action Control lets you adjust settings by tilting the camera; making it easy to operate with wet hands or if you're wearing gloves, and the Outdoor display mode ensures menus are easy to read in bright sunlight or underwater. The camera can even record your location with the electronic compass and your altitude or underwater depth with the dual altimeter/depth gauge. Nikon has created tough lenses to go with the 1 AW1, plus lots of other waterproof accessories.

Summary

A tough camera that lets photographers capture impressive images wherever they may be.

Technical data

Price	£749.99/$799.95 (with 11-27.5mm lens)
Megapixels (effective)	14.2
Max resolution (pixels)	4608 x 3072
Sensor information	13.2 mm x 8.8 mm CX-format CMOS sensor
Lens data	By lens
Zoom	By lens
Focus/macro	By lens
Shutter speed	1/16000sec – 30sec
ISO sensitivity	160-6400
Exposure modes	Auto, P, A, S, M
Metering options	M, CW, S
Flash modes	Auto, RE, SS, Fon, Foff, RC
Weight	313g (body only)
Dimensions (mm)	113.3 x 71.5 x 37.5
Batteries	Li-ion
Storage	SD/SDHC/SDXC
LCD	3" 921k-dot TFT
Viewfinder:	n/a

Bridge / Superzoom

Discover a versatile focal range in a compact camera that's perfect for your travels

Bridge cameras tend to be a little larger than compacts due to their impressive fixed lens that can usually stretch great distances to cover a large focal range. This is why these cameras are often also known as superzooms and is what makes them a great option for taking on holiday, because you can photograph a range of different scenes, from wide-angle landscapes to close-ups of distant action, without having to pack a variety of heavy lenses. So although bridge cameras can be quite bulky, they are still compact as a camera system because you only have one lens to worry about and it typically retracts into the camera body when not in use.

Superzooms also usually feature manual controls, making them a great upgrade from a simple point and shoot compact, or even a more portable alternative to a DSLR. Nikon offers several different bridge cameras to suit any budget.

"You can photograph a range of scenes, from landscapes to close-ups, without having to pack a variety of heavy lenses"

Electronic viewfinder
Like CSCs, there's no room for a mirror system, so you'll have to frame your shots via an electronic viewfinder or the camera's LCD screen

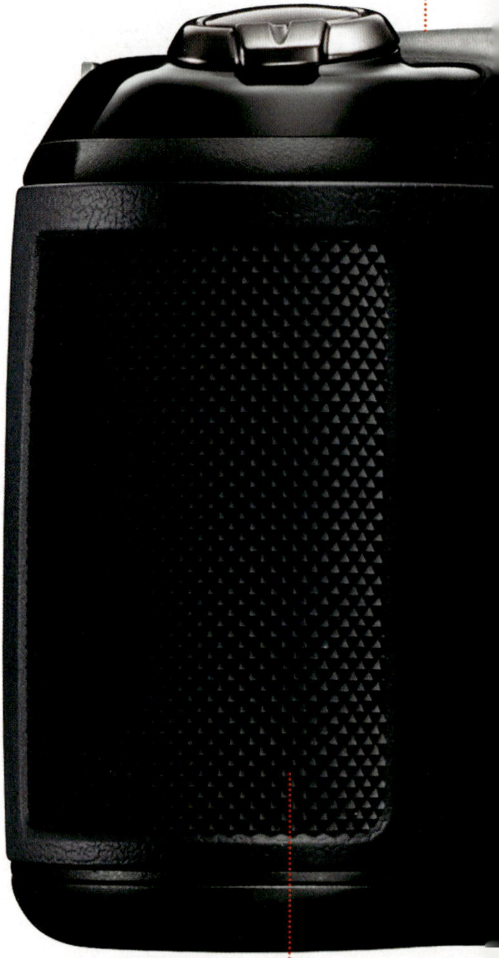

Added grip
Superzooms often have a large grip to help you hold the camera steady. This is particularly useful for avoiding blur

Large zoom
Bridge cameras tend to have a big optical and digital zoom that stretches great distances so you can get closer to the action

Image quality
The quality of images produced depends on the model of bridge camera, as different models have different sensor sizes and megapixel counts

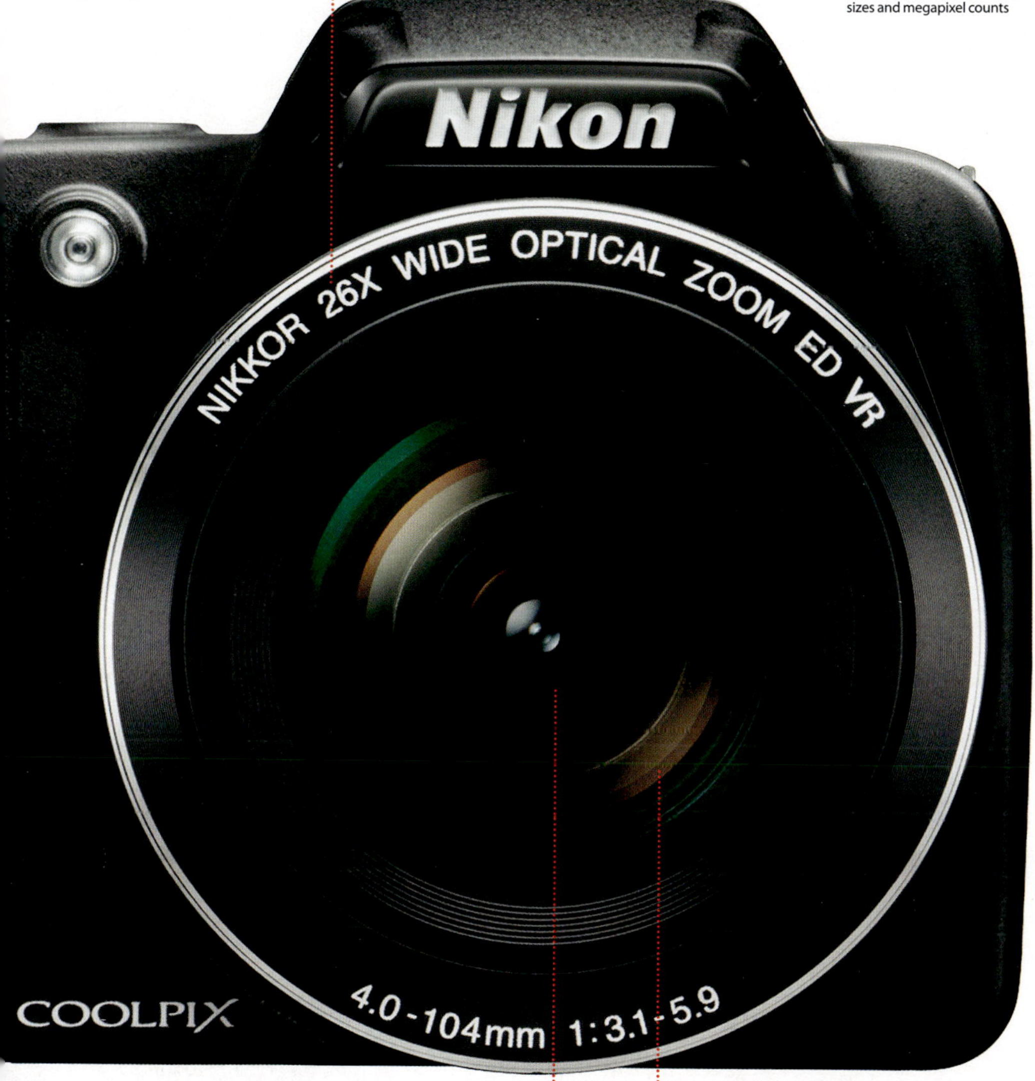

Advanced features
Bridge cameras give you lots of control over the look of your images, as you can adjust your exposure settings and other functions

Image stabilisation
Built-in image stabilisation is essential for preventing camera shake when using long focal lengths, as images tend to be blurry when shooting handheld

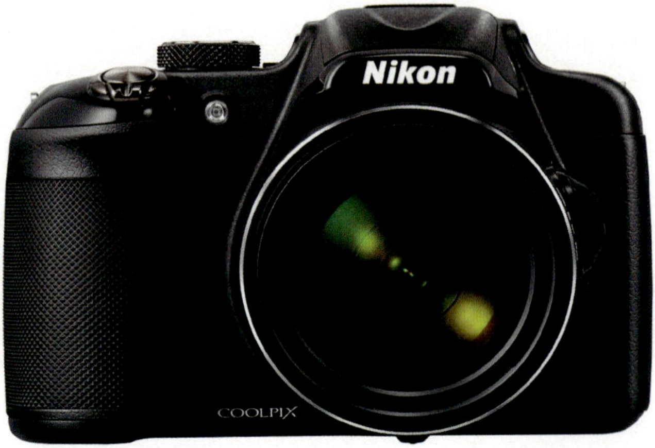

Nikon COOLPIX P600

Technical data

Price	£359.99/$499.95
Megapixels (effective)	16.1
Max resolution (pixels)	4608 x 3456
Sensor information	1/2.3-in. type BSI-CMOS sensor
Lens data	24-1440mm f3.3-6.5
Zoom	60x optical, 120x digital
Focus/macro	1cm – infinity
Shutter speed	1/4000sec – 15sec
ISO sensitivity	100-12800
Exposure modes	Auto, P, A, S, M
Metering options	M, CW, S
Flash modes	Auto
Weight	565g (with battery & memory card)
Dimensions (mm)	125 x 85 x 106.5
Batteries	Li-ion
Storage	SD/SDHC/SDXC/56MBint
LCD	3" 921k-dot TFT
Viewfinder:	0.2" 201k-dot EVF

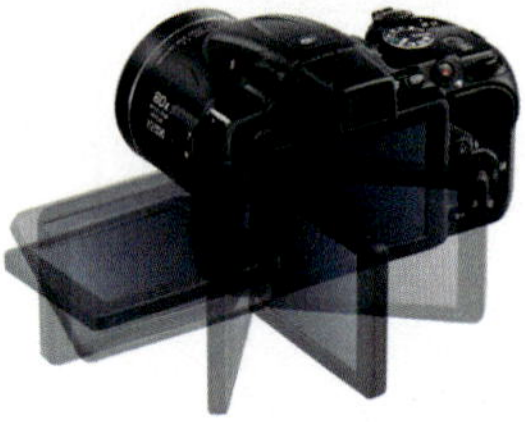

▲The P600's vari-angle LCD monitor makes it easy to frame your shots from high or low angles for a creative perspective

Nikon's P600 bridge camera features an impressive 60x optical zoom that is extendable to 120x with the digital Dynamic Fine Zoom. This gives a focal range of 24-1440mm which enables you to snap wide-angle landscapes as well as get close to subjects in the distance. Advanced Lens Shift Vibration Reduction helps prevent camera shake, and fast autofocus keeps subject sharp, even when moving. Fast-moving subjects are easy to capture thanks to continuous shooting mode which can shoot up to 7 shots at 7 frames per second and 200 shots at 1 frame per second. Plus, you can record your second shot whilst the first is still recording.

As well as 21 scene modes, there is also a built-in HDR mode that merges several exposures together and Panorama mode that lets you pan vertically or horizontally to record an 180 or 360 degree view. You can also use Macro mode to shoot just 1cm away from your subject for great close ups.

The built-in Wi-Fi lets you wirelessly transfer shots to your smartphone, and embed GPS data so you know exactly where they were taken. Plus you get 20GB of free online cloud storage with Nikon Image Space.

Summary

The P600 is a spectacular superzoom with an impressive focal range for shooting a wide variety of scenes.

Nikon COOLPIX P530

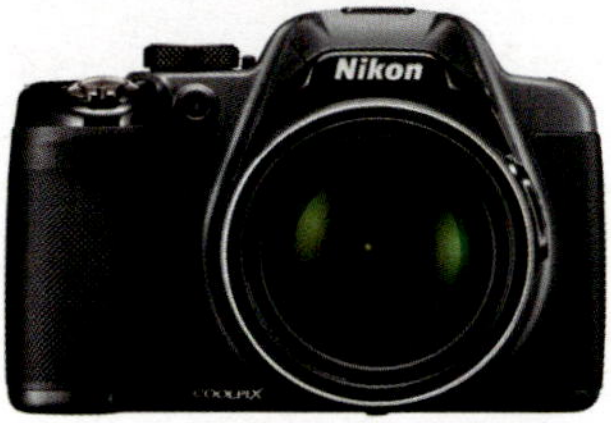

As well as its 42x optical zoom, the P530 also has an 84x digital zoom to extend its reach with a 24-1000mm focal range. Active mode and Advanced Lens Shift Vibration Reduction help to keep shots steady, plus you can frame them via the electronic viewfinder for even more stability. There are 21 scene modes on offer, including specialist presets for bird watching and taking high-contrast images of the moon so you can make full use of that impressive zoom.

Summary

The P530 is a well-equipped superzoom with a great range of advanced features.

Technical data

Price	£259.99/$449.95
Megapixels (effective)	16.1
Max resolution (pixels)	4608 x 3456
Sensor information	1/2.3-in. type CMOS
Lens data	24-1000mm f3-5.9
Zoom	42x optical, 84x digital
Focus/macro	1cm – infinity
Shutter speed	1/4000sec – 15sec
ISO sensitivity	100-12800
Exposure modes	Auto, P, A, S, M
Metering options	M, CW, S
Flash modes	Auto
Weight	494g (with battery and memory card)
Dimensions (mm)	122.8 x 84.1 x 98.2
Batteries	Li-ion
Storage	SD/SDHC/SDXC/56MBint
LCD	3" 921k-dot TFT
Viewfinder:	0.2" 201k-dot EVF

Nikon COOLPIX L830

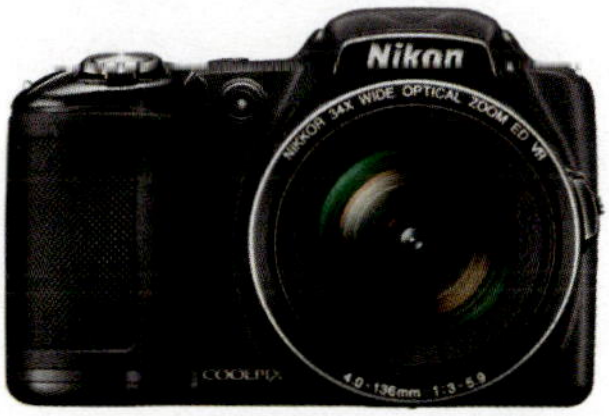

The L830 is a compact superzoom with a 36x optical and 68x digital reach, giving you a versatile focal range of 22.5-765mm. The Hybrid Vibration Reduction combines Lens Shift and Electronic VR for enhanced stability and the side zoom lever gives you easy access to the powerful zoom. The camera is very simple to use, with 18 scene modes, a Smart Portrait system for taking perfect people shots and Easy Auto Mode which picks the best settings for you.

Summary

The L830 is a very simple and easy to use bridge camera with an impressive zoom.

Technical data

Price	£229.99/$299.95
Megapixels (effective)	16
Max resolution (pixels)	4608 x 3456
Sensor information	1/2.3-in. type CMOS
Lens data	22.5-765mm f3-5.9
Zoom	34x optical, 68x digital
Focus/macro	1cm – infinity
Shutter speed	1/4000sec – 4sec
ISO sensitivity	125-3200
Exposure modes	Auto
Metering options	M, CW, S
Flash modes	Auto
Weight	508g (with battery and memory card)
Dimensions (mm)	111 x 75.8 x 91.2
Batteries	4x AA
Storage	SD/SDHC/SDXC/59MBint
LCD	3" 921k-dot TFT
Viewfinder:	n/a

Compact

Pocket-sized and simple-to-use, a compact can be taken anywhere so you never miss a shot

Compacts are the most portable of all the cameras, with some so slim that they can slip into your back pocket. This makes them a popular choice as a first step into photography, because you can keep the camera on you at all times to practice your skills. As you'll be in no danger of missing a great photo opportunity, compacts are also great for documenting everyday life and those special family moments.

Compacts come in all shapes, sizes and varieties. Some are simple point-and-shoot cameras that only feature basic auto modes, while others feature manual controls for added creativity. You can even buy specialist tough compacts that are waterproof, shockproof and freezeproof, so you can carry on shooting no matter where you are. The compact market may be struggling a little with increasing competition from camera phones, but Nikon has a wide range of COOLPIX compacts to suit everyone.

"Some are simple cameras that only feature auto modes, while others feature manual controls for added creativity"

Easy-to-use
Even the more advanced compact cameras are usually quite simple to use as they are designed for complete beginners with no knowledge of photography

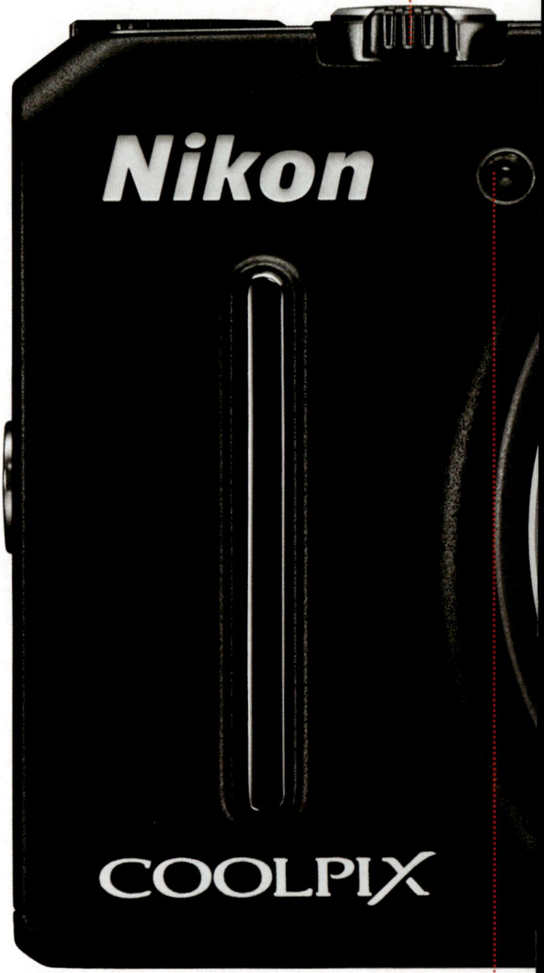

Image quality
Compacts tend to have quite small sensors, but can still produce great images that are suitable for printing and sharing online

Simple system
There's not much opportunity to expand your compact's functionality, as they usually don't have a hot shoe for attaching accessories such as an external flashgun

LCD screen
Compact cameras don't tend to feature any sort of viewfinder, so framing and viewing shots is left to the LCD screen on the back

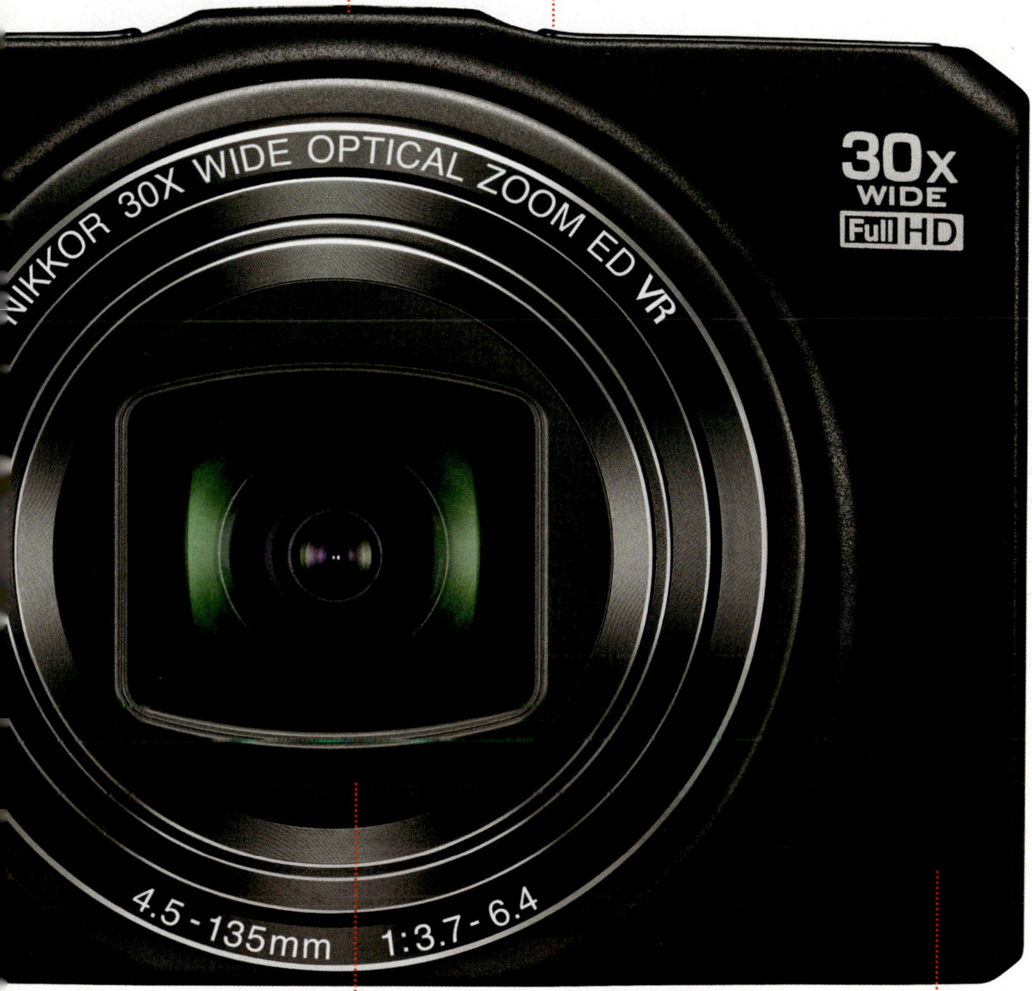

Fixed lens
The focal range and optical zoom differs from camera to camera, but most models have an average range to suit the needs of the average photographer

Slim and sleek
Compact by name and compact by nature, most have a slim-line body that can easily fit in your pocket or bag so you can take it everywhere

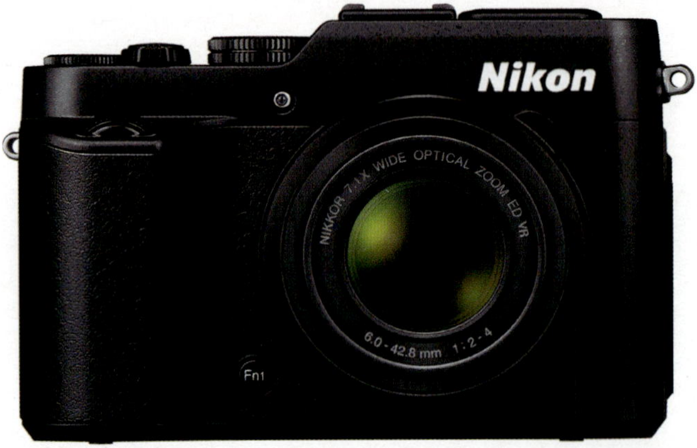

Nikon COOLPIX P7800

The P7800 is a premium compact camera that features manual control and plenty of other advanced features not commonly found on compacts. There's a built-in electronic viewfinder as well as a vari-angle LCD screen for framing shots, plus the camera can record images in the RAW file format, which allows you to process them yourself for more control when editing.

The 7x optical zoom lens has a bright maximum aperture of f2 at its shortest focal length, creating beautiful background blur to make your subject stand out. Action shots are also made easy with the continuous shooting mode that can take up to 8 high-resolution images per second.

With two command dials and a Quick Menu button for accessing the camera's main functions, it is quick and easy to take shots. To speed operation up even further, there are three User Modes and two Function buttons that can be customised.

COOLPIX Picture Control is also on hand to help create perfect images, as you can use the Quick Adjust option to balance settings automatically, make manual adjustments or create a Custom Picture Control to use again. You can also add creative filters to your shots in live view, previewing the various effects before you shoot.

Technical data

Price	£499.99/$549.95
Megapixels (effective)	12.2
Max resolution (pixels)	4000 x 3000
Sensor information	1/1.7-in. type CMOS
Lens data	28-200mm f2-4
Zoom	7.1x optical
Focus/macro	2cm – infinity
Shutter speed	1/4000sec – 60sec
ISO sensitivity	80-6400
Exposure modes	Auto P, A, S, M
Metering options	M, CW, S
Flash modes	Auto
Weight	399g (with battery and memory card)
Dimensions (mm)	118.5 x 77.5 x 50.4
Batteries	Li-ion
Storage	SD/SDHC/ SDXC/86MBint
LCD	3" 921k-dot TFT
Viewfinder:	0.2" 921k-dot EVF

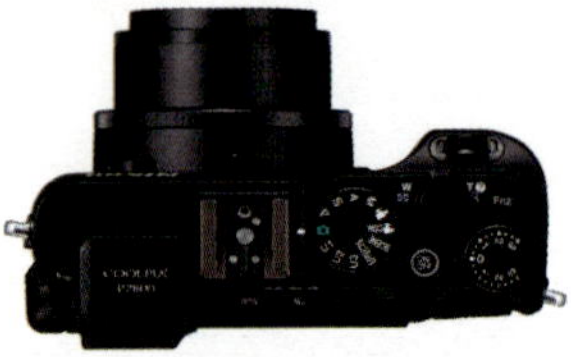

▲The Nikon P7800 has a hotshoe for attaching additional accessories and a separate dial for quickly adjusting your exposure compensation to brighten or darken shots

Summary

The P7800 is a professional-standard compact offering users decent manual control in a portable body.

Nikon COOLPIX S810c

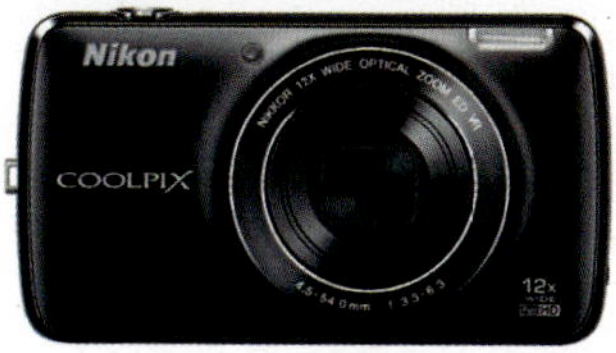

The S810c runs the latest Android operating system, which means you can download apps from the Google Play store straight onto the camera. This opens up shooting, editing and sharing possibilities, as well as allowing you to play games on the go. Built-in Wi-Fi lets you share shots to social networks or upload them to cloud storage sites for safe-keeping, and the large touch screen makes controlling the camera a breeze. There's even a headphone socket for listening to music.

Summary

The S810c is a very well connected compact with downloadable apps that expand its potential.

Technical data

Price	£249.99/$349.95
Megapixels (effective)	16
Max resolution (pixels)	4608 x 3456
Sensor information	1/2.3-in. type BSI-CMOS
Lens data	25-300mm f3.3-6.3
Zoom	12x optical, 24x digital
Focus/macro	2cm – infinity
Shutter speed	1/4000sec – 4sec
ISO sensitivity	125-3200
Exposure modes	Auto, P
Metering options	M, CW, S
Flash modes	Auto
Weight	216g (with battery and memory card)
Dimensions (mm)	113 x 63.5 x 27.5
Batteries	Li-ion
Storage	microSD/ microSDXC/1.1GBint
LCD	3.7" 1229k-dot TFT
Viewfinder:	n/a

Nikon COOLPIX AW120

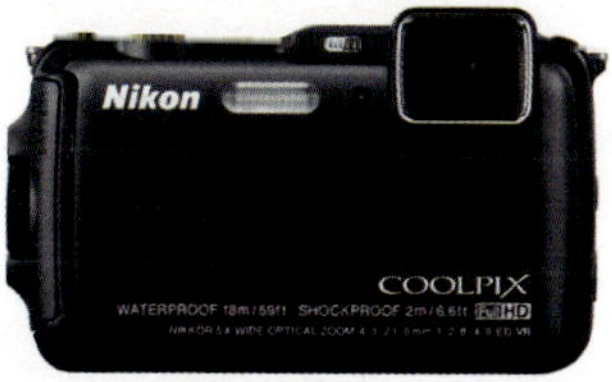

The AW120 is a tough compact that is waterproof to 18m, shockproof to a 2m drop and freezeproof down to -10°C, so you can truly take it anywhere. The 5x zoom is capable of shooting a range of scenes and Action Control lets you adjust your settings by tilting the camera for easy underwater or wet weather operation. Built-in Wi-Fi is on hand for sharing your shots whilst on the go, and you can record the location, altitude, depth, atmospheric pressure and water pressure of your images, too.

Summary

The AW120 is an action-packed camera for taking travel snapshots no matter where you are.

Technical data

Price	£269.99/$349.95
Megapixels (effective)	16
Max resolution (pixels)	4608 x 3456
Sensor information	1/2.3-in. type CMOS
Lens data	24-120mm f2.8-4.9
Zoom	4x optical, 10x digital
Focus/macro	1cm – infinity
Shutter speed	1/4000sec – 4sec
ISO sensitivity	125-6400
Exposure modes	Auto
Metering options	M, CW, S
Flash modes	Auto
Weight	213g (with battery and memory card)
Dimensions (mm)	110.1 x 66 x 25.5
Batteries	Li-ion
Storage	SD/SDHC/ SDXC/329MBint
LCD	3" 921k-dot OLED
Viewfinder:	n/a

Set up your Nikon

Everything you need to get more from your new Nikon camera

Whether it's an upgrade or your first step into the world of photography, a new camera is an exciting purchase. However, a shiny new Nikon camera with all its buttons and dials can be a little overwhelming, leaving you wondering how to get started.

In this guide, we will take you through the process of setting up your camera from the moment you take it out of the box. Once it's ready, continue to the other guides and discover how lenses work, what the modes do, how to take different styles of photos and finally what to do with your shots once you have taken them. So what are you waiting for? Lift the lid and let us help you get started!

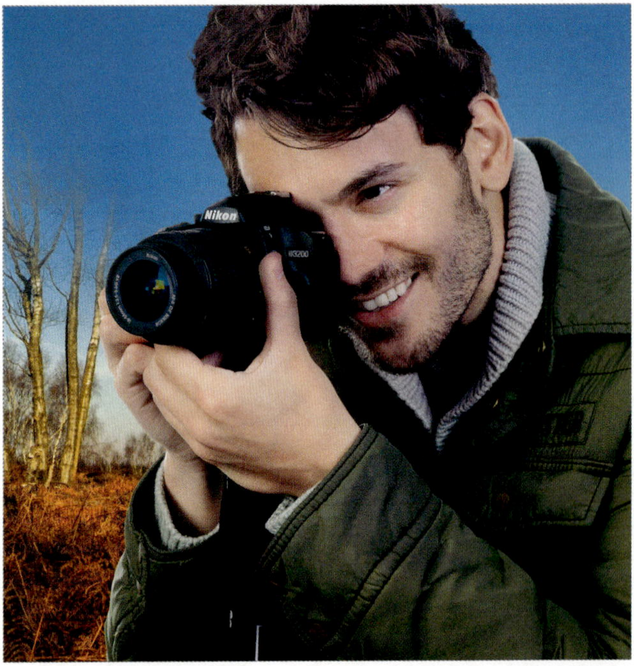

What you'll need Essential extras for your camera

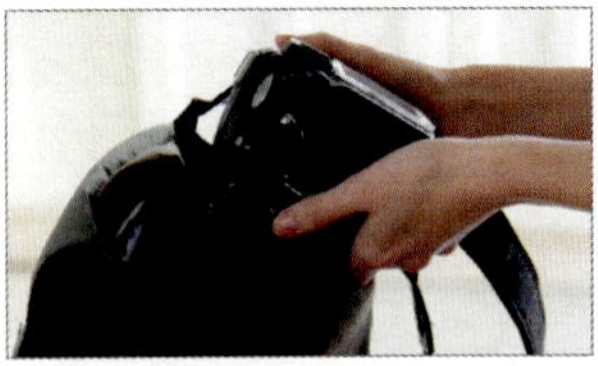

Camera bag

A camera bag helps keep your kit safe and secure on the go. There are many types available, from shoulder bags to backpacks, all of varying sizes.

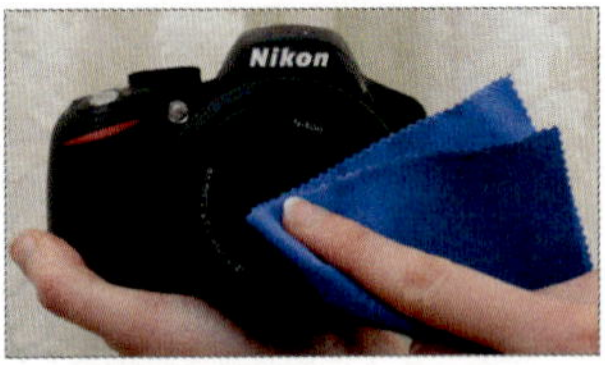

Cleaning cloth

Dust and smudges on your lens can show up in your photos. Carry a microfibre cloth and use it to keep your LCD screen clear, too.

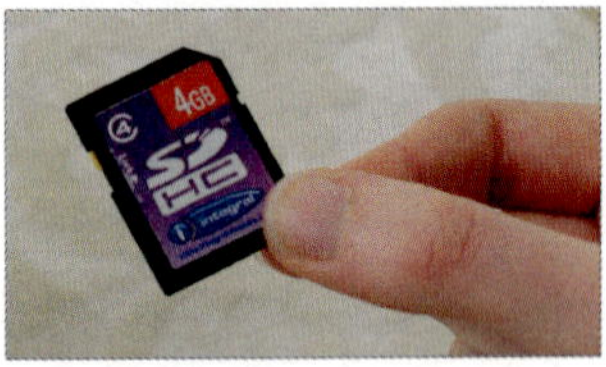

Memory card

Check whether your camera requires an SD, SDHC or SDXC card or a micro version, and buy one for your camera to store your photos on.

What's in the box? Learn about the important bits supplied in the box

1 Use the supplied camera strap to reduce the risk of dropping your camera.

2 Keep hold of the manual, as you'll need it to learn about your specific camera.

3 Take off any protective film covering the LCD screen before you get started.

4 If you've purchased a CSC or DSLR, then it will probably come with a kit lens.

5 New cameras usually come with a digital copy of the manual and editing software.

6 Plug your camera into the charger for a few hours before you start setting up.

7 You should be supplied with cables for connecting your kit to other devices.

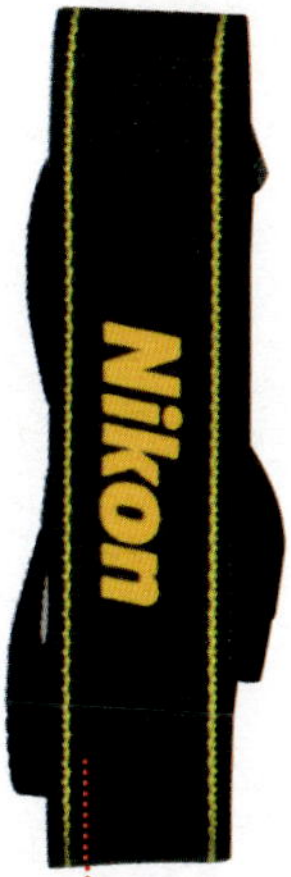

1 Strap

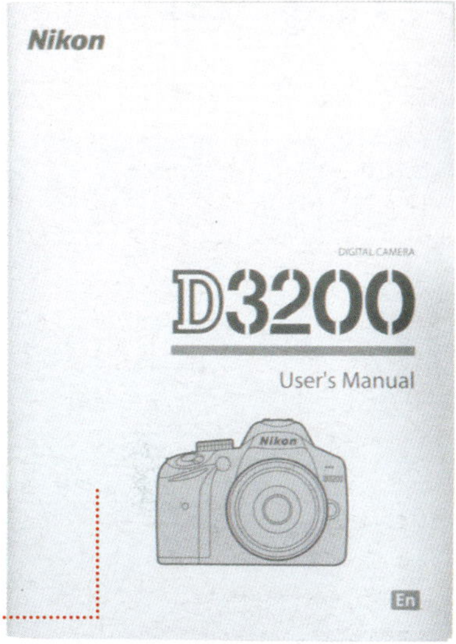

2 Manual

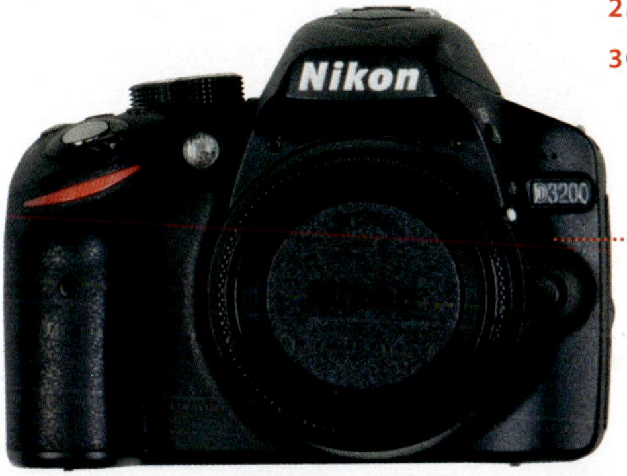

3 Camera

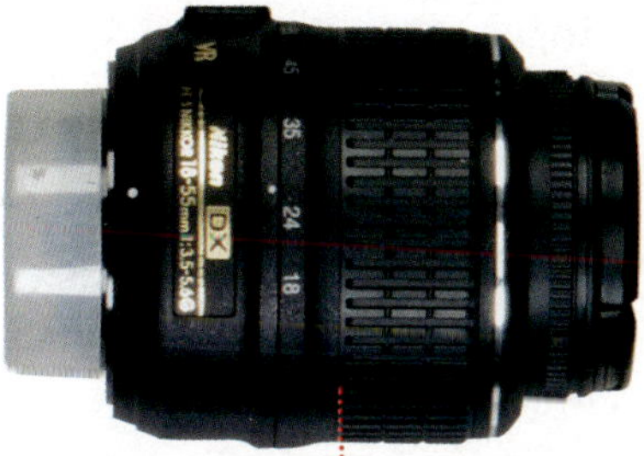

4 Lens

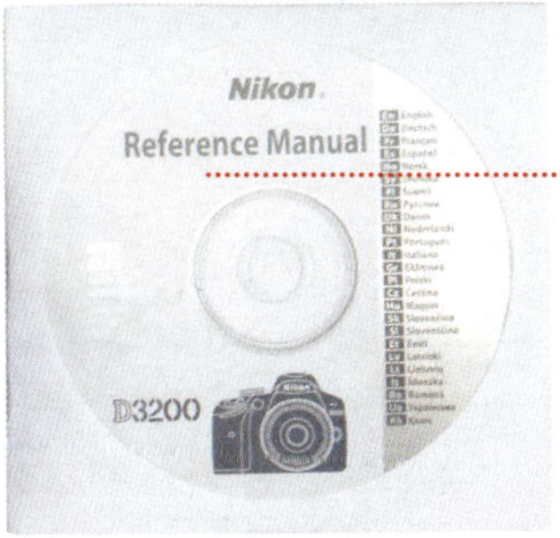

5 Software

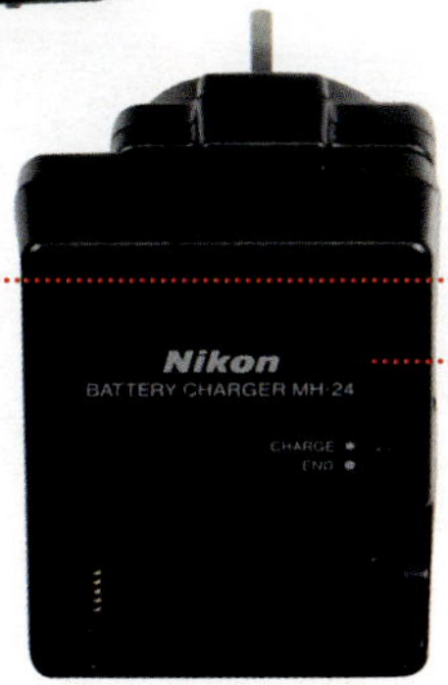

6 Battery charger

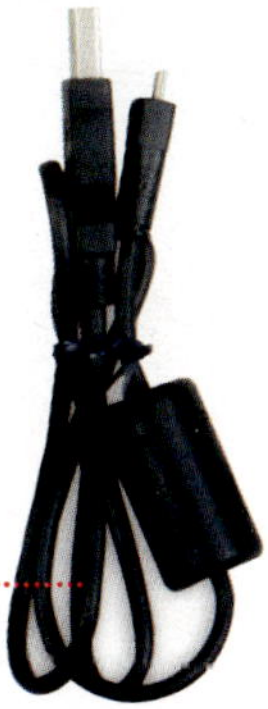

7 USB cables

Prepare your Nikon

Set up your new Nikon the right way to start shooting your best-ever shots

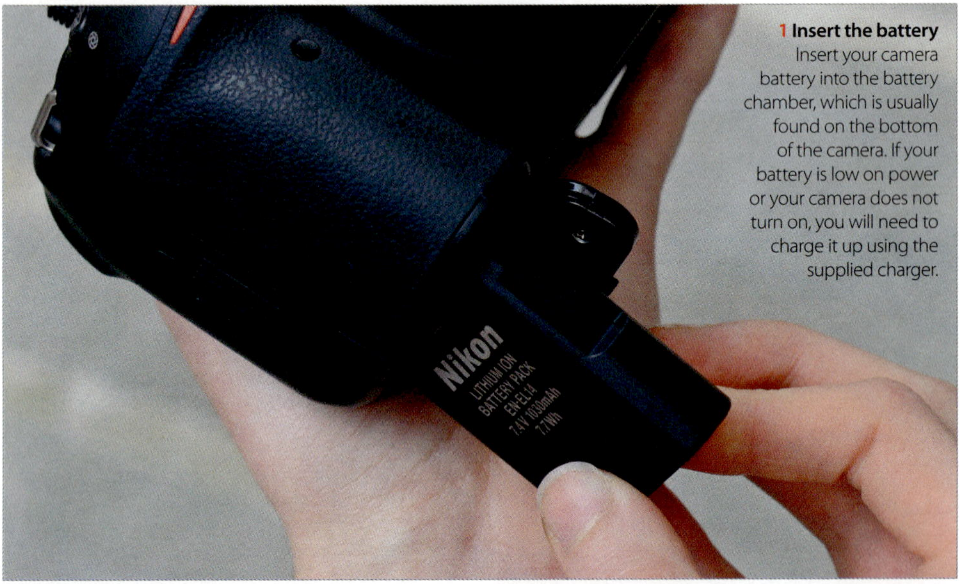

1 Insert the battery Insert your camera battery into the battery chamber, which is usually found on the bottom of the camera. If your battery is low on power or your camera does not turn on, you will need to charge it up using the supplied charger.

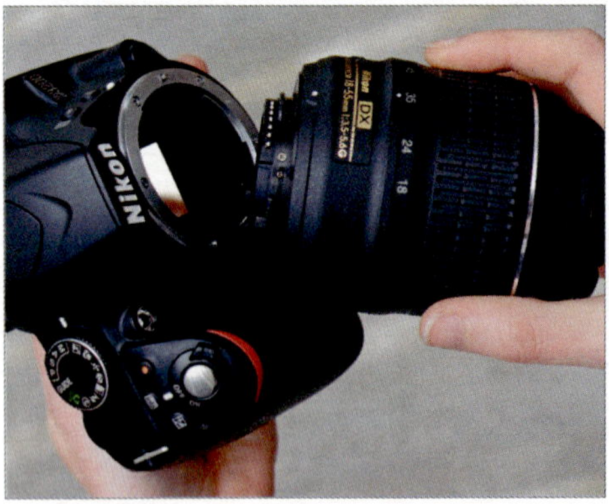

2 Attach the lens If you have an interchangeable lens camera, remove the cap on the front of your camera and the cap on the bottom of the lens. Align the markings on the lens and camera and turn the lens clockwise to lock it.

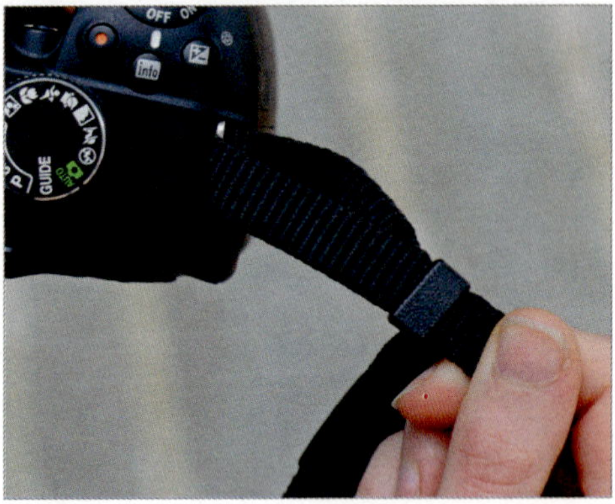

3 Attach the strap Feed each end of the strap through the lugs on either side of the camera and then secure it into place. Adjust the length so that it's comfortable for you to carry around and hold when you are out shooting.

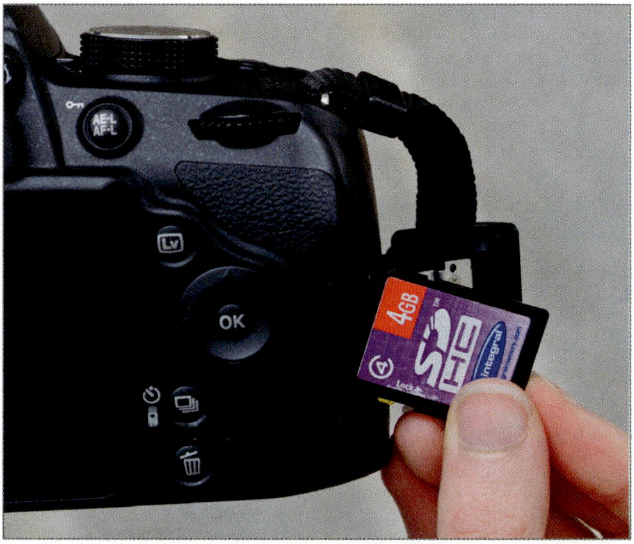

4 Insert the memory card Before you start shooting, insert a memory card to store your photos on. The memory card slot can usually be found on the bottom or side of the camera and will show you which way round to insert it.

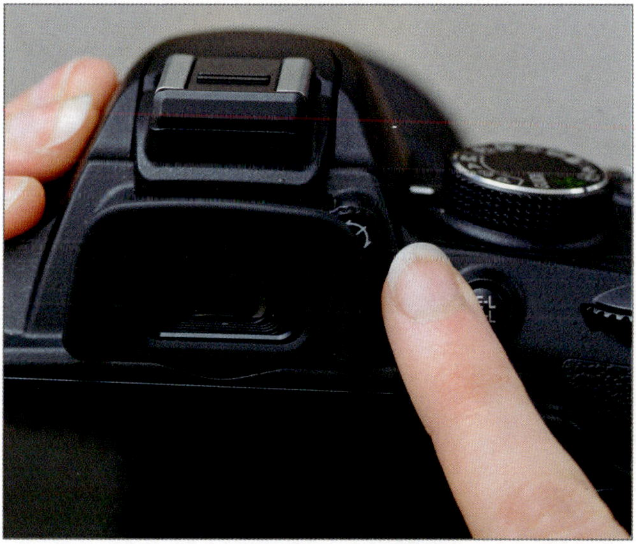

5 Focus the viewfinder If your camera has an optical viewfinder, then you will need to focus it correctly so that you have a clear view of what you're shooting. Rotate the dioptre dial next to the viewfinder until the view appears sharp.

Delve into your camera's menu

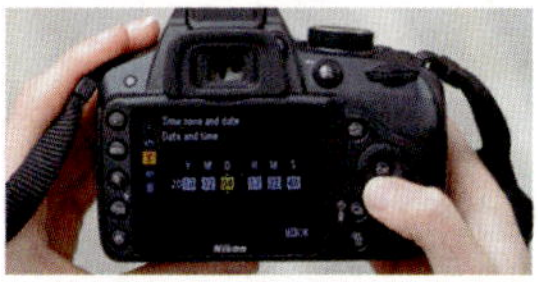

1 Set the date and time Input the correct time and date so this information will be recorded with your photos, making them easier to organise. You will find this option in the Settings menu.

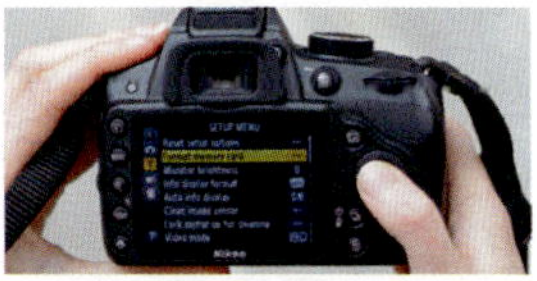

2 Format the card Formatting your memory card will set it up for your camera and improve performance. It will also delete any content on the card, so back everything up first.

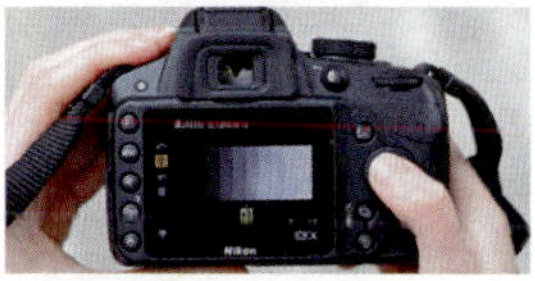

3 Adjust the LCD Ensure the LCD screen is lit enough to see your shots. Some cameras adjust brightness automatically, or you can do it from the menu.

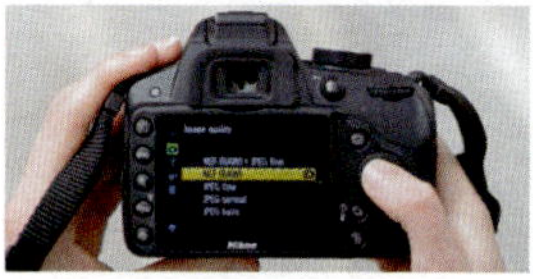

4 Choose a file type In the Quality section, set the type and size of files. JPEG is standard, but some cameras can shoot RAW, which you have to process.

Pick the right Nikon lens

Discover which lenses you need to capture the shots you want

The beauty of DSLRs and CSCs is the ability to change the lens depending on the mood, occasion or subject. For shooting sweeping vistas and landscapes, photographers plump for a focal length of 28mm or lower. For portraiture a standard or 'normal' telephoto is required carrying a focal length of between 35 and 85mm because this is what the eye is used to seeing. Medium telephotos of 100 to 300mm are prized by wildlife and action enthusiasts, whereas super-telephotos of 300mm gift sports fans with the kit they need to reach the heart of the action. In this complete guide to lenses you'll discover everything you need to know about choosing the right lens for the job, as well as tips for getting a perfect shot.

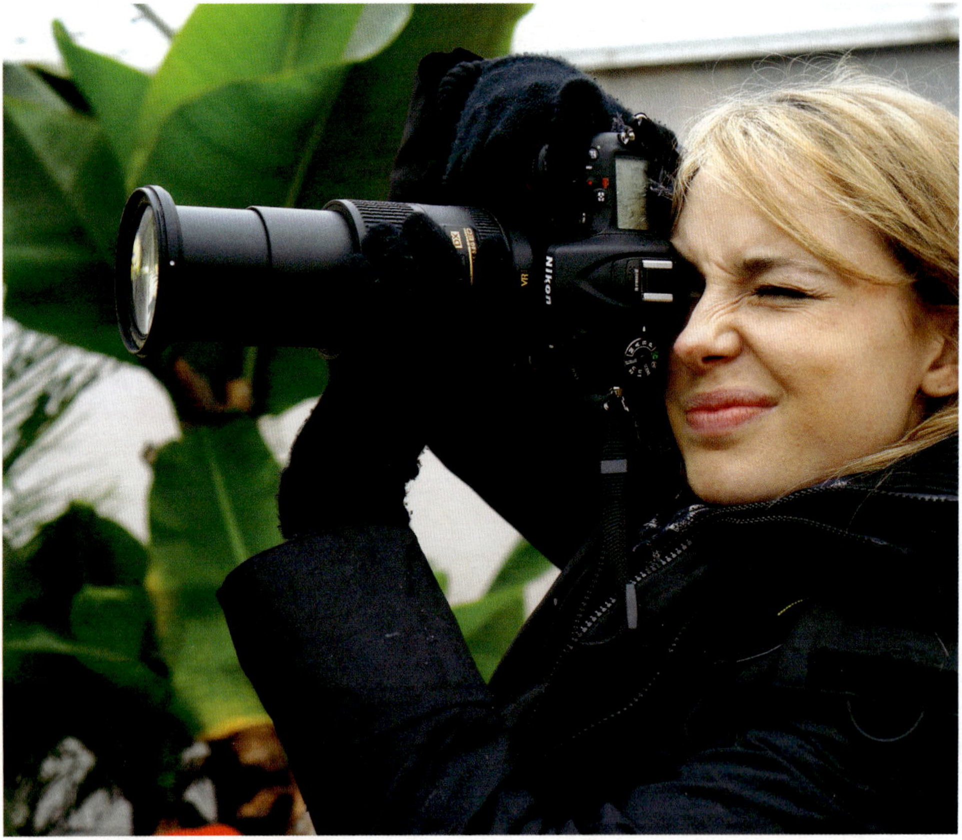

Landscape

Leading lines
Landscape photographers use lines within their compositions to lead the viewer into the focal point of image, for example a pier, a bridge, a pathway, a hedge, a railway track etc

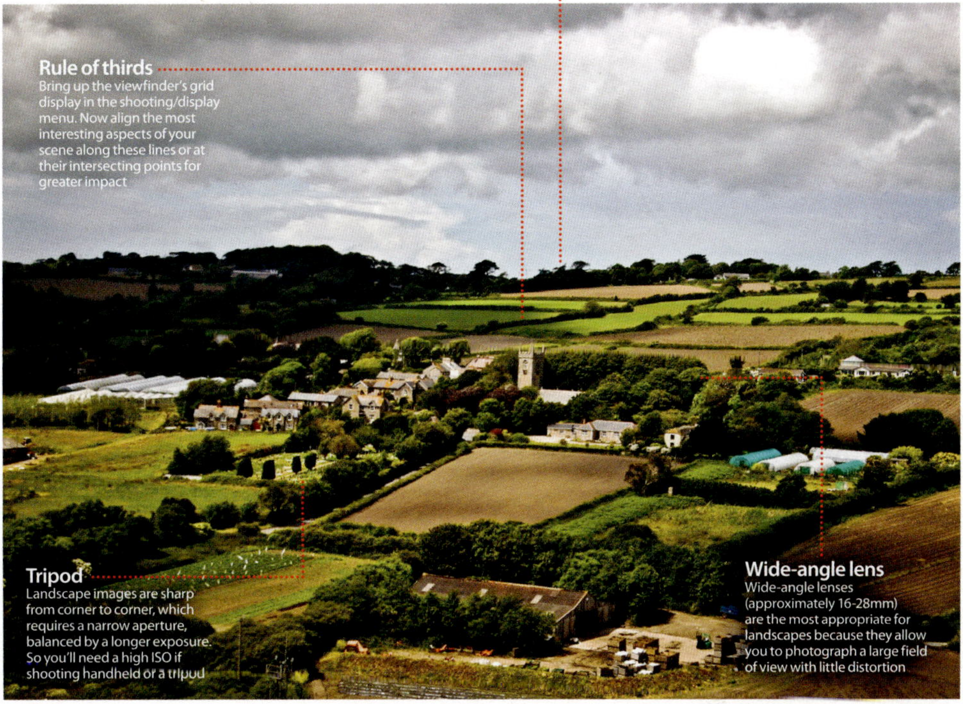

Take a look Top lenses for stunning landscape shots

AF Fisheye-NIKKOR 16mm f/2.8D

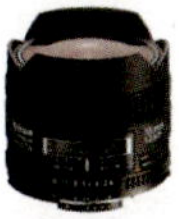

A slightly more unusual lens, perhaps best suited to the avant-garde, journalistic or adventurous landscape shooter. The FX-format boasts an attractive ultra-wide, fixed focal length, which may not appeal to everyone, but it is a remarkable lens for capturing large swathes of land, sea or sky, particularly in low-light thanks to its fast maximum aperture.

Price	£762/$999.95
Web	http://europe-nikon.com

AF-S NIKKOR 16-35mm f/4G ED VR II

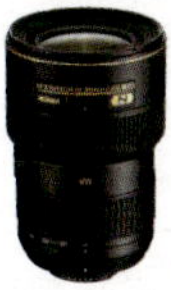

The ultra wide-angle zoom lens has become a common weapon of choice for lovers of landscape photography, thanks to its suitable and versatile focal range with constant f/4 aperture. Aimed at prosumers and the serious enthusiast, the FX-format lens adopts two focus modes (M/A and A) and also provides a Nano Crystal Coat for ghost and flare reduction.

Price	£1,071.99/$1,260
Web	http://europe-nikon.com

AF-S NIKKOR 24mm f/1.4G ED

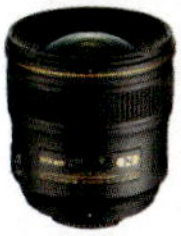

The prized AF NIKKOR 24mm f/1.4G ED is a class-leading wide-angle prime lens with an ultra-fast aperture of f1.4. It boasts a superior optical DNA that delivers sharp images even in low-light and is a popular choice with professional landscape shooters. Its wide aperture results in a brighter viewfinder image and makes it a superb choice for night landscapes in particular.

Price	£1,991/$2,199.95
Web	http://europe-nikon.com

Portraits

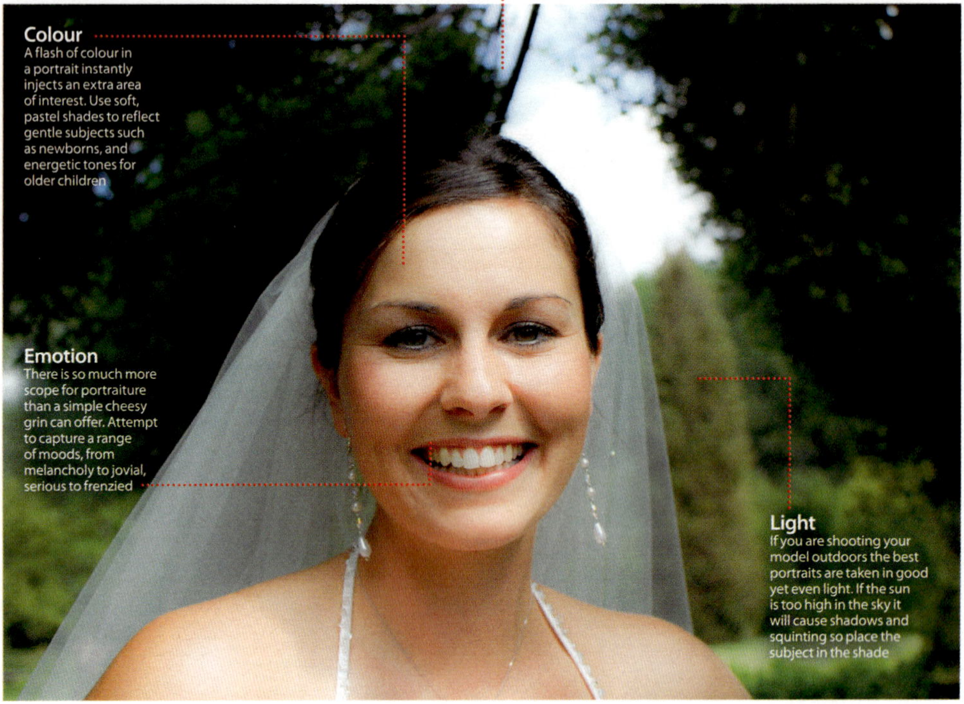

Take a look Quality lenses to make your portraits shine

AF-S DX NIKKOR 18-55mm f/3.5-5.6G VR II

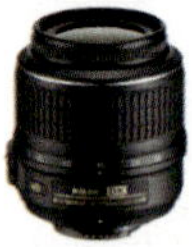

Nikon calls this its 'walk-around' zoom lens thanks to its incredibly lightweight construction. Its focal range is a popular choice for portrait fanatics who don't want to be stuck with one focal length, as is the case with prime lenses. Its attractive price point puts this lens towards the front of the brand's most inexpensive lenses.

Price	£156/$249.95
Web	http://europe-nikon.com

AF-S NIKKOR 50mm f/1.8G

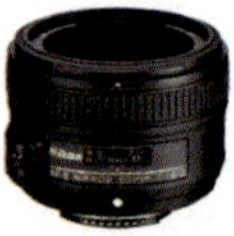

This lens is a special edition of the popular 50mm f1.8 NIKKOR lens and brags a lightweight, compact build, not to mention a fashionable retro-design. Its fast aperture makes the lens a great candidate for low-light shooting or when a shallow depth of field is called for. Its DNA coupled with its impressive results make it the perfect portrait lens for a photographer on a budget.

Price	£199.99/$279.95
Web	http://europe-nikon.com

AF-S NIKKOR 85mm f/1.4G

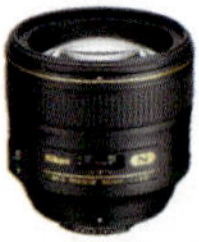

This stunning professional medium telephoto prime lens is designed for use with FX-format cameras. Its outstanding optical performance in part is due to its wide aperture of f1.4, which not only makes it appropriate for low-light portraits but also those where the photographer wishes to generate soft creamy edges and backgrounds; such as those associated with newborn photography.

Price	£1,531.99/$1,699.95
Web	http://europe-nikon.com

Travel

The witching hour
Cities are transformed at night so it's worth returning for a second shoot. Use a tripod for lengthy exposures or balance the camera on a wall, and then trigger the shot with the timer

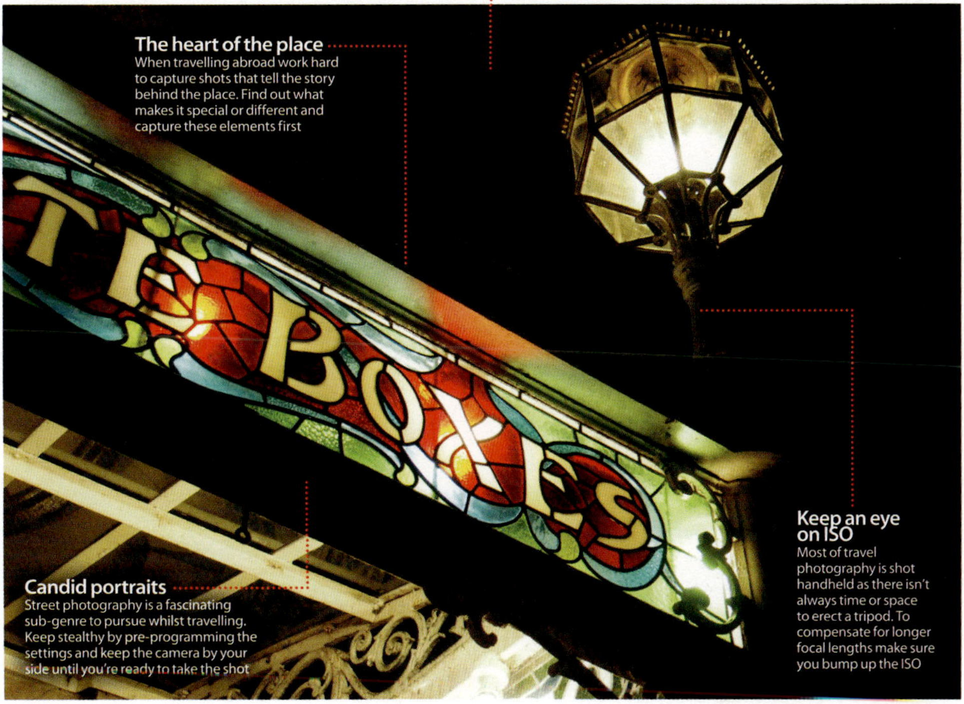

The heart of the place
When travelling abroad work hard to capture shots that tell the story behind the place. Find out what makes it special or different and capture these elements first

Keep an eye on ISO
Most of travel photography is shot handheld as there isn't always time or space to erect a tripod. To compensate for longer focal lengths make sure you bump up the ISO

Candid portraits
Street photography is a fascinating sub-genre to pursue whilst travelling. Keep stealthy by pre-programming the settings and keep the camera by your side until you're ready to take the shot

Take a look Explore these lenses to take on your travels

AF-S NIKKOR 24-85mm f/3.5-4.5G ED VR

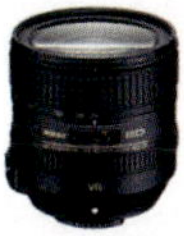

This high-performance, FX-format travel lens is more compact than some of the other suggestions here, which makes it ideal for those seeking a transportable lens. Its focal length covers the most commonly used focal lengths from wide-angle to normal-telephoto which makes it suitable for those mainly shooting travel landscapes and portraits.

Price	£519.99/$599.95
Web	http://europe-nikon.com

AF-S DX NIKKOR 18-140mm f/3.5-5.6G ED VR

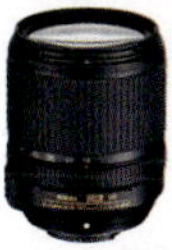

This compact, lightweight and versatile DX-format zoom lens is perfect for holidays and expeditions as it covers a broad focal range gifting travel connoisseurs with a 7.8x zoom. The affordable all-rounder's focal range of 18-140mm makes it an attractive choice for those hoping to snap a variety of subjects including: landscapes, portraits, street, wildlife, documentary and action.

Price	£579.99/$499.95
Web	http://europe-nikon.com

AF-S DX NIKKOR 18-300mm f/3.5-6.3G ED VR

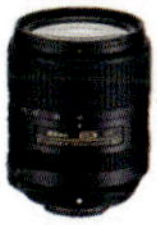

This DX-format, ultra high-power zoom lens with VR and zoom lock is an ideal accompaniment to any travel photographer's kit bag. With its 16.7x zoom, travellers can scan distances from 18-300mm making it perfect for shooting a range of popular holiday subjects such as landscapes and portraits, plus the long telephoto range opens the door for wildlife and action shots too.

Price	£629.99/$8.99.95
Web	http://europe-nikon.com

Macro

Rain or shine
Macros work whatever the weather so don't be afraid to shoot in the rain. Closely cropped shots of delicate rain drops on a cobweb or flower petal can be extraordinary

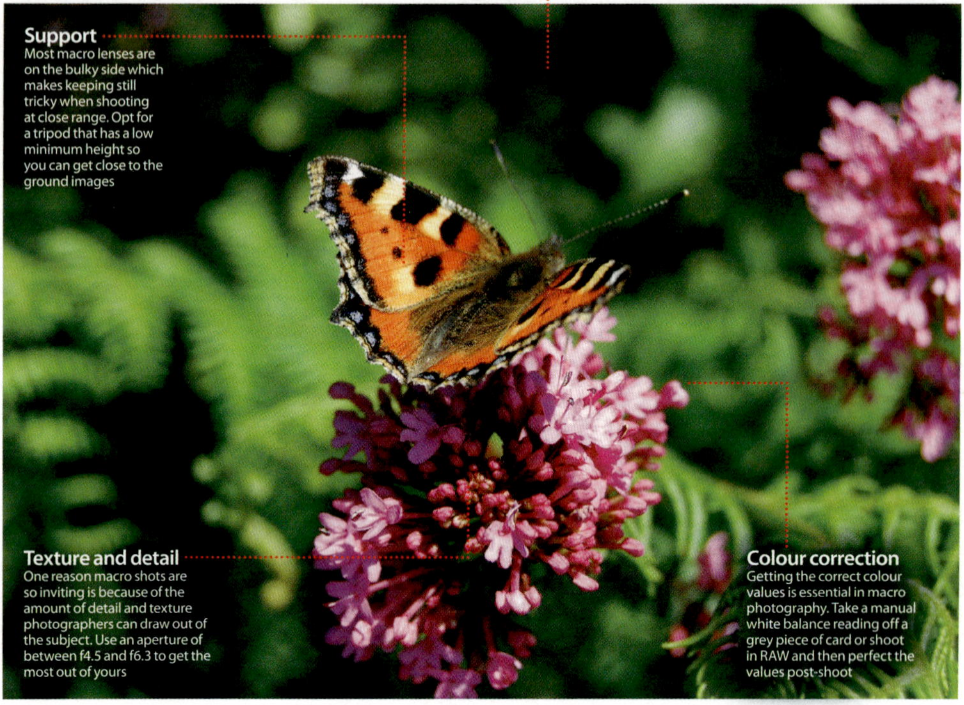

Support
Most macro lenses are on the bulky side which makes keeping still tricky when shooting at close range. Opt for a tripod that has a low minimum height so you can get close to the ground images

Texture and detail
One reason macro shots are so inviting is because of the amount of detail and texture photographers can draw out of the subject. Use an aperture of between f4.5 and f6.3 to get the most out of yours

Colour correction
Getting the correct colour values is essential in macro photography. Take a manual white balance reading off a grey piece of card or shoot in RAW and then perfect the values post-shoot

Take a look Revel in the detail with these lenses

AF-S DX Micro NIKKOR 40mm f/2.8G

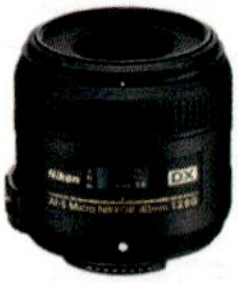

The 40mm DX-format macro lens offers a fast maximum aperture of f/2.8 and a 1:1 reproduction ratio making it a perfect choice for close-ups. Its Silent Wave Motor ensures quiet autofocus so that you can get as close to your subject as possible without scaring it off; ideal when shooting insects and flighty animals.

Price	£249.99/$279.95
Web	http://europe-nikon.com

AF-S Micro NIKKOR 60mm f/2.8G ED

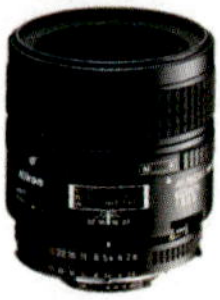

Currently Nikon's most compact Micro lens, this versatile product, which weighs 440g, also provides macro-enthusiasts with an essential 1:1 reproduction ratio. What's more the lens offers close range correction (CRC) a system that delivers stellar focusing performance at close range and far off distances.

Price	£499.99/$599.95
Web	http://europe-nikon.com

AF-S VR Micro NIKKOR 105mm f/2.8G IF-ED

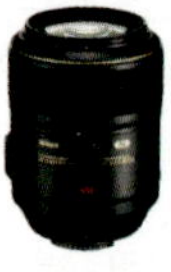

The AF-S VR MICRO NIKKOR 105mm f/2.8G IF-ED presents vibration reduction in a macro lens package. Its body incorporates a Silent Wave Motor for quieter capturing plus its lens is enhanced with an extra-low dispersion (ED) glass elements for minimising chromatic aberrations. The lens offers users a 154mm working distance for near 1:1 reproduction.

Price	£782/$984.95
Web	http://europe-nikon.com

Action

Short, sharp shots
To capture the action you'll need to use a very fast shutter speed. To do this try raising the ISO to take that speed to the next level

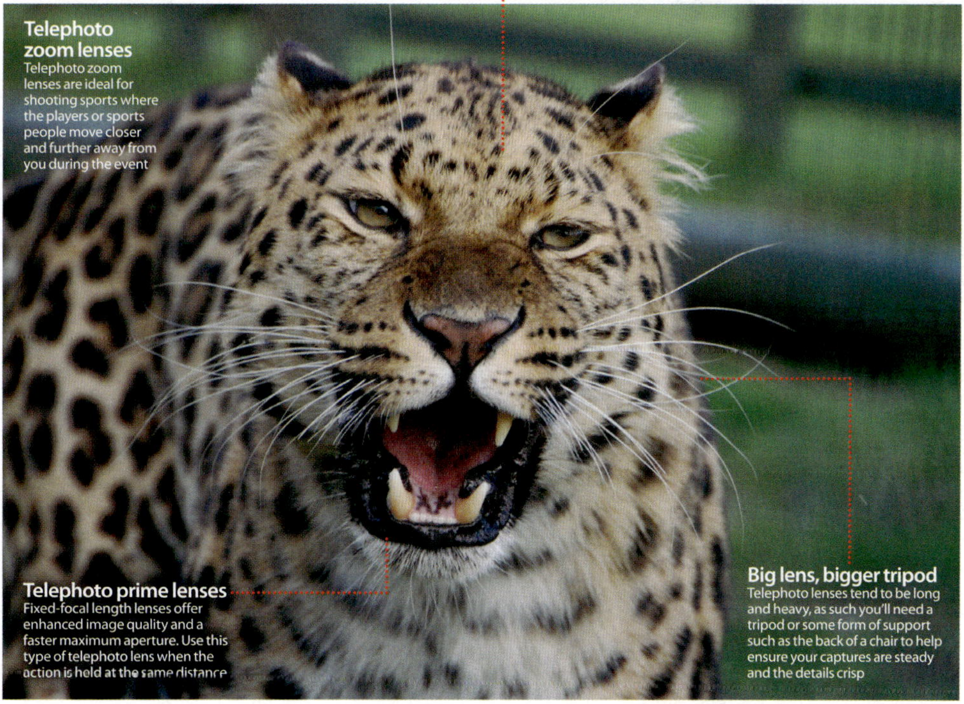

Take a look Capture all of the action using these lenses

AF-S DX NIKKOR 18-300mm f/3.5-5.6G ED VR

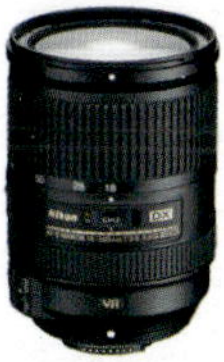

This high-powered DX-format zoom lens is a great find for sports enthusiasts thanks to its vast super-telephoto reach; offering stunning close ups from a distance. The zoom delivers an ideal focal range of 18-300mm and is considered an affordable option for entry-level DSLR users

Price	£849.99/$999.95
Web	http://europe-nikon.com

AF-S NIKKOR 70-200mm f/4G ED VR

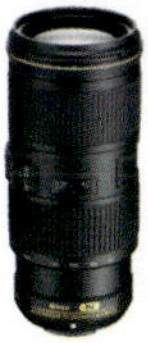

A lovely compact and lightweight lens designed for FX-format cameras, capable of delivering an impressive focal range from 70 to 200mm. A Nano Crystal Coat has been applied to reduce ghosting and flare, and its VR is essential for minimising camera shake as it gifts users with the equivalent of a shutter speed 4.0 stops faster.

Price	£1,172.99/$1,399.95
Web	http://europe-nikon.com

AF-S NIKKOR 200-400mm f/4G Ed VR II

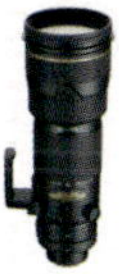

A world-class high-end lens designed for professional sports, action and wildlife shooters. The FX-format compatible super telephoto zoom lens is constructed from 24 elements in 17 groups and presents four ED glass elements for minimising chromatic aberrations. Its VR systems, designed to combat camera shake, raises the equivalent shutter speed by 3.0 stops.

Price	£6,383/$6,999.95
Web	http://europe-nikon.com

Essential kit

Improve and expand your photography experience with these must-have items

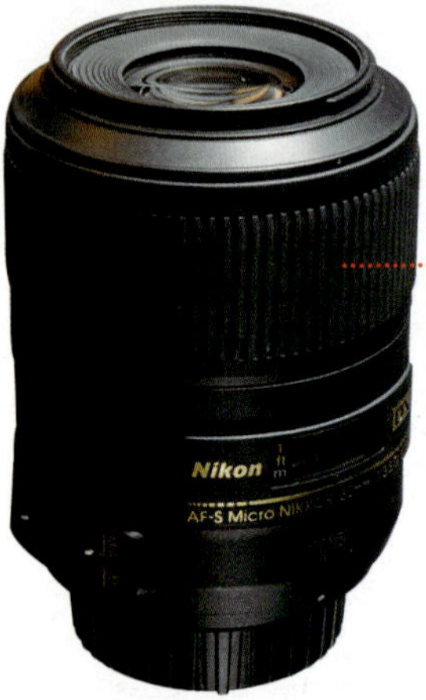

Lenses

The wider the selection of lenses a photographer has at their disposal, the more genres of imagery they can produce. As a general rule of thumb use a focal length of less than 28mm for landscapes, 35 to 85mm for portraits, and anything over 100mm for zooming into the action such as sports, wildlife or documentary

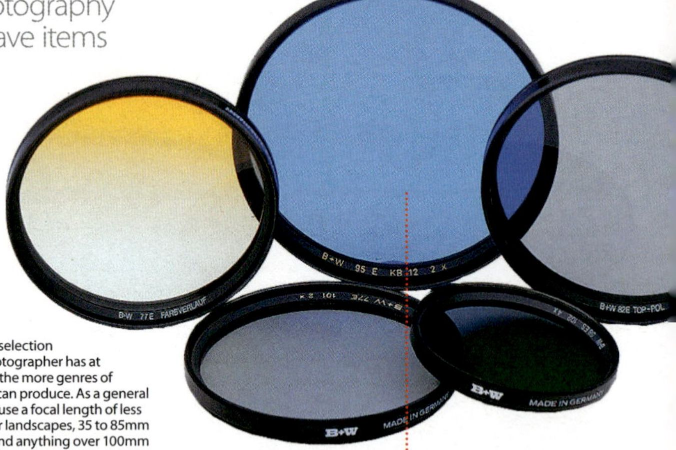

Filters

A UV or skylight filter acts as a simple protective piece of transparent glass that safeguards your lens against smears, knocks and smashes. It is widely considered essential, particularly if the lens is expensive. An ND grad is used in landscapes and can help to 'trick' the camera's image sensor when you want to manipulate exposures. A polariser filter can minimise glare caused by reflections, boost colours and heighten contrast

Camera bag

With so much kit to carry it's wise to invest in a rugged camera bag. The best bags feature removable padded separators for protecting your equipment; they can be pulled out and reattached by their Velcro strips to suit the style and shape or your own equipment. Also look for one that is waterproof, lightweight, has plenty of smaller pockets and a strap for attaching your tripod to

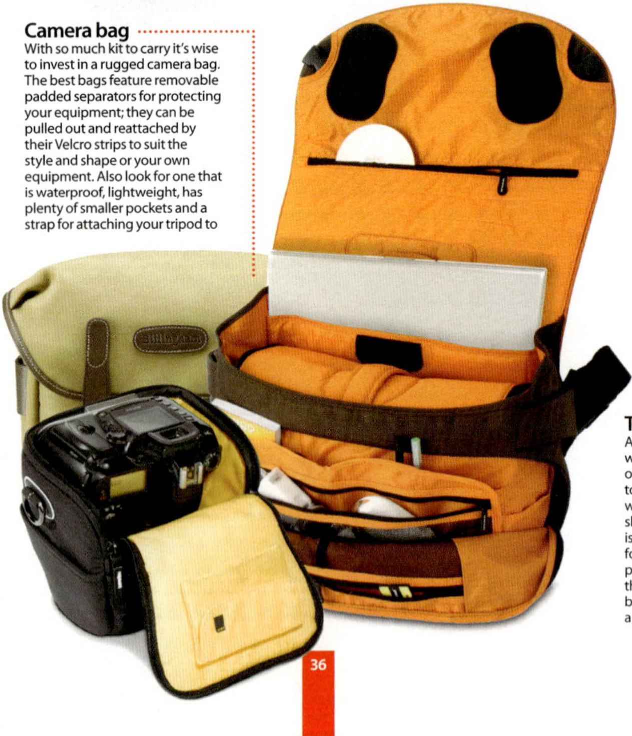

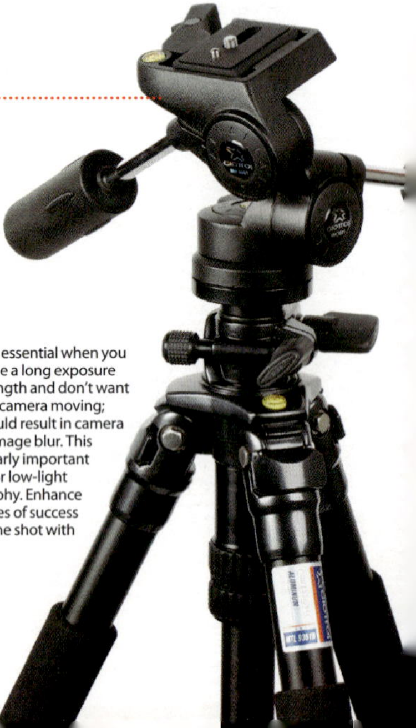

Tripod

A tripod is essential when you want to use a long exposure or focal length and don't want to risk the camera moving; which would result in camera shake or image blur. This is particularly important for night or low-light photography. Enhance the chances of success by firing the shot with a timer

Lens pen or cloth

Lens spots and dust motes are an expected annoyance when using lenses on a regular basis. Trust in a reliable make of lens cloth or pen to wipe away marks and stains before you begin capturing your subject. This will save you hours upon hours of time later on, cloning and removing the blemishes in an editing suite

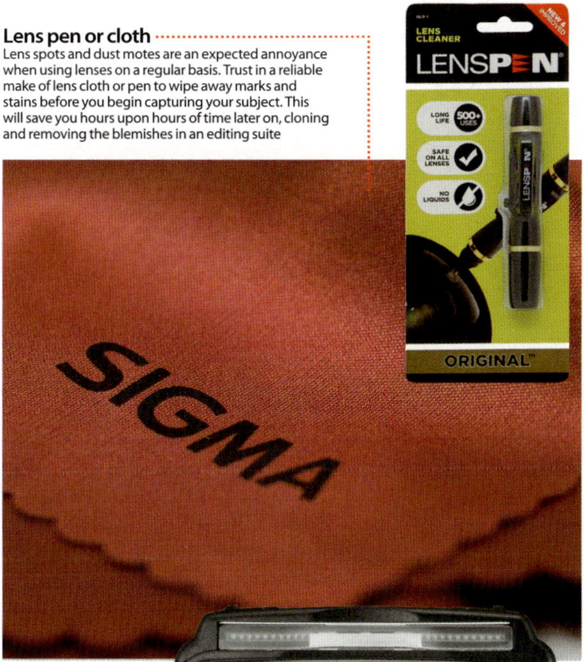

Memory card

Unless your camera has a particularly large internal memory you'll need a memory card to record your images on. The most common formats used today are SD/SDHC and SDXC. Opt for several smaller cards (4-16GB) rather than one large card (32GB) in case that card is lost, stolen or damaged

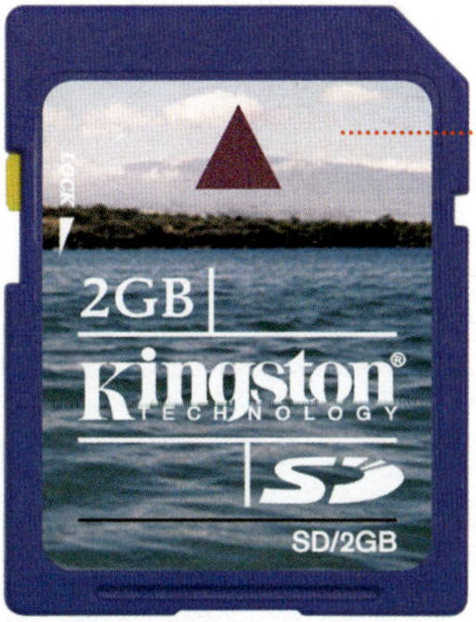

Remote control

If you enjoy shooting landscapes, seascapes or nightscapes you may want to invest in a remote control. These type of shots call for longer exposures and as such any movement the camera and tripod experience will be captured in your shot. Using the camera's self-timer or even better; a tethered or wireless remote control will eradicate this

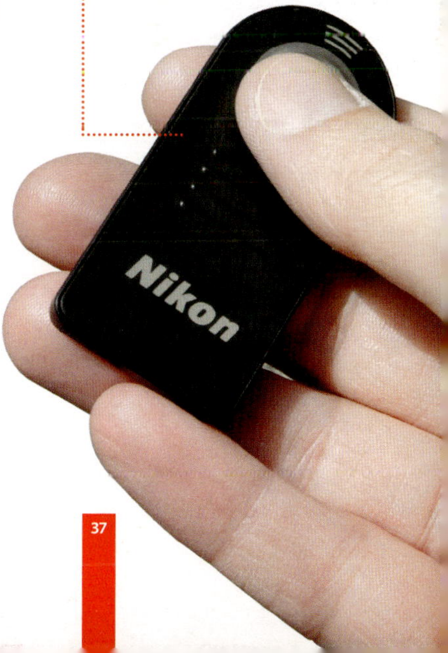

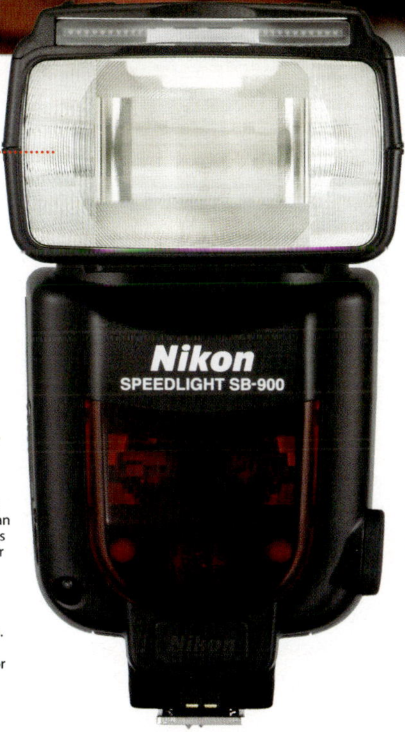

Flash

A portable flash is a wise investment for anyone shooting above a beginner level. This type of flash grants the photographer more creativity because portrait, fashion, event and wedding photographers can bounce the flash off ceilings and walls to generate softer more flattering effects to illuminate the subjects, which are much more natural than those of the camera's own pop-up flash. Flash is also useful when it comes to shooting action or sports photography

Cleaning your Nikon

If you want to keep your Nikon camera in pristine condition and working its best, you need to learn how to clean it

Giving your Nikon a good clean will help to prolong its life and ensure it is performing to its best ability. Marks on the lens can show up in your shots and general dirt on the camera body can find its way into the inner workings, so it is in your best interest to keep it spotless. The outer body of your camera is easy to clean yourself at home, but when it comes to cleaning the very delicate sensor, it is best to send it away to be dealt with professionally. Here's how we recommend you go about it...

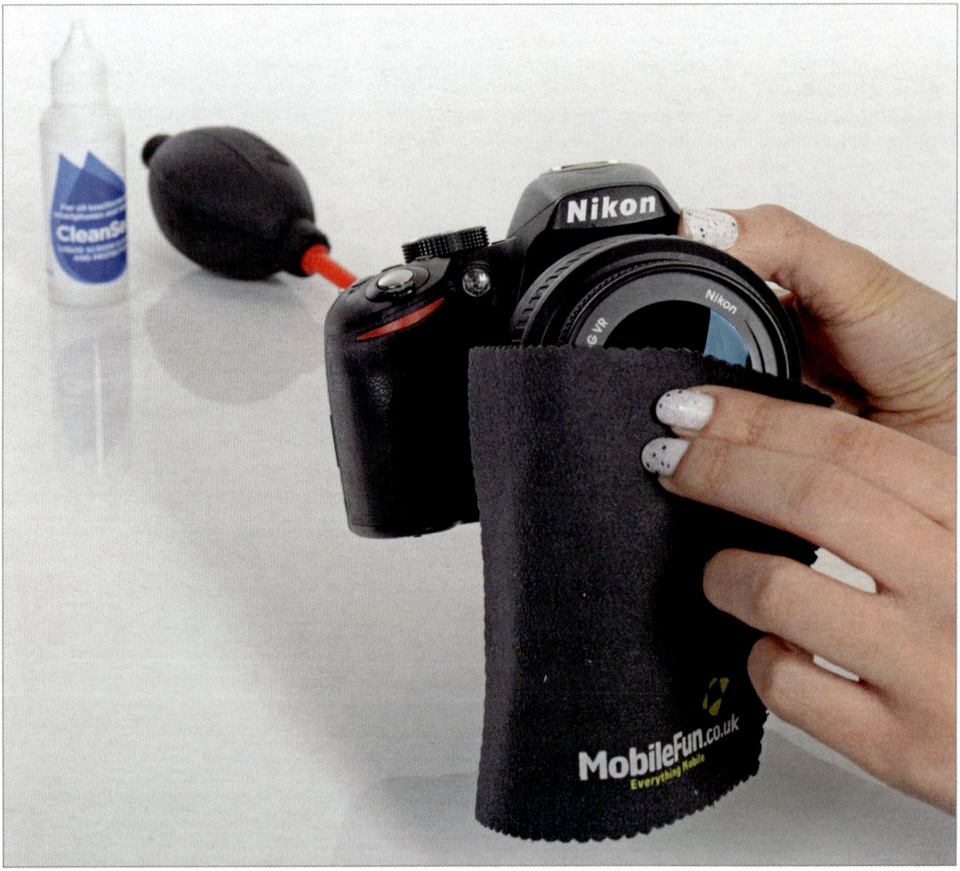

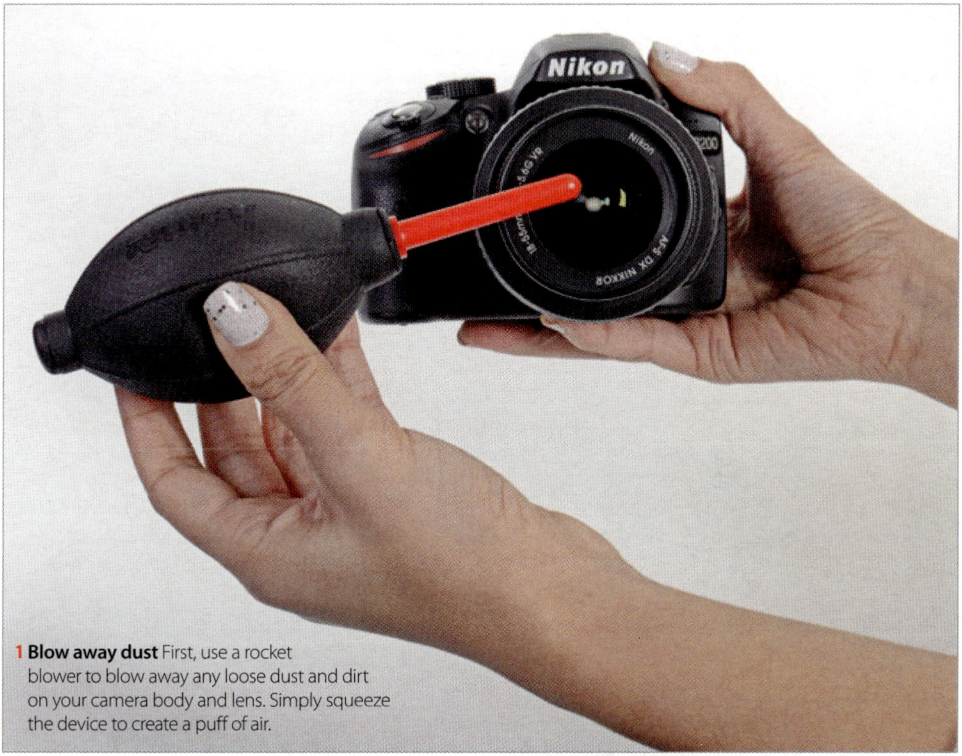

1 Blow away dust First, use a rocket blower to blow away any loose dust and dirt on your camera body and lens. Simply squeeze the device to create a puff of air.

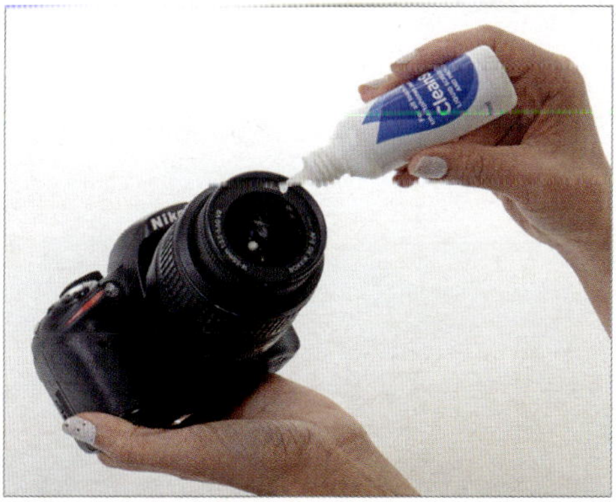

2 Apply cleaning solution An alcohol-based lens cleaning fluid will help you remove any stubborn marks and smudges on your lens. Apply to the lens and wipe with a microfibre cloth.

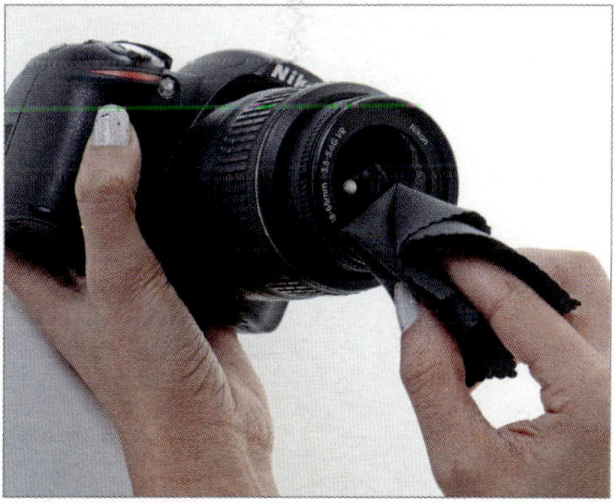

3 Use a microfibre cloth A microfibre cloth is the best option for lens cleaning as it will really lift away any dirt. Just make sure you wash your cloth regularly to keep it as clean as possible.

The Nikon buttons

Get to know our way around your Nikon camera by learning what all those buttons do and learn to identify them easily

When you first get your Nikon camera, or even when you've had it for quite some time, you might not know what all of those fiddly buttons do. What are their functions? This guide aims to inform you about what all of them do. You'll be an expert in no time!

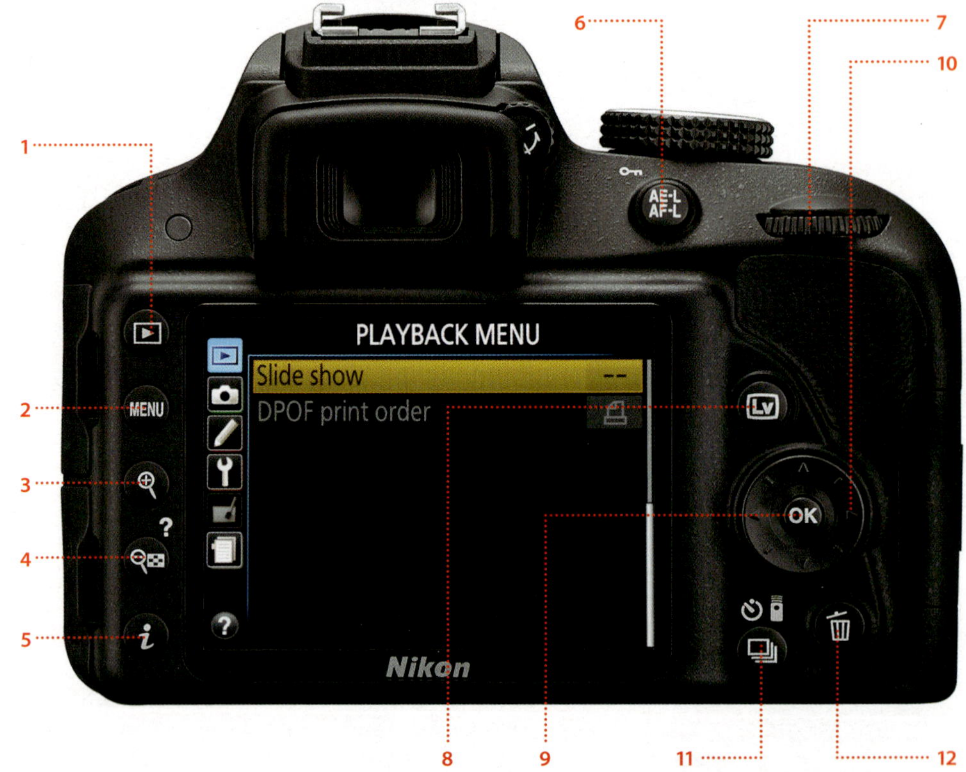

1 Playback The Playback button will bring up all the stills and video footage recorded on the memory card or internal memory.

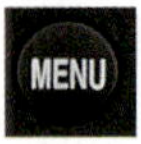

2 Menu In order to adjust the majority of settings you'll need to press this Menu button to find the option you want to change.

3 Playback zoom Sometimes you need to examine an image closely. To scroll in to your captured images for a closer inspection, use this button.

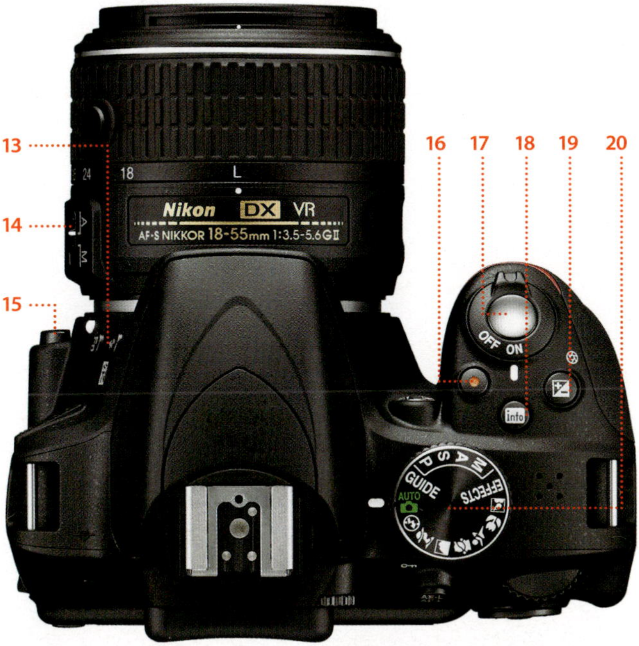

4 Thumbnail/Playback zoom out/Help Three commands here; to show images as thumbnails, zoom out of an image or bring up the help screen.

5 Information If your camera doesn't have an info LCD screen, use the info button to discover what settings you currently have programmed in.

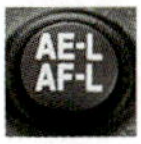

6 AE-L/AF-L The AutoExposure-Lock holds the current exposure. AutoFocus-Lock stops the camera finding a new object to focus on.

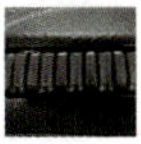

7 Command dial The command dial is used to affect settings, for example it can widen the aperture or slow down shutter speed.

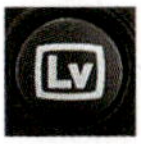

8 Live View Instead of composing through the viewfinder, you can use the LCD screen instead (Live View). This is ideal when recording movies.

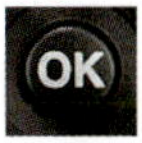

9 OK button When you want to change a setting or action a command you'll use the OK button in order to confirm the instruction.

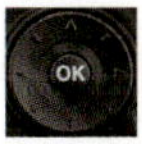

10 Multi selector This refers to the ring or area around the OK button. Photographers use these arrows to navigate the menu.

11 Burst mode/self-timer Photographers can make use of these controls to alter how many shots a fired in one go, or to utilise the camera's self-timer.

12 Delete When you're reviewing images in Playback mode, use this delete button to erase unwanted or imperfect captures.

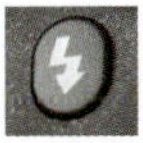

13 Pop-up flash This lightning bolt icon symbolises the pop-up flash. Simply hit it when a bit of extra illumination is required.

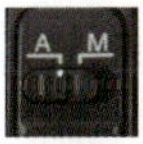

14 Manual/Autofocus switch To control the focus yourself push this switch to M for manual, otherwise let the camera do the work with Autofocus.

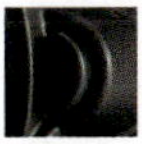

15 Lens release Hold down this button and gently pull away the lens to remove it. Change lenses quickly to avoid dust and debris collecting on the sensor.

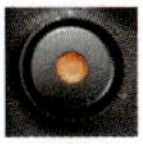

16 Movie record Shown as a small red dot, the shortcut movie record button fast tracks movie-makers into the dedicated recording mode.

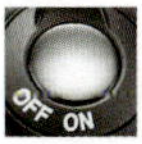

17 Shutter button The most important and probably obvious button on the camera. It's the shutter button which you press to fire the shot.

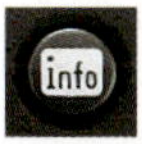

18 Metering Choose between the camera's metering options, usually this is the option of Spot, Evaluative/Matrix or Centre Weighted.

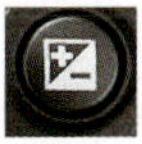

19 Exposure compensation This lets you override the suggested settings, allowing you to quickly underexpose or overexpose.

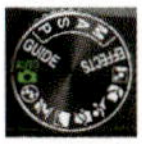

20 Mode dial The palette of modes gifts photographers with the manual and semi manual options as well as commonly-used scene modes and auto.

The Nikon menus

Discover all there is to know about Nikon's menu system

Granted, Nikon's camera menu system doesn't sound like the most glamorous or scintillating facet of the device, but in actual fact understanding how to use it, and how to use it well, can really enhance your photography.

By exploring, learning and changing the menu options, photographers have the ability to take control away from the camera and hand themselves the reigns to execute stronger, more dynamic and interesting imagery. What's more, photographers who understand how to manipulate the in-camera system will be in a better place to challenge themselves in tricky lighting conditions or in more complex shooting situations. So are you ready to learn more? Let's get started…

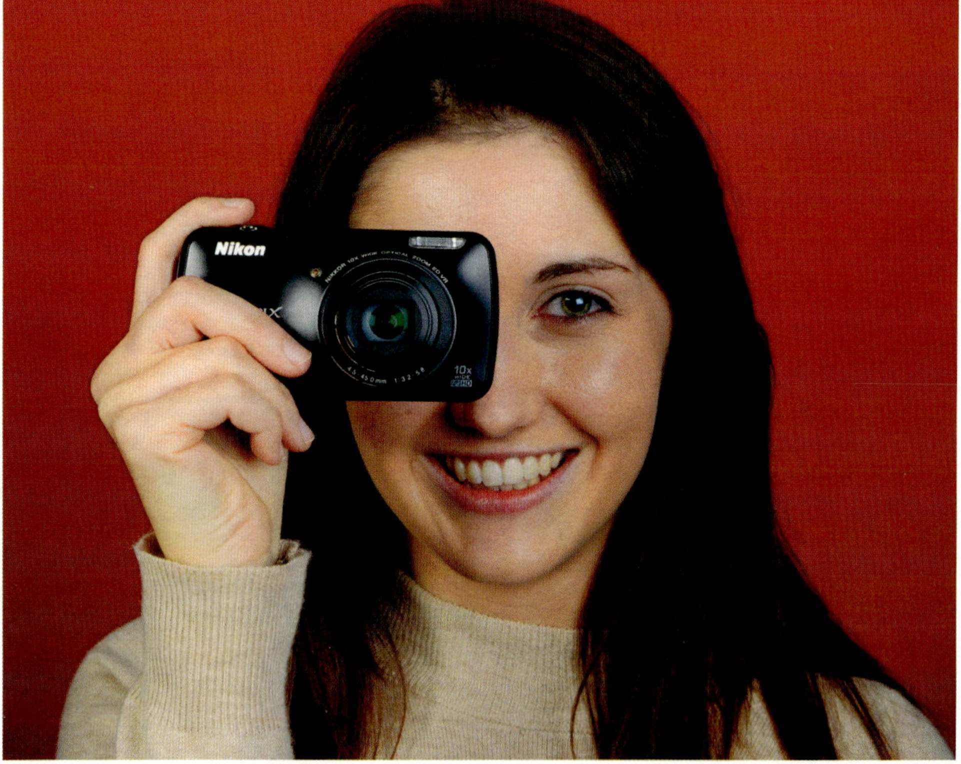

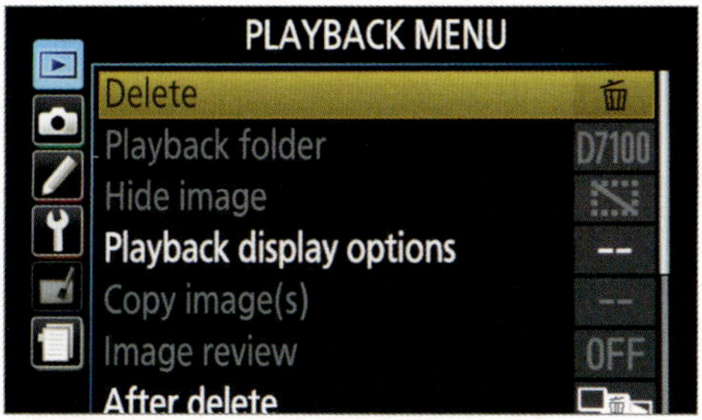

Playback

Nikon's first, but often overlooked menu in its portfolio is the Playback menu. It allows users to make changes to how images are presented in review mode.

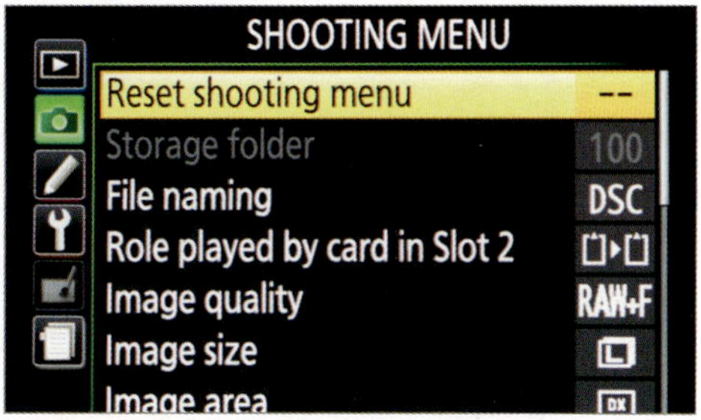

Shooting

This is arguably one of the most frequented and thus important menus in the camera. It holds settings that optimise how the image is recorded.

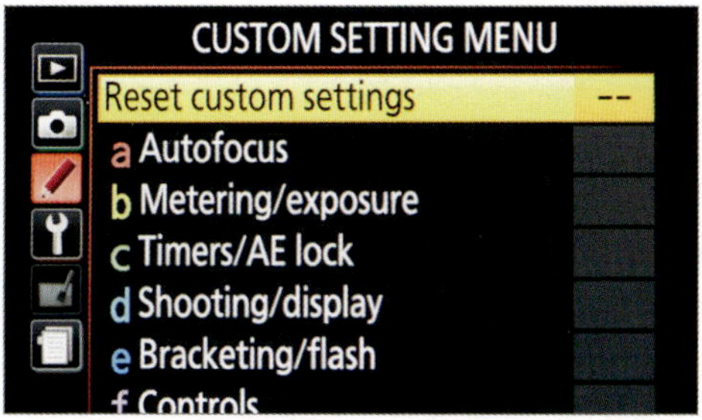

Custom Shooting

This holds many sub-menus, which are: Autofocus, Metering/Exposure, Timers/AE lock, Shooting/Display, Bracketing/Flash and Controls.

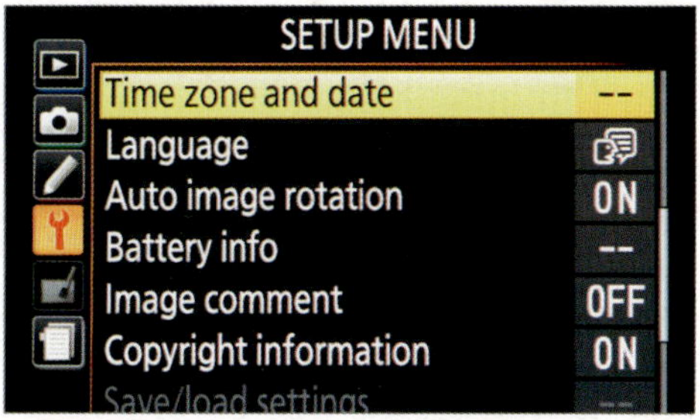

Set Up

The Set Up menu contains a portfolio of helpful housekeeping options such as LCD brightness, Clean Image Sensor, Time/Date, GPS activation, language and more.

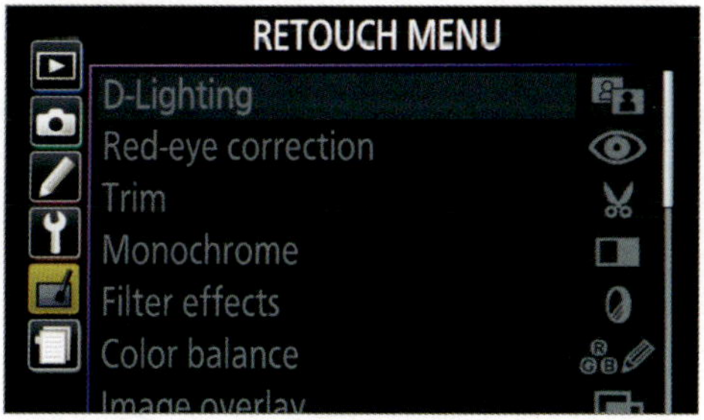

Retouch

If you're unhappy with an image or just want to get creative, travel into the Retouch menu to jazz it up. The original will remain unchanged.

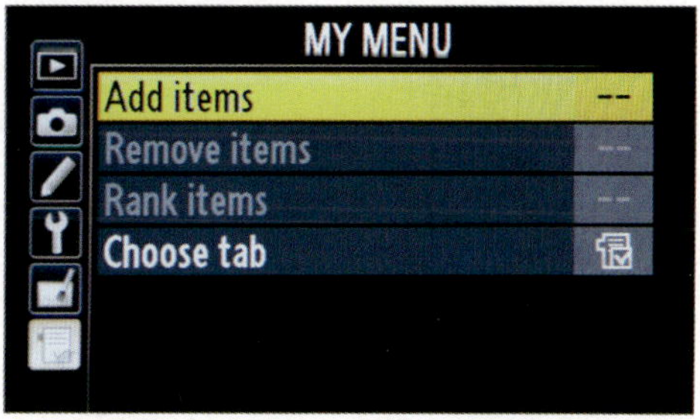

My Menu

This area of the menu system is for you to create a customisable list of settings to your own liking and can contain up to 20 items.

Ultimate guide to shooting modes

Get to grips with your Nikon's mode dial and discover how to improve your shooting skills and take better images

Your Nikon's mode dial features a whole host of fantastic shooting modes that can help you develop from a budding beginner to experienced enthusiast in no time at all. Whether you want to simply point and shoot in Auto and Scene modes, or take more control over your exposures in semi-automatic (P, A, S) or full Manual mode, in this practical guide we'll take you through all you need to know about using each one.

Most Nikon cameras feature what's known as a mode dial on the top plate, which gives you quick access to your shooting modes, and some require you to adjust your shooting mode via the menu interface. Explore what options you have available and then join us as we take you around the mode dial from Auto to Manual and explain what each shooting mode does and what it can be used for. There are plenty of practical tips along the way too, including some great tutorials you can sink your teeth into, so start experimenting with your shooting modes today and find out what your camera really has to offer.

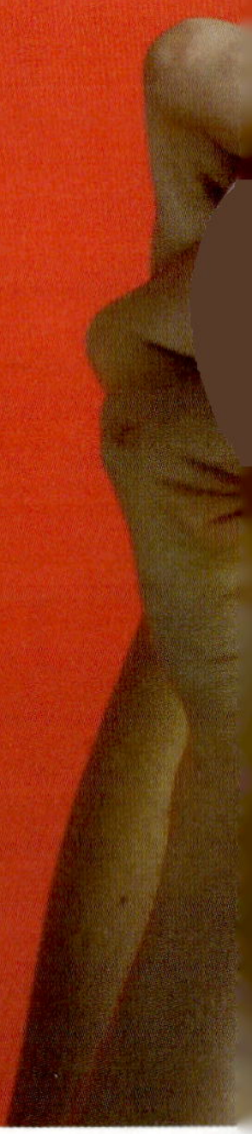

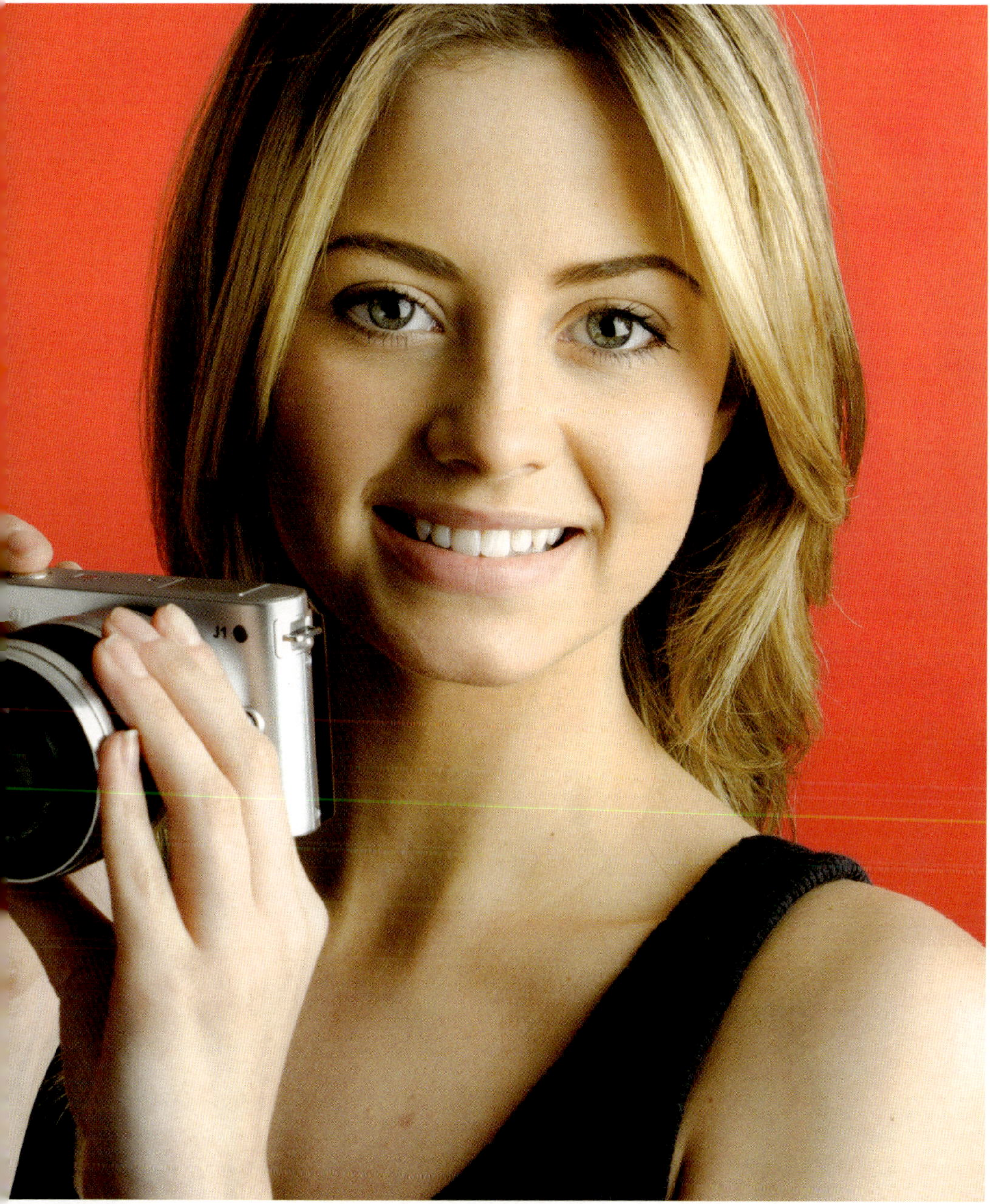
J1

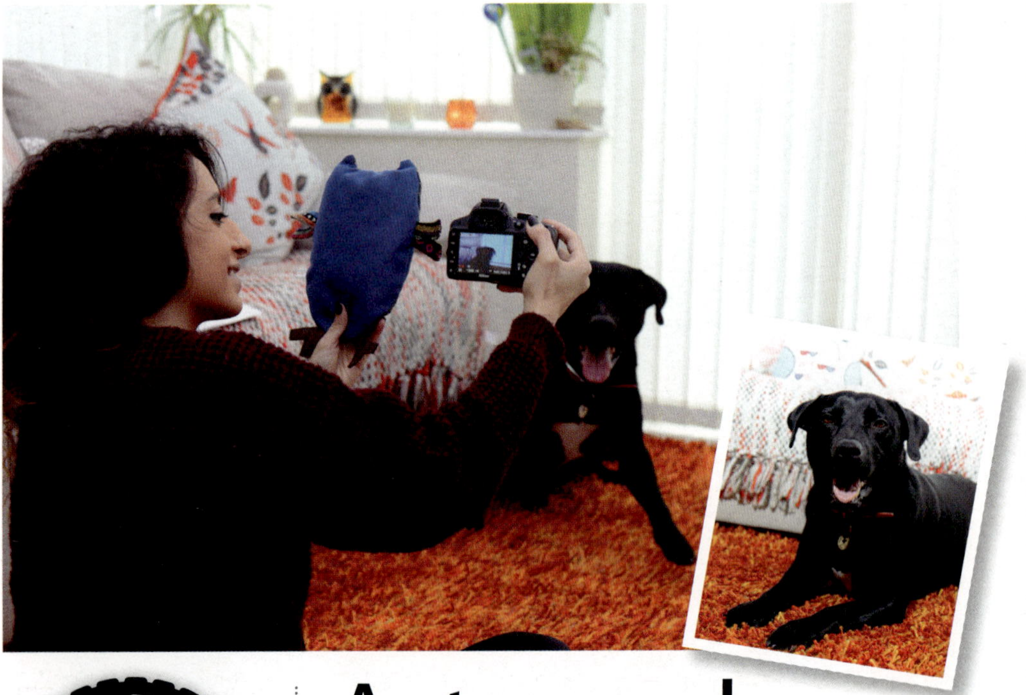

▲ **Go Auto** Switch to Auto mode to capture quick shots on the go without having to master your camera manual

Auto mode

Discover more about your Nikon's beginner-friendly Auto mode

Auto mode is known for being a straightforward, no-fuss point and shoot setting. It's also easy to identify on your Nikon's mode dial and features within almost all of its camera models, only with the exception of professional-level DSLRs. Beginners who are keen to get stuck into their photography can sometimes overlook this powerful setting and head straight for the scene modes or semi-automatic (P, A, S) settings. However, Auto is a great place to start developing your skills, and in fact as a shooting mode it has the capacity to capture some really great images indoors and out.

As a setting, Auto mode is designed to essentially take care of the exposure for you, which means you won't have to learn the ins and outs of how aperture and shutter speed work together right away.

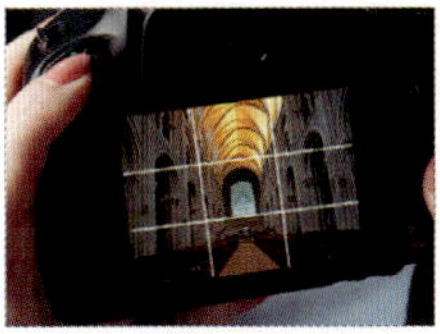

If your Nikon offers Live View select it in Auto and use the on-screen grid to compose better images

It also determines the best focus, white balance and ISO settings for the scene for you. Newer camera models, however, can offer slightly more advanced Auto modes that are able to detect the type of scene you're shooting in order to determine the best settings for the shot. Most also enable you to turn the flash off, which is handy if you're shooting a low-light landscapes, and some even give you the option to select continuous or burst mode so that you can capture a series of action shots quickly.

Although on the surface Auto may seem a little limiting in terms of creative control, there are benefits to letting the camera take care of all the settings for you, as it means you can focus on developing basic skills in other important areas of photography first, such as mastering composition.

Composition is a key element in any great image and being able to recognise what would work well as photograph can take some practise. Use your camera's Auto mode as you advance your skills in this area and turn to page 62 to find out more about composition.

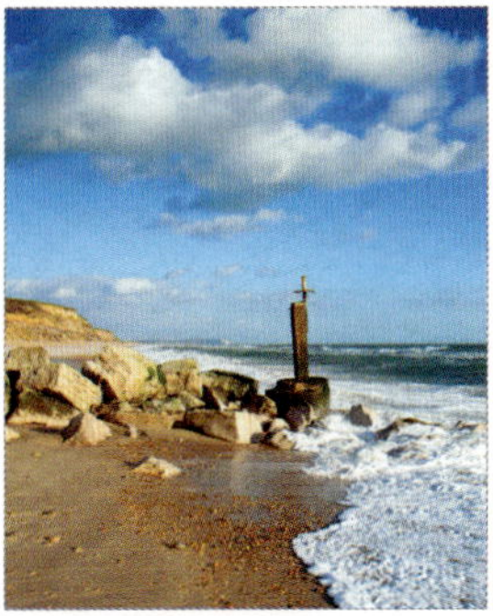

▲ **No-fuss results** Although a simple point and shoot mode, Auto is still capable of capturing great, even exposures without you having to fuss over settings

▼ **Go further** Explore your camera's semi-automatic modes for more creative control over the outcome of your images

◀ **Great results instantly** Auto is great for straightforward shots and particularly useful if you want to simply point and shoot

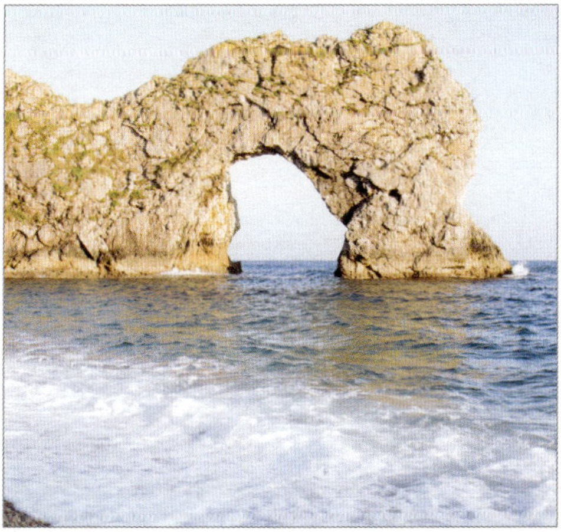

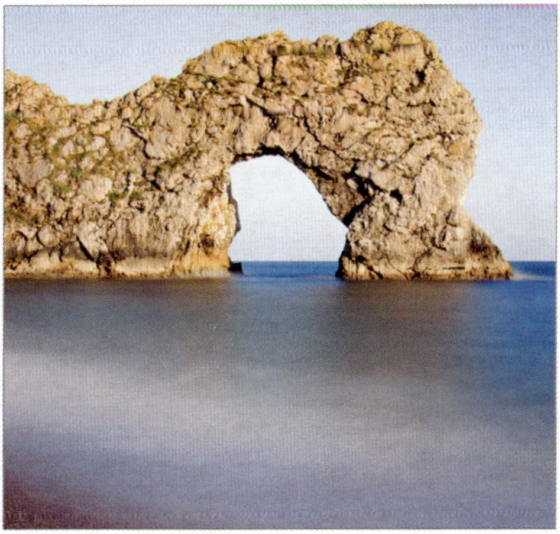

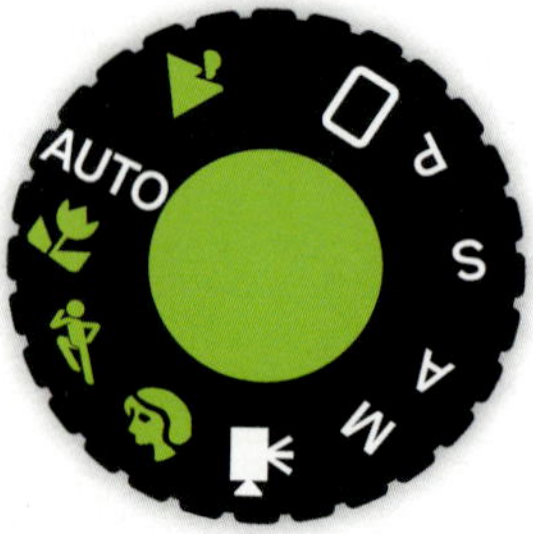

Scene modes

Switch to scene modes and capture impressive images of specific subjects

Scene modes are a lot like your Nikon's Auto mode in that they take care of exposure settings so you can focus solely on framing the shot. Most cameras offer an array of scene modes, with some of the most common being, portrait, landscape, close-up and action.

Unlike your Auto mode, however, scene modes are considered slightly more advanced, and are designed to shoot using the best combination of settings for your chosen subject. For example, by selecting the Portrait scene mode, which is represented by a face icon, the camera will automatically set a wider aperture (large f-number between f2-f5.6) in order to increase depth of field so that the background softly blurs out, making your model the main focus point. Other scene modes make similar adjustments in order to

▼ The right mode for the job Most cameras offer a selection of scene modes to suit almost all photographic subjects

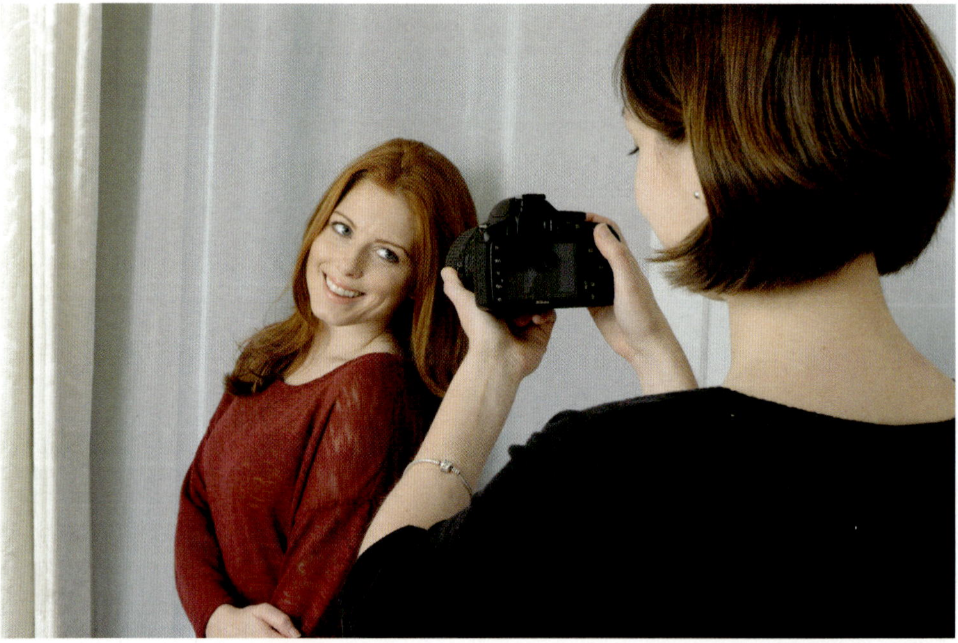

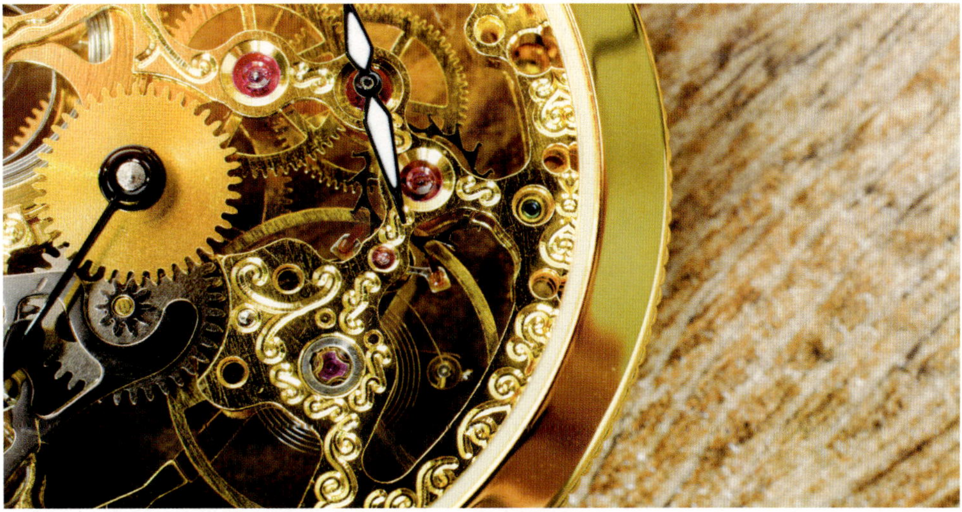

▲ **The best options** Scene modes are fantastic for specific subjects as they select the best settings for the scene

optimise images, including increasing colour vibrancy and contrast for Landscapes and setting faster shutter speeds for capturing action in the Sports mode.

The amount of scene modes you have is dependant on your camera type; however, most cover all of the main photographic genres. Selecting a scene mode is quick and easy; simply rotate the mode dial to the icon that best represents the scene or subject you're shooting. You can even control the use of on-camera flash with most scene modes and can select burst mode for continuous capture. Some even enable you change your white balance setting so you ensure your shots are free from colour casts.

Scene modes are a fantastic starting point for those who want to step up from Auto. However, you may find at times you don't get the exact results you were after, which is a great sign that you're ready to rotate the mode dial round to more advanced settings that can give you much more creative control over your captures.

"Scene modes are designed to shoot using the best combination of settings for your chosen subject"

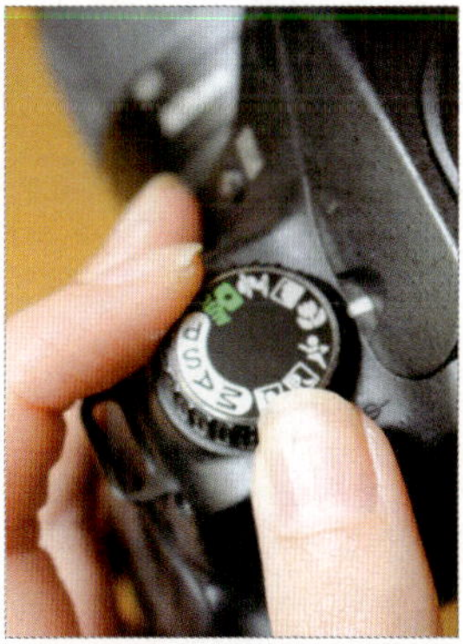

▲ **Pick the scene** Scene modes appear as illustrated icons. Select one that best represents your scene or subject

Portrait mode

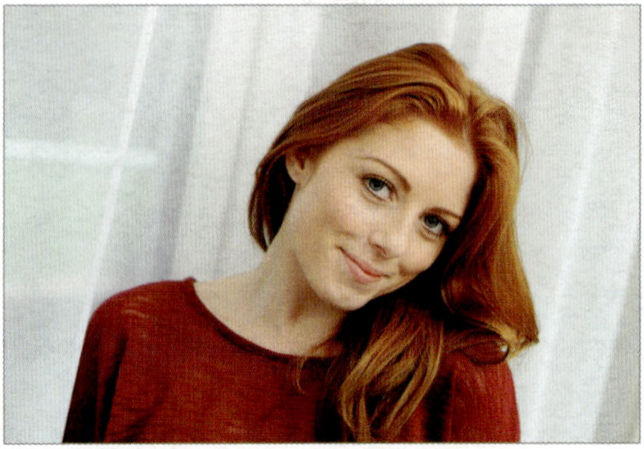

Use the Portrait mode to take picture-perfect shots of yourself, a family member or even a group shot of friends. The Portrait scene mode will automatically set a wider aperture so the background will appear slightly blurred, which is a great way to isolate your subject and ensure they're the focus point. This also means you'll get professional-quality portraits without having to master aperture settings. Some portrait scene modes even automatically enhance the shots for you by smoothing skin.

Landscape mode

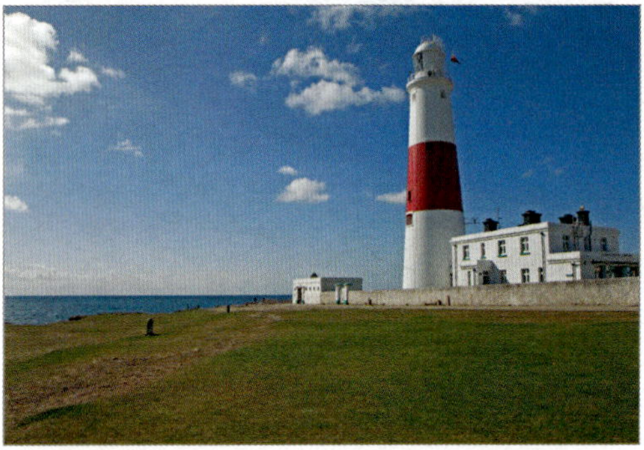

Switch to the Landscape scene mode, represented as mountains, if you want to capture vibrant vistas. Landscape scene mode is designed to enhance contrast and bring out the blue and green colour tones. It will also set a narrow aperture to increase depth of field so that more of your photo appears in focus. Some newer Nikon cameras even offer a dedicated panorama mode, enabling you to shoot a sweeping landscape vista, which the camera then automatically stitches together.

Close-up mode

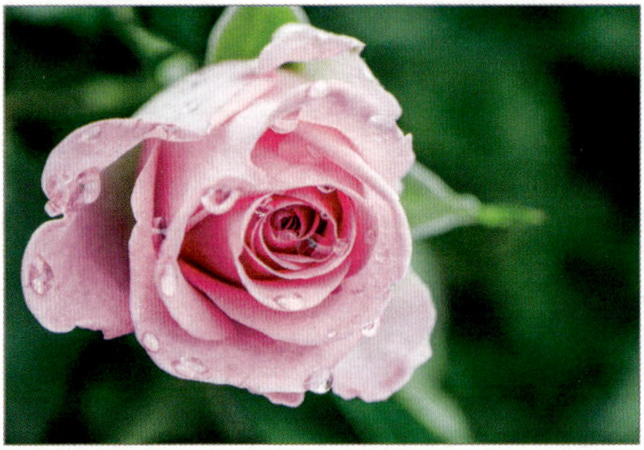

If you want to capture incredible close-ups, select the flower icon. Using this setting, your camera will let you focus much closer to your subject than it would in regular Auto mode, which means you can capture more intricate and abstract details. It's great for photographing flowers, insects, food and many other interesting items. Close-up mode also sets wider apertures (large f-number) to isolate your focus point within the image, which means distracting and busy backgrounds are softly blurred out.

Sport mode

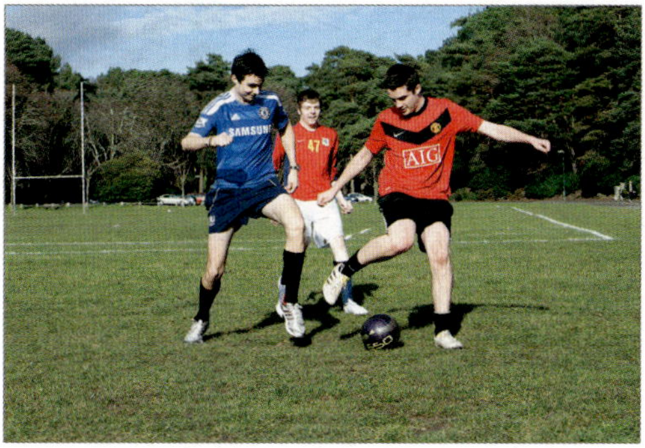

If you're struggling to capture sharp shots of moving subjects, select the Sport scene mode, which appears as a running man icon on the mode dial. In this mode, your camera will prioritise fast shutter speeds, which means you won't miss capturing a moment of the action. For particularly fast-moving subjects, use the Sport mode in conjunction with your camera's burst or continuous drive mode setting so that you can capture multiple shots at speed and then pick the best of the bunch.

Child mode

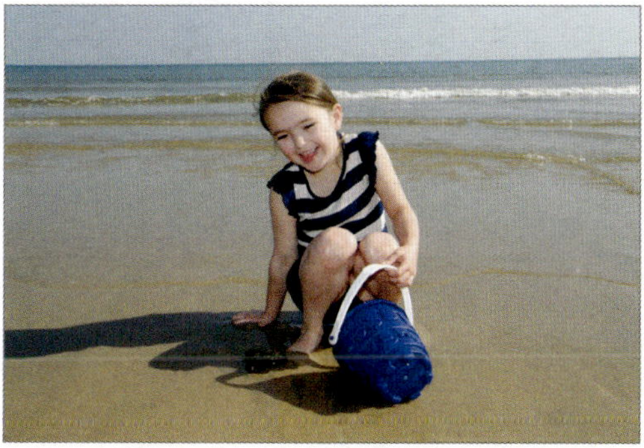

Child scene mode is an extension of the Portrait and Sport modes. It's designed to capture sharper shots of moving subjects, which makes it ideal when photographing kids at play. It automatically sets faster shutter speeds to freeze action but you'll need to be mindful that fast-paced movement, such as children on bikes, can be too quick, which is when you would need to favour Sport mode. Child mode also optimises skin tone, but stick to Portrait mode for sharp stationary close-ups.

Night mode

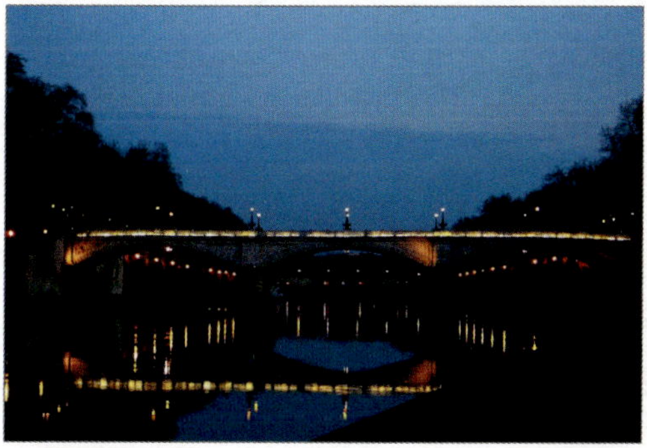

The Night mode is ideal when you're faced with shooting in low-light situations. It automatically selects the best combination of aperture, shutter speed and ISO, in order to increase the camera's sensitivity to light. Some Nikons may even offer two Night modes; one for portraits and another for landscapes. This is due to the camera favouring flash for low-light portraits and slower shutter speeds for landscapes, which is a result of the on-camera flash not being powerful enough to illuminate an entire scene.

Program mode

Take more control over your images using your Nikon's semi-automatic Program mode

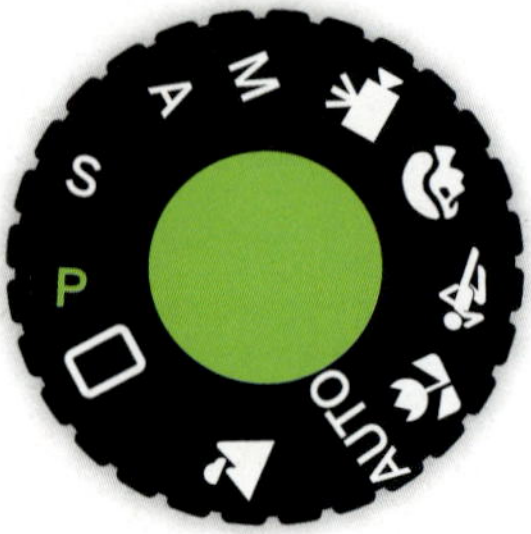

▼ **Get more from your shots** Select Program mode to get a little more creative in-camera using aperture and shutter speeds without ruining your shots

Program mode (P) appears alongside other semi-automatic modes (A, S) and full manual control (M) on the Nikon mode dial. It may seem much more advanced, and to an extent it is, but it's still a straightforward shooting mode, even for beginners. In fact, it's a great starting point for those keen to learn more about their exposure settings without making mistakes and missing a shot.

On the surface Program mode is a lot like your camera's Auto setting as it calculates the best shutter speed and aperture setting. Unlike Auto however, Program can be much more flexible as it also enables you to adjust other settings, which can each have a creative impact on your images, such as metering modes, flash, ISO, white balance, focusing modes and even exposure compensation. Each

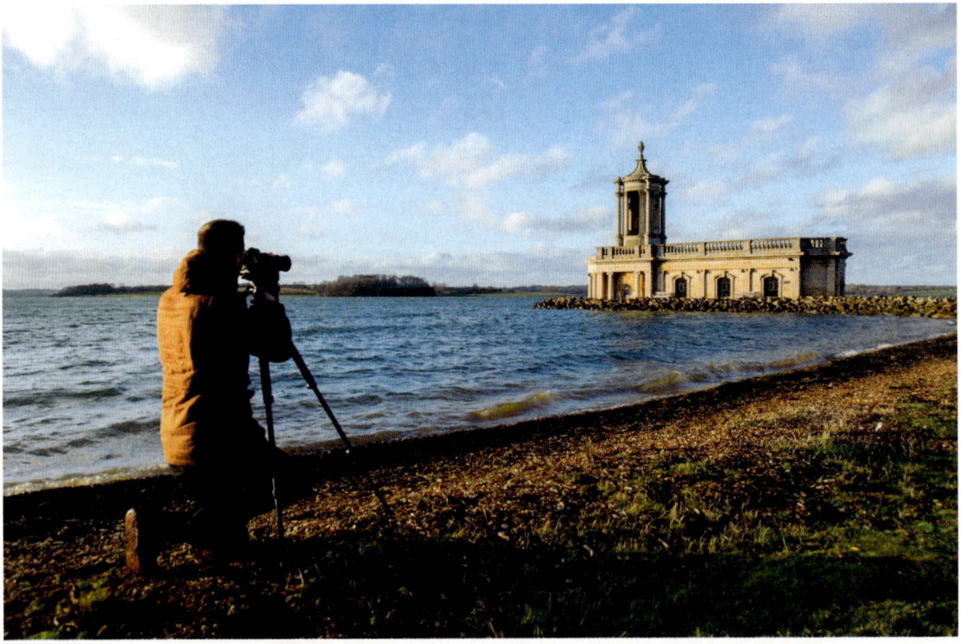

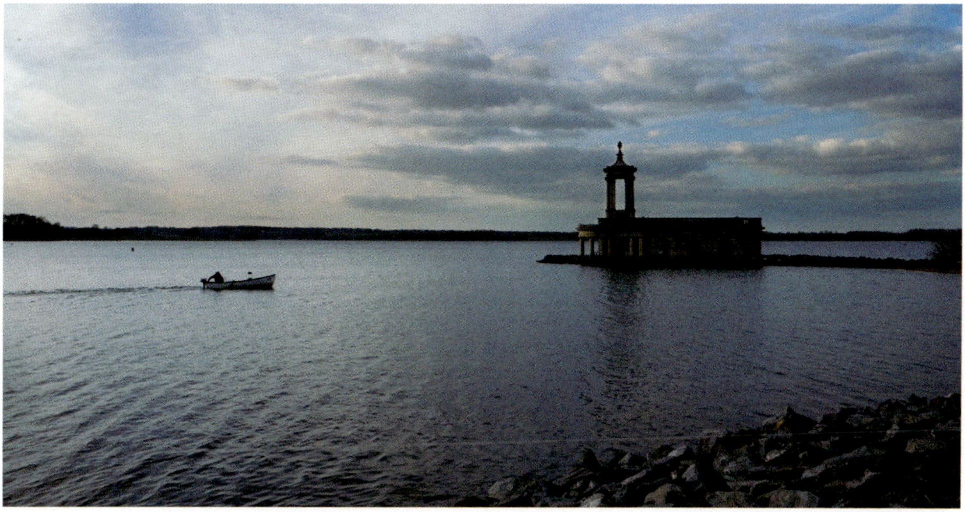

of theses can affect the combination of aperture and shutter speed your camera decides to select, which means you're able to take much more control over the outcome of your images.

You can take things a step further too, as Program mode enables you to shift and override the combination of settings that the camera chooses. This means that if the camera has decided to set a narrow aperture for example, but you would like to shoot with a wider aperture, you can adjust the aperture and the shutter speed will automatically align itself with your chosen setting. This works in the same way with shutter speed.

Program mode is a safe setting to learn more about the relationship between shutter speeds and aperture, as you'll be able to see exactly what combinations the camera favours when adjusting one setting over the other. This is a great guideline for when you're ready to start experimenting in the more advanced modes later on.

"Program mode is a safe setting to learn more about the relationships between shutter speeds and aperture"

▲ **Flawless exposure** Program mode is a safe setting to learn about exposure as it will select the best exposure settings based on the scene and camera lens you're using

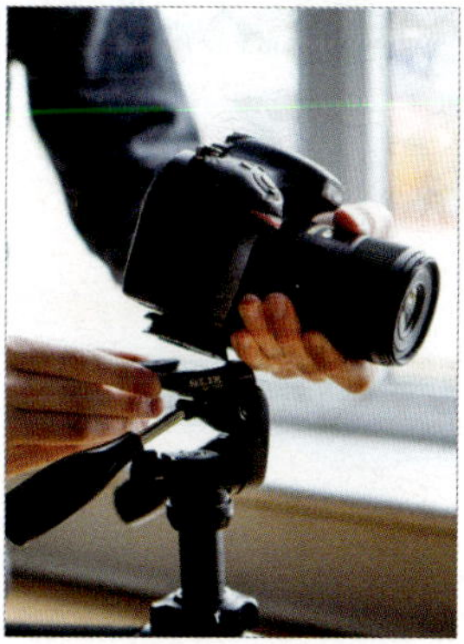

▲ **Keep a tripod to hand** Program mode will always assume you're shooting handheld; if your camera selects a shutter speed slower than 1/80sec use a tripod or adjust the shutter speed so that the camera will amend the aperture

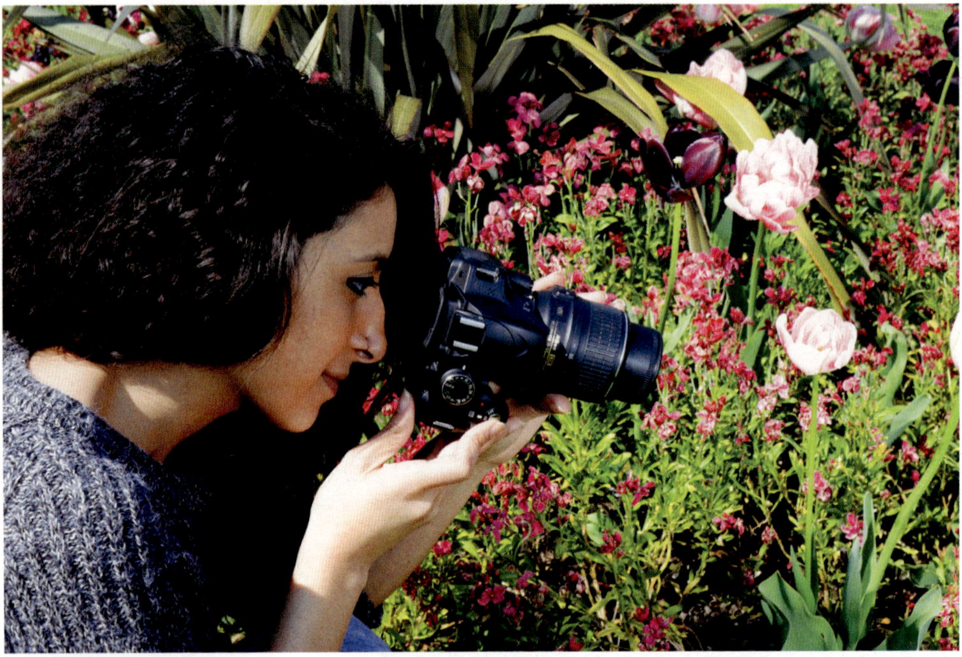

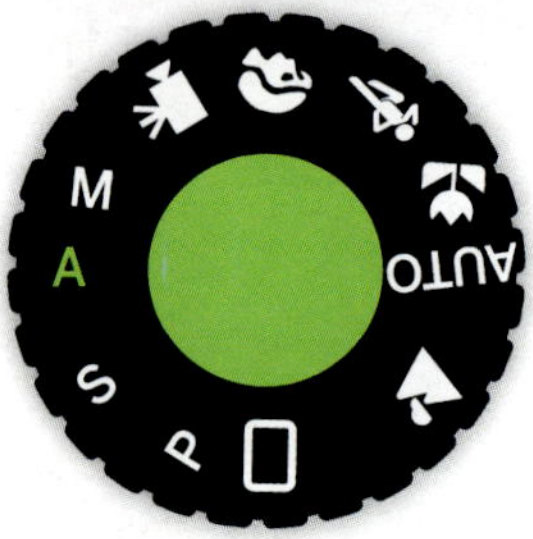

Aperture Priority mode

Take control of exposure and discover more about depth of field with Aperture Priority mode

▲ **Concentrate on one thing** Aperture Priority enables you to select your desired aperture settings whilst the camera controls shutter speed

▶ **Soft and bright** Aperture Priority mode is great if you're shooting subjects up close, portraits or in low-light conditions as it softens the background and brightens the exposure

Control the creative outcome of your images by selecting the Aperture Priority mode, represented by an A symbol. Aperture Priority is a semi-automatic mode as it enables you to set your own aperture setting whilst the camera determines the best shutter speed based on your selection and the scene you're shooting. It's ideal if you're keen to experiment with depth of field and is commonly used for portraits, macro, still life and low-light shots.

To get a shallow depth of field, which essentially blurs the background of your image, you can select a wide aperture setting

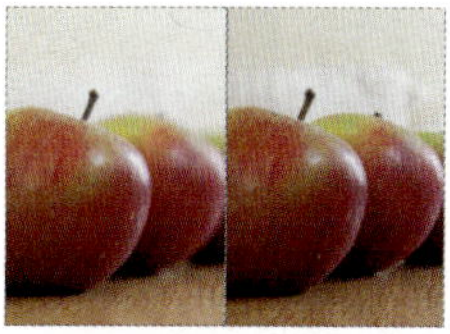

Use wide apertures for shallow depth of field, and narrow apertures to increase depth of field

(f1.4-f5.6). Provided you focus your camera on the subject in the foreground correctly, they should appear sharp while the rest of the image blurs out. Wide apertures make the opening inside the lens much larger which means more light is let in; the camera will counter this by selecting a faster shutter so that your image won't be overexposed. Selecting a narrow aperture, however (f8-22) increases depth of field, which means more of the image will appear sharp and in focus. This is why narrow apertures are selected for landscape photography. Of course, narrow apertures shrink the size of the opening inside the lens so less light is let in. To avoid underexposing images the camera will set a slower shutter speed. You'll need to be particularly mindful of this if you're shooting indoors or when light is low, as a slower shutter speed will make your shots more susceptible to camera shake or blur.

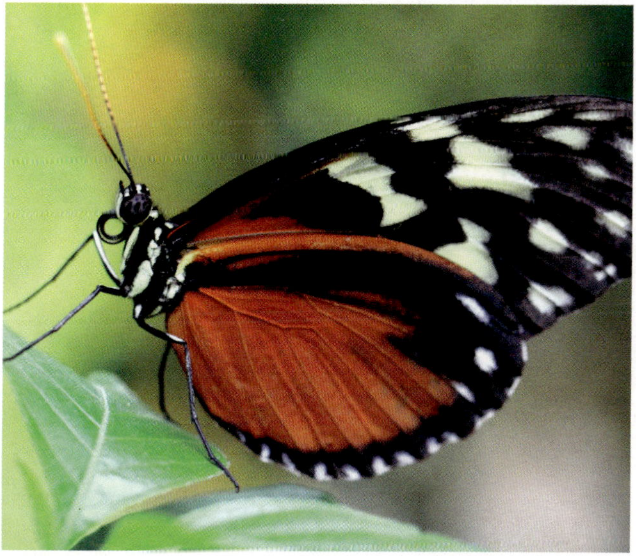

Take stunning portraits

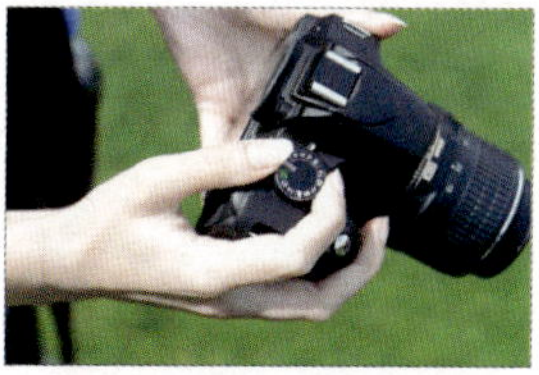

1 Select Aperture Priority Set the mode dial to A and using the scroll wheel, set aperture to f4 for background blur.

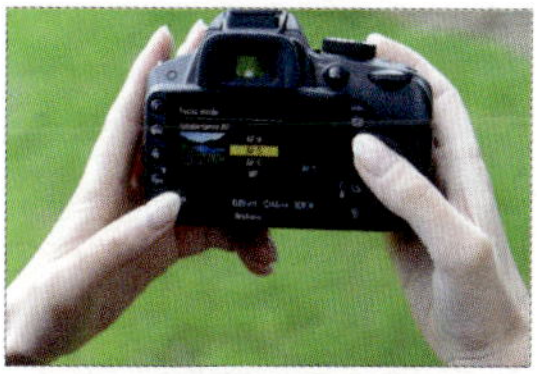

2 Set your focus mode Stick to autofocus and select the Single-Servo AF mode. Position the focus point over the face.

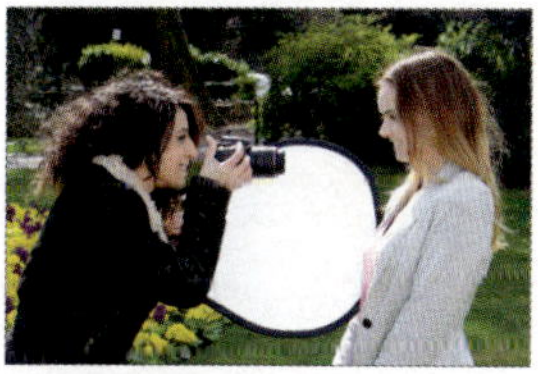

3 Frame and shoot Compose your image and half depress the shutter button to focus. Use a reflector to bounce light.

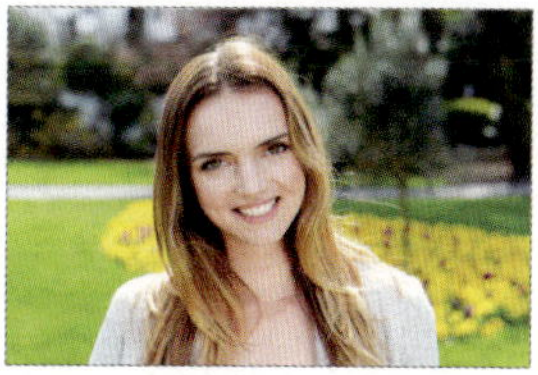

4 Picture-perfect portraits The wide aperture ensures the model's face appears sharp, with a blurred background.

Shutter Priority mode

Learn how Shutter Priority mode can control movement in your shots for better effects

Shutter Priority mode gives you the control your Auto and Sport scene mode can't. It follows the same principle as Aperture Priority and is marked as an S on the mode dial. Select Shutter Priority mode in order to control how fast or slow your shutter opens and closes. Your camera will then calculate the best aperture setting based on your selection.

Shutter Priority gives you freedom to capture more noticeably creative images in camera and is most commonly used when photographing fast-moving subjects or scenes that require long

▶ **Experimental shots** Position your camera on a tripod and experiment with slow shutter speed settings for stunning effects in camera

▼ **Sharp shooter** Switch to Shutter Priority mode for more creative shots of movement or sharper shots of action

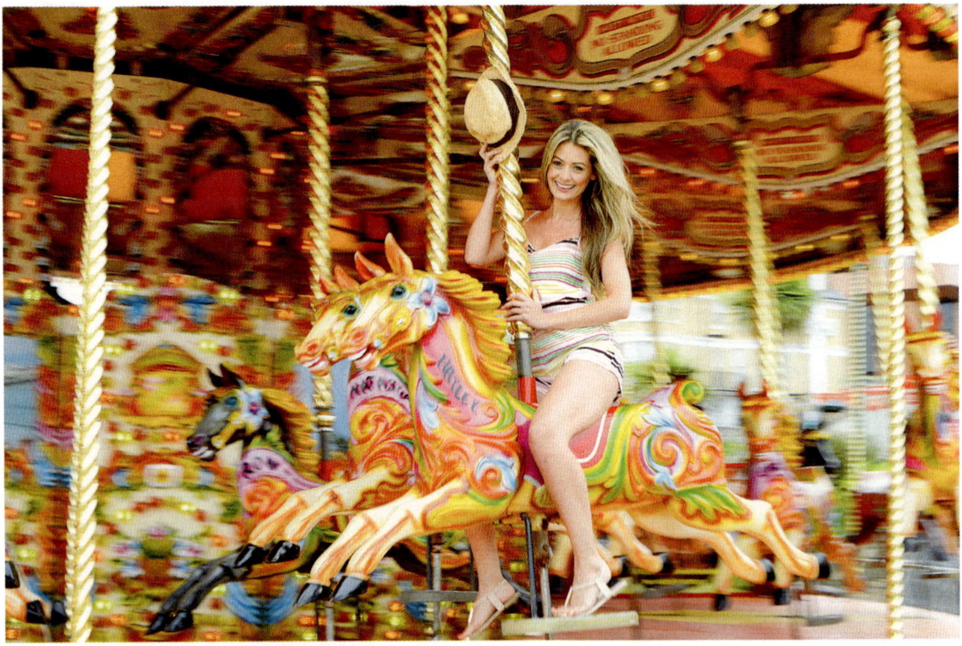

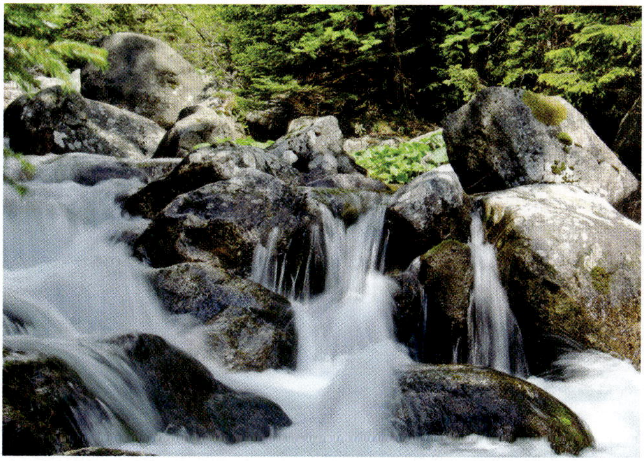

exposures. Inputting faster shutter speeds (1/250 and above) is great for capturing high-energy action shots of sport, and because you're able to determine the exact speed of your shutter in this mode, you can also shoot sharp images of children at play, pets and wildlife.

Slower shutter speeds are used for capturing creative long exposure effects. Bear in mind, however, that steadying your camera on a tripod is essential if you're shooting with shutter speeds slower than 1/80sec handheld, otherwise your images will noticeably suffer from camera shake. Use long exposures to photograph stationary subjects in low light such as indoor still life or landscapes at sunrise or sunset. You can even use slow shutter speeds to create a sense of motion in your shots. This is ideal for blurring moving water in a seascape or waterfall image. Panning is another great long-exposure technique that enables you to incorporate motion into your shots. With the right settings, you'll be able to ensure your subject appears sharp in motion whilst the slow shutter blurs the background; we'll show you how in our step by step.

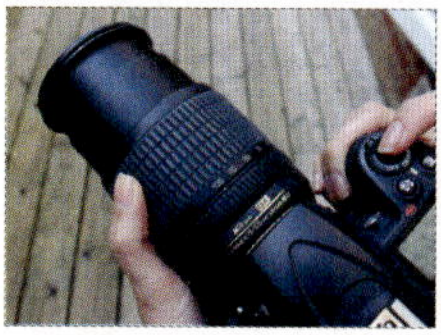

Set your shutter speed to a value that matches your focal length to avoid camera shake

Master panning

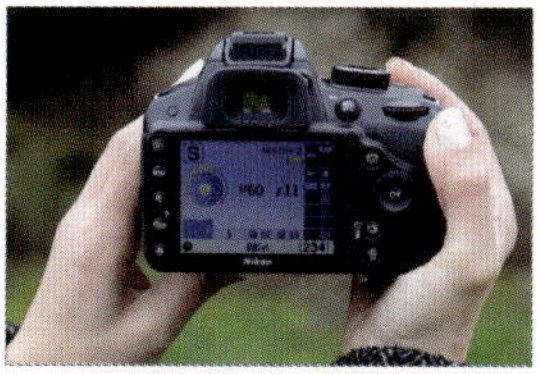

1 Select Shutter Priority Pick the S on the mode dial and set a slow shutter speed of around 1/60sec or slower.

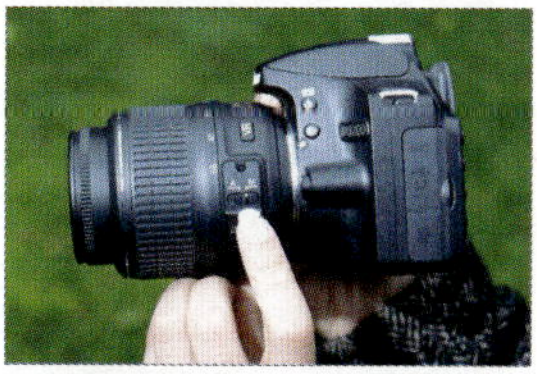

2 Set your focus Focus on a point that is roughly the same distance away as your moving subject and switch to manual.

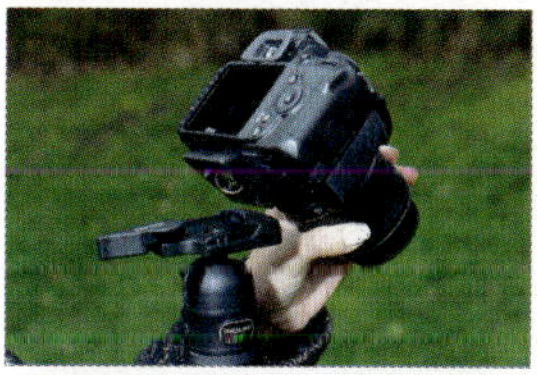

3 Steady your camera Use a monopod for support. When your subject comes into view, press the shutter button.

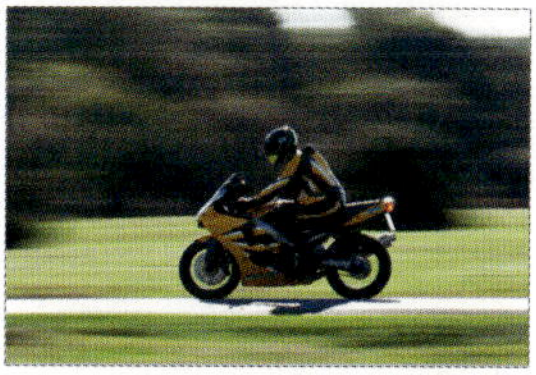

4 Impressive panning shots By moving the camera whilst the shutter is open, you can capture a shot that shows speed.

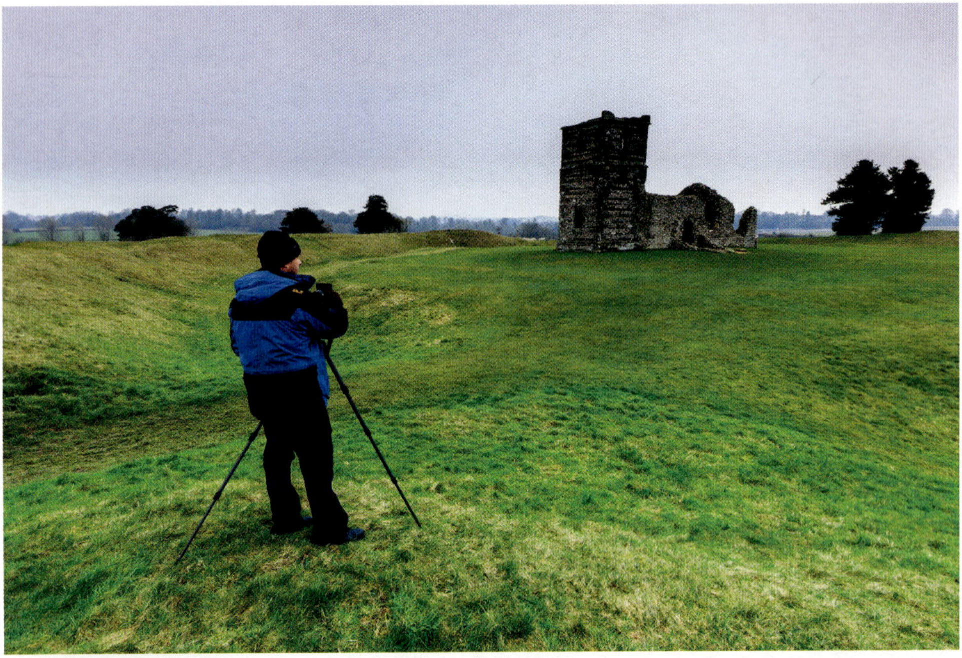

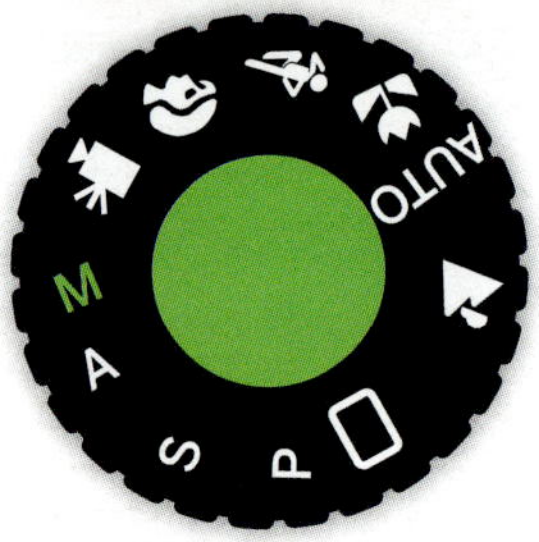

Manual mode

Discover how Manual mode gives you complete creative control over your exposures

▲ **Exposure control** Switch to M on your mode dial and select your own exposure settings for the shot

▶ **Total freedom** Manual mode gives you complete control, which means you can use it to photograph any subject or scene

Of all the modes available, Manual mode (M) is by far the most advanced. This setting quite simply, gives you complete control over your exposures, which means you can adjust settings such as white balance, metering and focusing alongside your ISO, shutter speed and aperture. Unlike Aperture and Shutter Priority mode, where the camera helps to balance an exposure based on the setting you've selected, in Manual the stabilisers are off and all the decisions regarding exposure are up to you.

Manual is a great mode for experimenting but avoid rushing into using this setting if you simply want to grab a quick shot. To get great results in Manual mode, you need to have a clear understanding of how exposure works, which is something you can

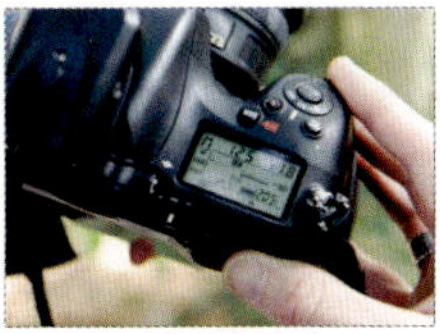

Adjust the shutter speed by rotating the scroll wheel and the aperture via the front wheel

start to pick up on using the more supportive Program, Aperture and Shutter Priority modes first. When using these semi-automatic settings, pay attention to how the camera assists your exposure and apply similar principles when you're ready to explore full Manual mode. Although mastering Manual mode can be a trial and error process, taking some time to really experiment with it, even as a beginner, is definitely worthwhile.

With plenty of practise however, you'll soon start to feel confident in Manual mode, which is when it's really worth experimenting with different combinations of aperture and shutter speed. Help is at hand too, as all cameras come with a light meter, which you can preview inside the viewfinder or on your LCD screen when using Live View to shoot. The light meter will give you a good indication as to whether your image will be under- or overexposed based on the settings you've selected. The marker should appear central at 0 for an evenly exposed image; if it sits to the right your image may be underexposed or overexposed if it's to the left.

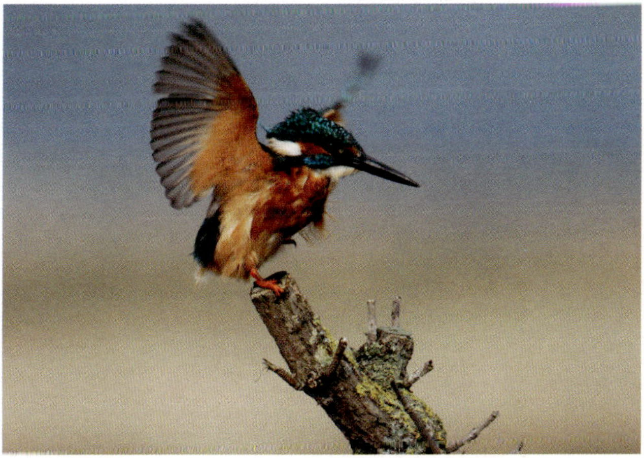

Shoot stunning sunsets

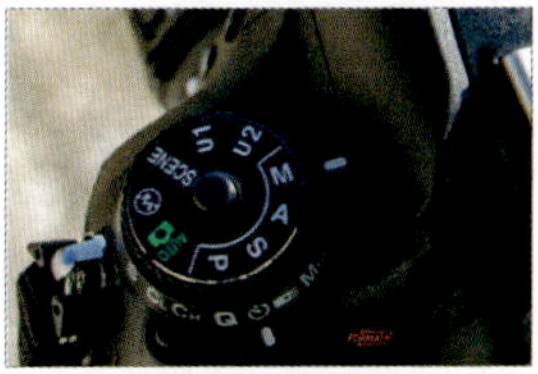

1 Switch to Manual mode Rotate to M and select self-timer or remote shutter release to reduce camera shake.

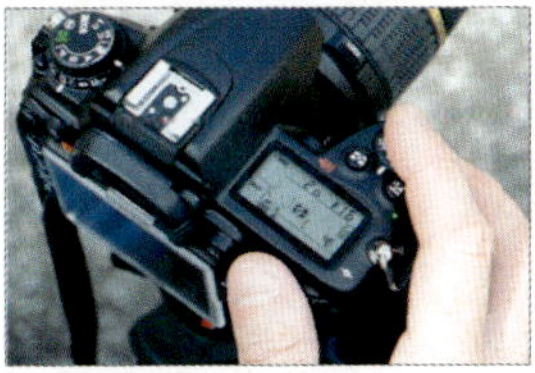

2 Adjust your settings Set a narrow aperture for a sharp result and a slow shutter speed to avoid an underexposed shot.

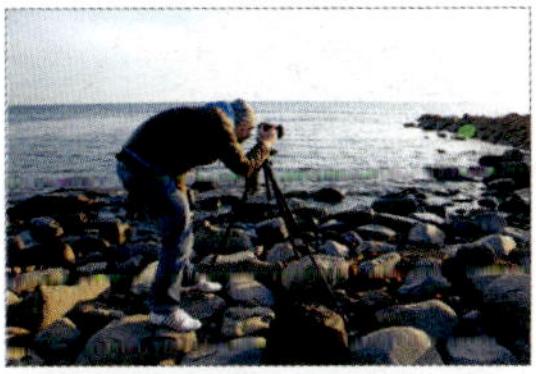

3 Compose the scene Use Live View and focus a third of the way into the frame. Release the shutter to activate the timer.

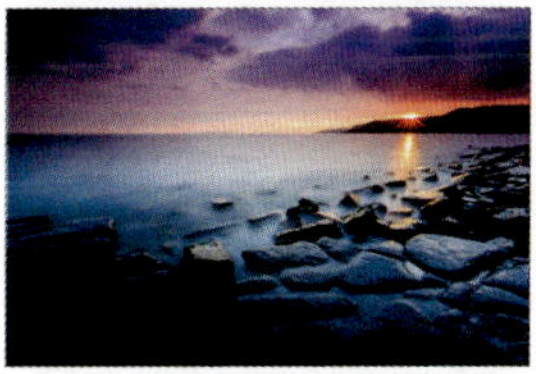

4 The result The slow shutter speed caught the moving water as mist and the narrow aperture means it is all sharp.

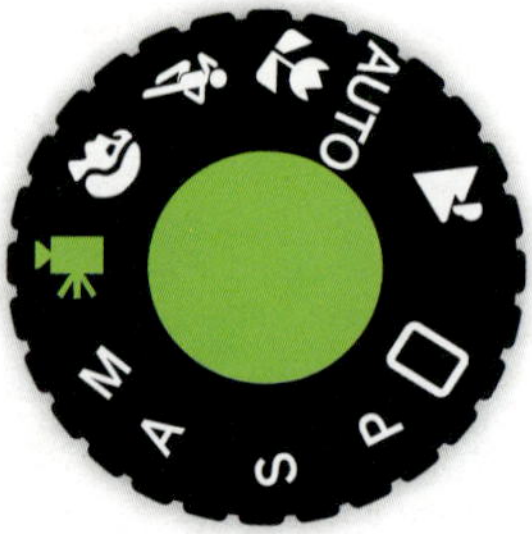

Video mode

Capture high-quality video with your camera using Nikon's dedicated Video mode

Nikon was the first camera manufacturer to introduce video recording into DSLRs with the launch of its D90 model. Due to its success, Video mode is now considered a staple feature in most cameras, including compacts. Being able to access stills and video capture in one camera means it's even easier to record precious family moments on the go.

If your Nikon camera offers Video mode, it may appear on the mode dial as a video camera icon or could be accessed via a switch that turns the camera from still to video on the back of the camera. On some models you may even have to select it via the menu interface. Check your Nikon manual to see if Video mode is available on your camera.

▶ **Pick and choose** Most Nikon cameras combine still capture with video these days, so you can seamlessly switch between shooting either format

▼ **Still from moving** You can grab high-quality stills from HD video footage, which is great if you want a single photographic frame of the action

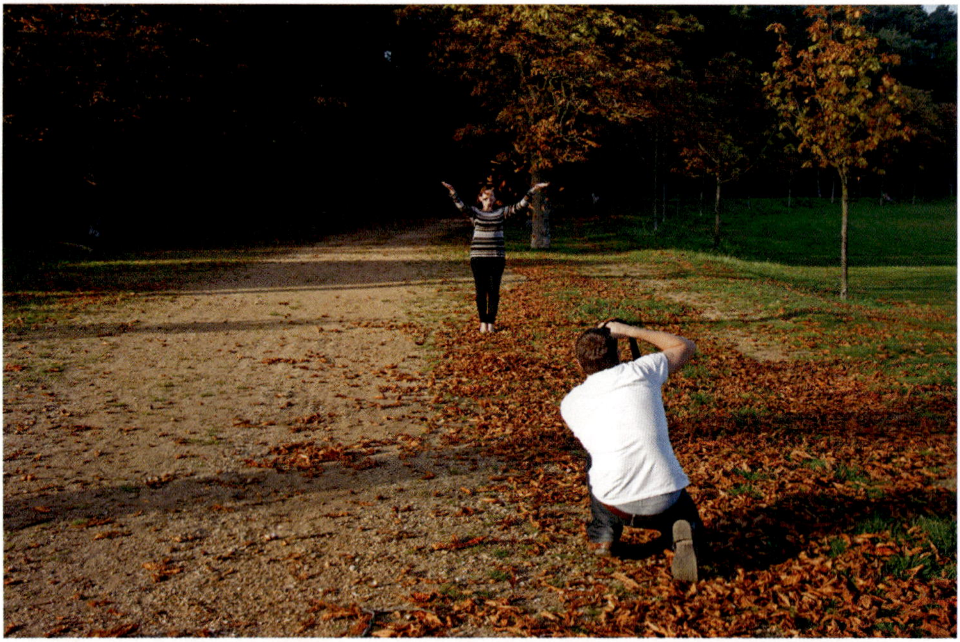

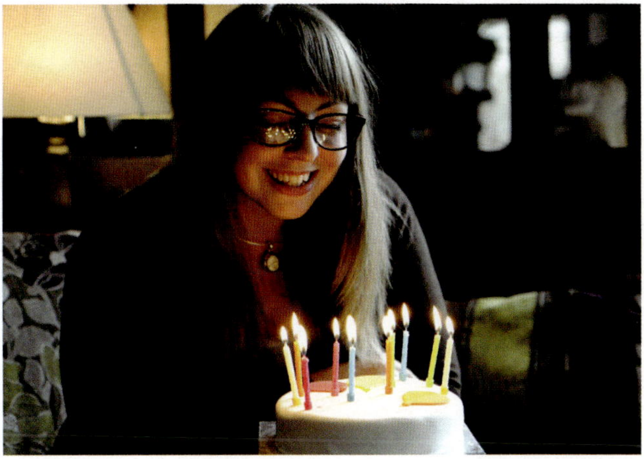

Once you've selected Video mode, switch to Live View in order to compose and record footage easily on the camera's back LCD screen. You'll also need to select the movie quality and frame size prior to recording, which is accessible via the main menu interface. Almost all Nikon cameras offer HD video recording at either 720p or full 1080p, alongside smaller frame sizes, which can be useful if you want to upload video online without having to edit it first.

All Nikon cameras that offer Video mode come with built-in microphones but you can purchase an external mic for some Nikon models that enables you to record better quality sound. Alternatively, switch sound off altogether and shoot a silent movie.

As you're recording you can also take full control over your camera settings, which is great if you want to adjust depth of field using aperture or introduce creative colour casts with white balance. You can also choose to focus manually or use select autofocus modes, which include a tracking feature that ensures moving subjects remain sharp in your video.

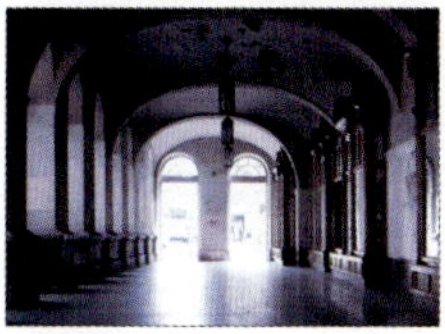

Experiment with your white balance setting if you want to illustrate a mood in your movies

Activate Video mode

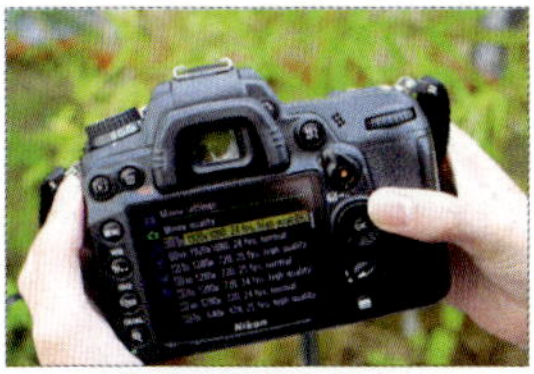

1 Select your frame size Select the Movie Settings menu and click on Movie Quality. Set the size of your video to 1080p.

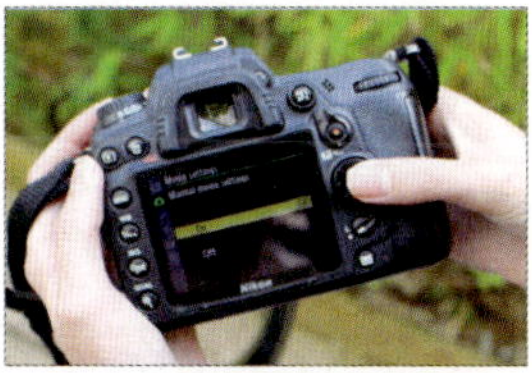

2 Input your settings Within the Movie Settings menu, turn on the Manual movie settings icon, for more creative movie effects.

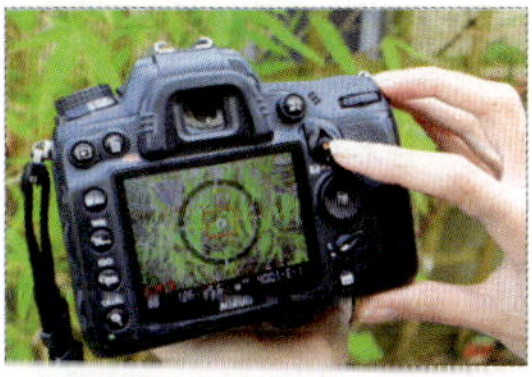

3 Turn on Live View Input your white balance and aperture settings and select Live View before you begin recording.

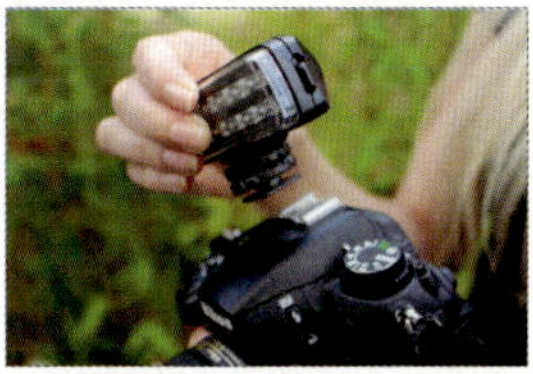

4 Add light If light is a little low, attach an LED light source to ensure footage is bright. Press record and press it again to stop.

Composing your shots

Anyone can take an okay shot, but to take a really great shot you need to master the skills of composition

Composition is one of most basic yet important skills for creating images, and is used by artists and photographers alike. It describes what is included within the frame and where it is positioned, with the aim of creating the most engaging and visually pleasing image possible. How you compose a photo can have a big impact on how it is interpreted, so it is one of the first things you should learn about in photography. In this guide we will take you through some simple tips for creating stunning images every time, no matter which Nikon you own.

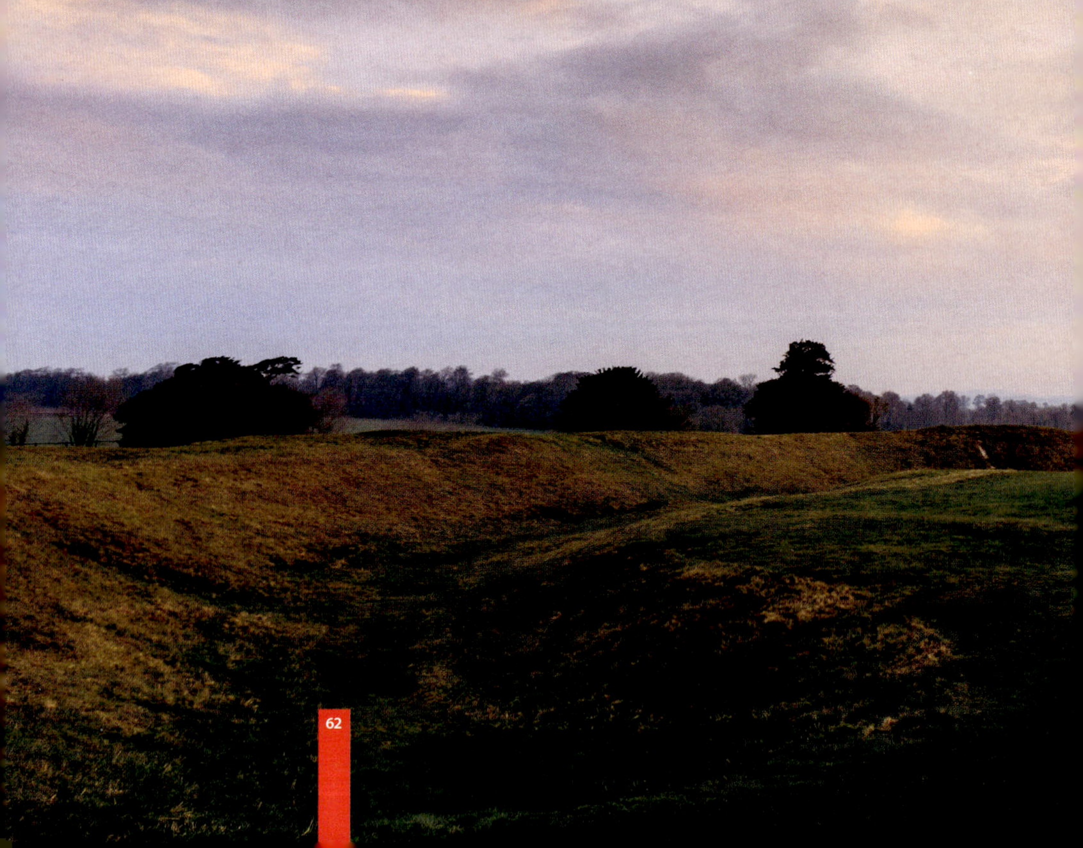

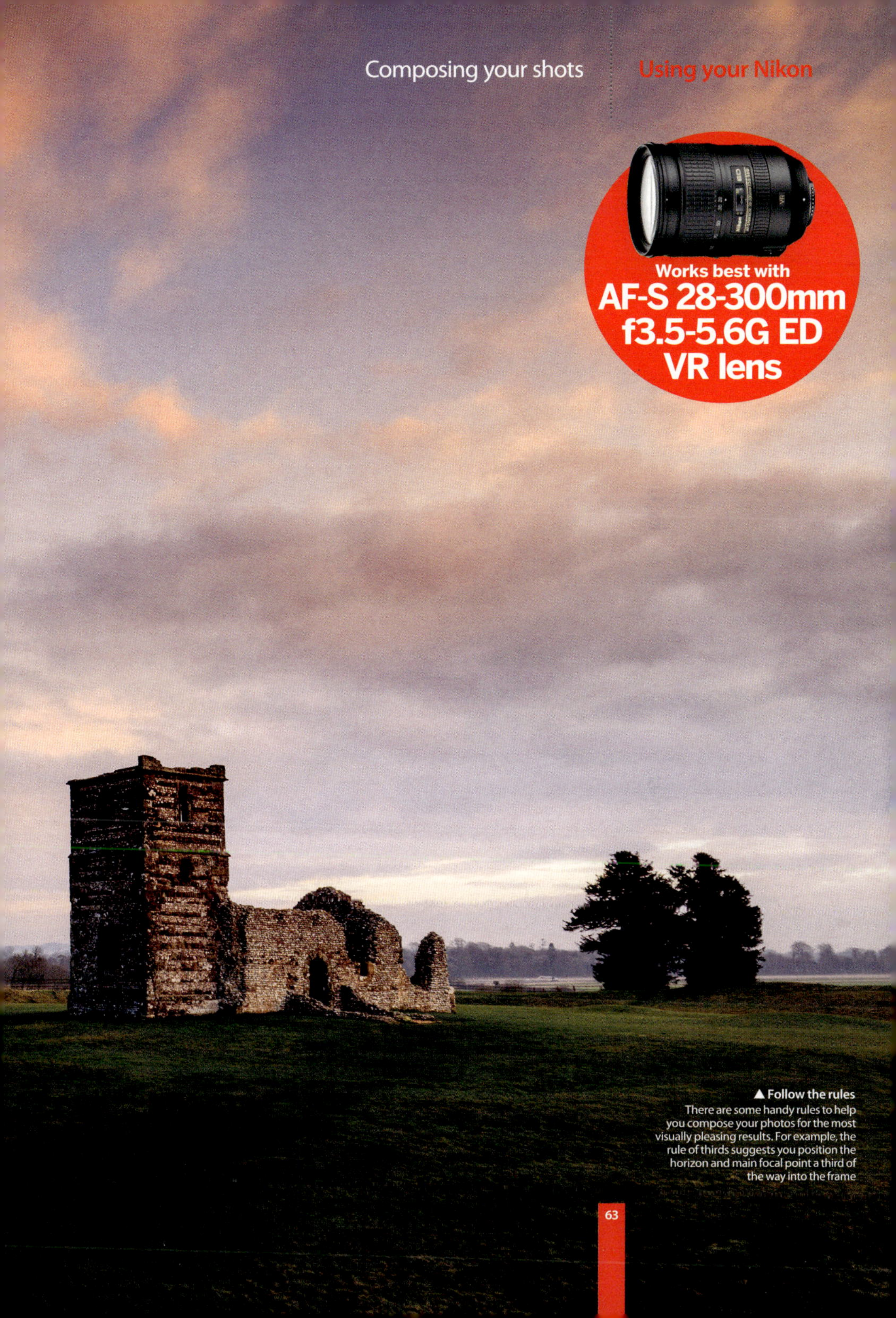

Works best with
AF-S 28-300mm f3.5-5.6G ED VR lens

▲ Follow the rules
There are some handy rules to help you compose your photos for the most visually pleasing results. For example, the rule of thirds suggests you position the horizon and main focal point a third of the way into the frame

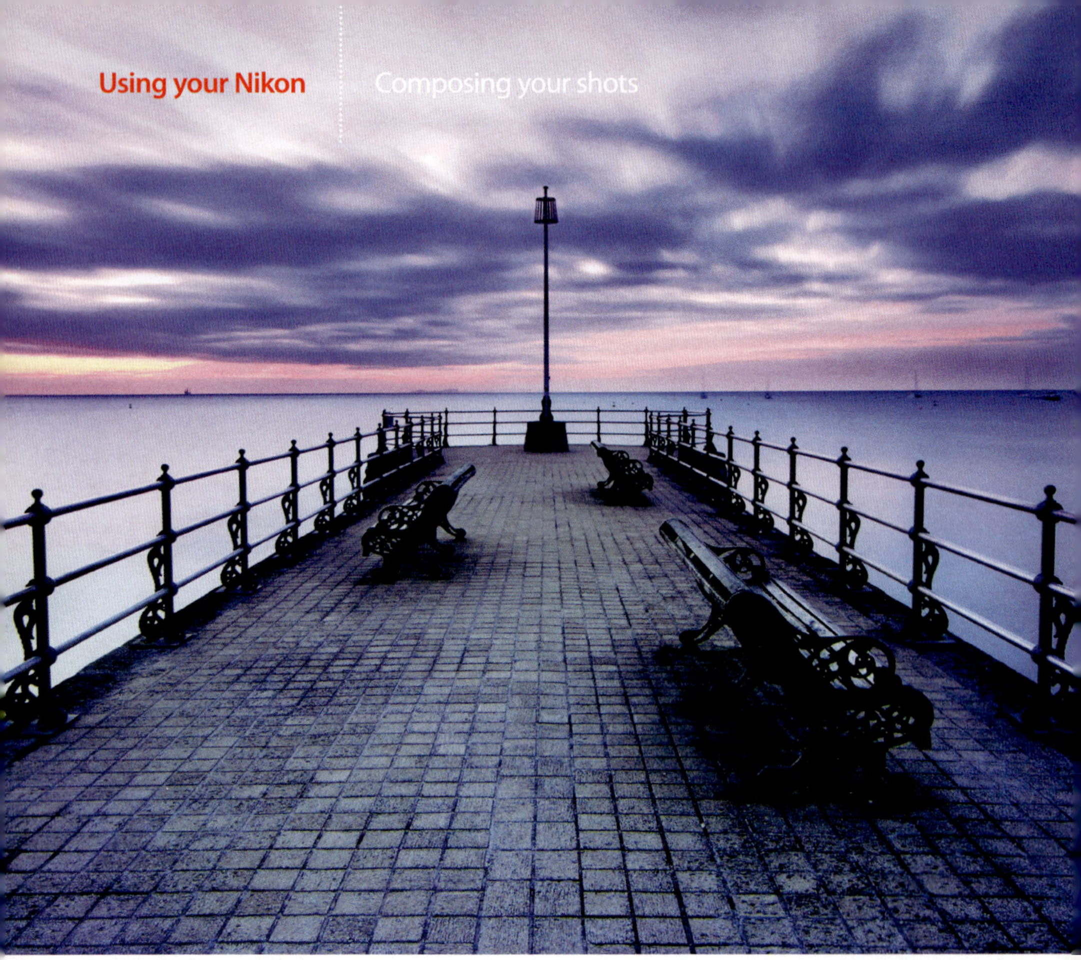

▲ Lead the eye
Including natural lines in your photos helps to guide the viewer through the shot. Look out for fences, paths and rivers that will direct your viewer's gaze, but make sure that they don't lead them out of the frame

When taking a photo of any scene, it can be tempting to simply point and click so you can move on to the next shot. However, taking your time over an image will allow you to consider more carefully the best way to capture it and how you want others to interpret it. By putting more thought into how you compose your shot, you can convey the message you want and create an image that is more appealing to the eye.

There is no definitive rule for what makes a great photo, however, there are a few tried and tested techniques that will give you a good starting point when composing your photos. The most basic thing to remember is to keep it simple, as an overly-cluttered photo will leave the viewer not knowing where to look first. Ideally, you want to guide their eye through the photo so that they can explore the entire scene in a logical order. One of the best ways to

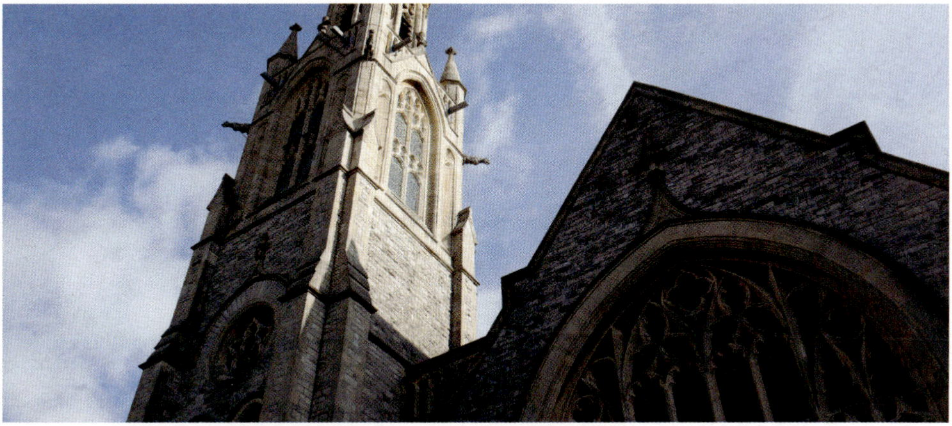

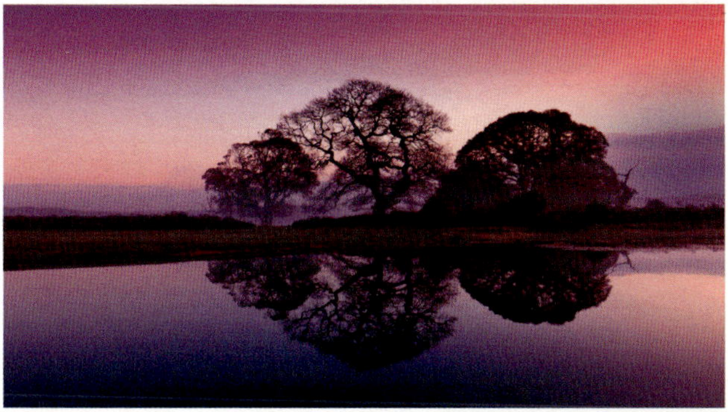

▲ Experiment with angles
Once you've taken a shot, try taking it again from a different angle to get a new perspective. Low angles work well for shooting tall buildings as they will make the structure look even more dramatic and imposing

◀ Look for symmetry
Symmetrical subjects are pleasing to the eye so make for great photos. Reflections are great for creating symmetry and also allow you to break the rules of thirds, as it's best to position the horizon through the middle of the frame

▼ Leave some space
With moving subjects, leave active space in front of them to show where they are going. Otherwise you will lead your viewer out of the frame

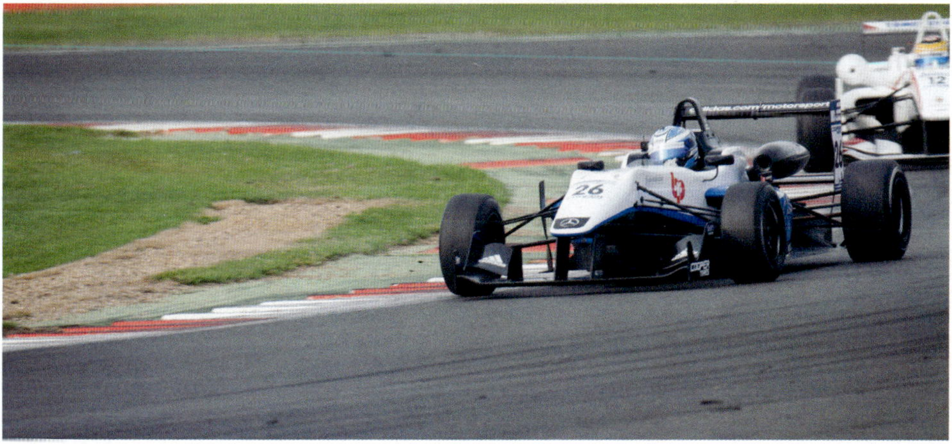

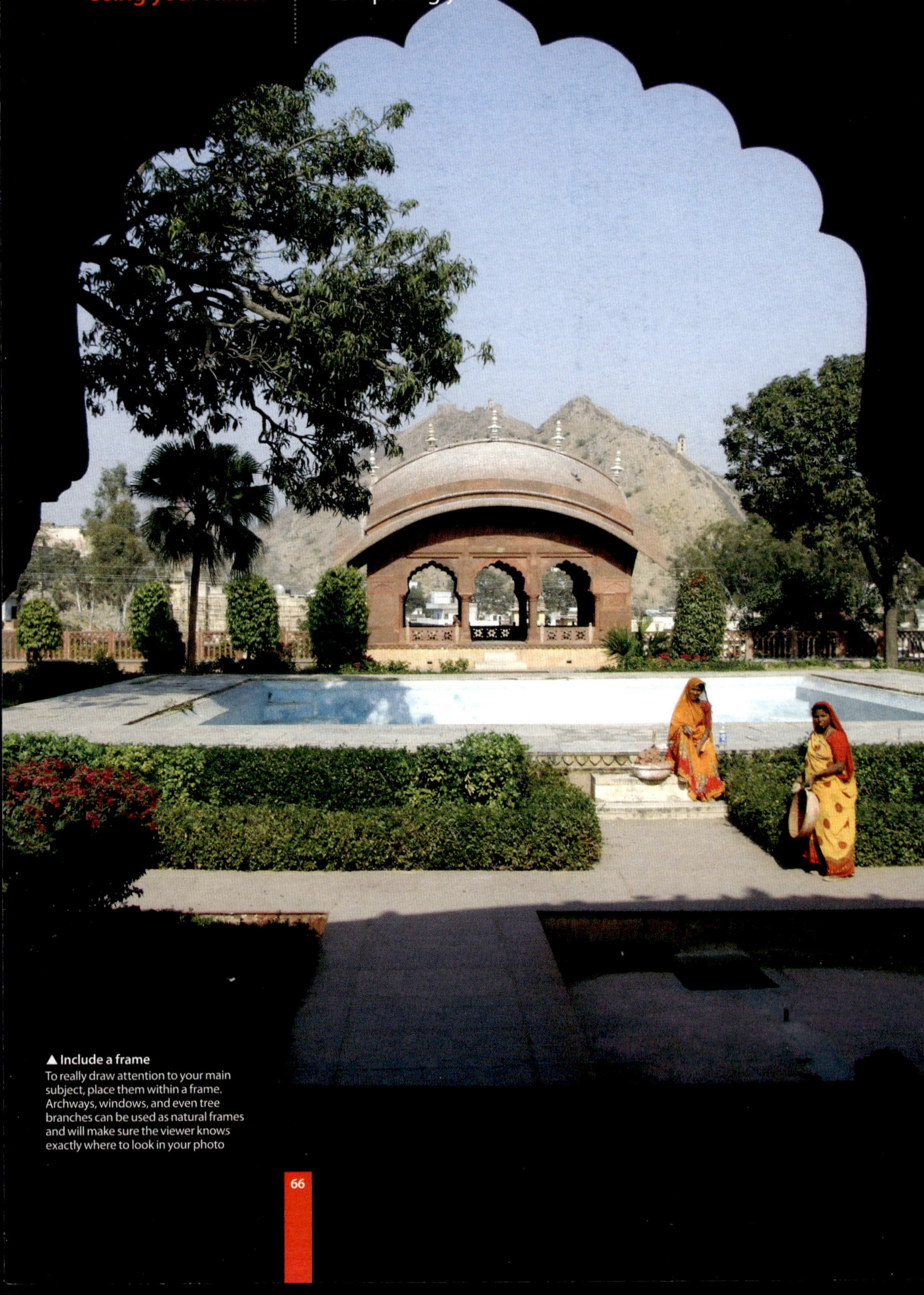

▲ Include a frame
To really draw attention to your main subject, place them within a frame. Archways, windows, and even tree branches can be used as natural frames and will make sure the viewer knows exactly where to look in your photo

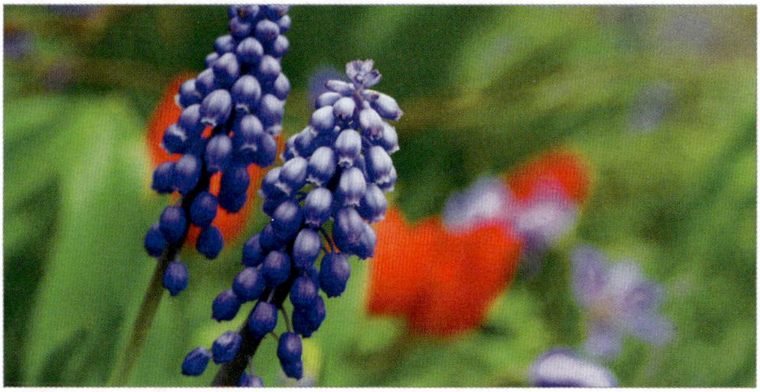

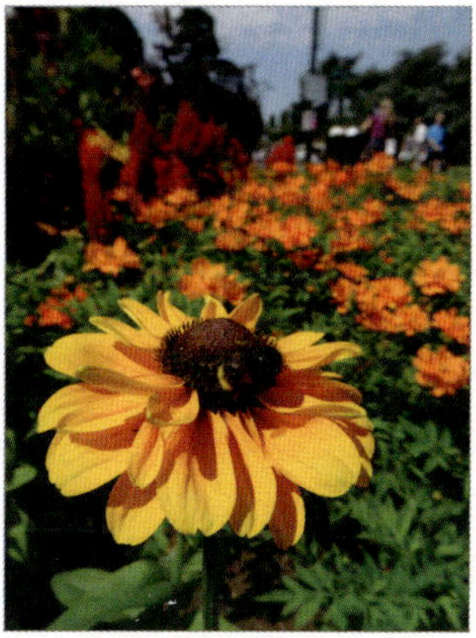

▲ **Compose with colour**
Bright colours will add impact to your shots and grab people's attention. To prevent a cluttered photo, try to include no more than three different colour tones in the frame and make sure that all the colours complement each other

do this is with the 'rule of thirds'. This is a technique typically used by painters, but it works for digital photography, too. It involves dividing the scene into a grid with nine equal parts and then positioning the main focal point along one of the lines or intersecting points. The idea is that the image will be more engaging if the main subject is positioned off-centre rather than in the middle of the frame, as this is where the viewer is likely to look first. You could simply imagine a grid over the scene, or see if your camera has a gridline display that you can use instead.

Another great way to guide your viewer through your photo is with lines. This could be a line of trees, a pathway or fence, or even a river or road. Position the line so that it leads towards your main subject rather than out of the frame, as this will keep the viewer engaged with the image. The same can be said for moving subjects or ones that are looking at something; you should have them facing into the shot with some space in front of them so as not to lead the viewer out of the frame.

Of course, all of these 'rules' of composition can be broken if you think a different approach will work better for a particular image. For example, you could choose to centre your main subject to give your shot some symmetry, or get your portrait subject to look away from the lens for a more candid feel to the photo.

"The image will be more engaging if the main subject is positioned off-centre rather than in the middle of the frame"

Choose your focal length

Focal length can have a big effect on the look of your photos. A short focal length will allow you to fit more into your photos, creating a sense that you could simply step into the scene. However, this can also cause your images to appear distorted, as short focal lengths tend to exaggerate that which is closest to the lens, and stretch the rest off into the distance. Zoom in to bring everything closer together and create a more natural-looking image.

Focusing your Nikon

Learn how to keep your shots pin-sharp with the right focus mode, focusing tricks and some clever ways to avoid camera shake

Editing software has come a long way and now boasts some incredible tools to sharpen up soft shots. They can't save one that's simply out of focus, however, so it's vital to learn how to keep it sharp in-camera. The best way to do this is to learn the right mode for the job, as well as utilising tricks like pre-focusing, and selecting your AF point. Read on to explore these methods further but to begin with we'll take you through the very basic method of focusing your camera – just half-press the shutter-release button to focus, then fully press it to take the shot. It's as simple as that!

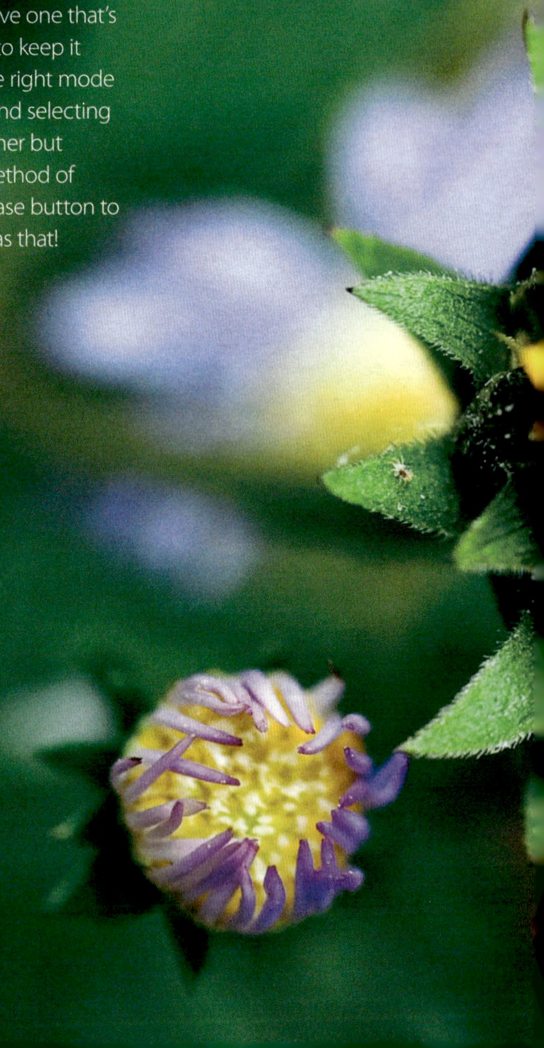

▲ Keep it sharp
At close distances, only a small portion of the shot will be in focus so it's important to be accurate with your technique, and often manual is the best mode for macro. Using a tripod to stop movement back and forth will help too

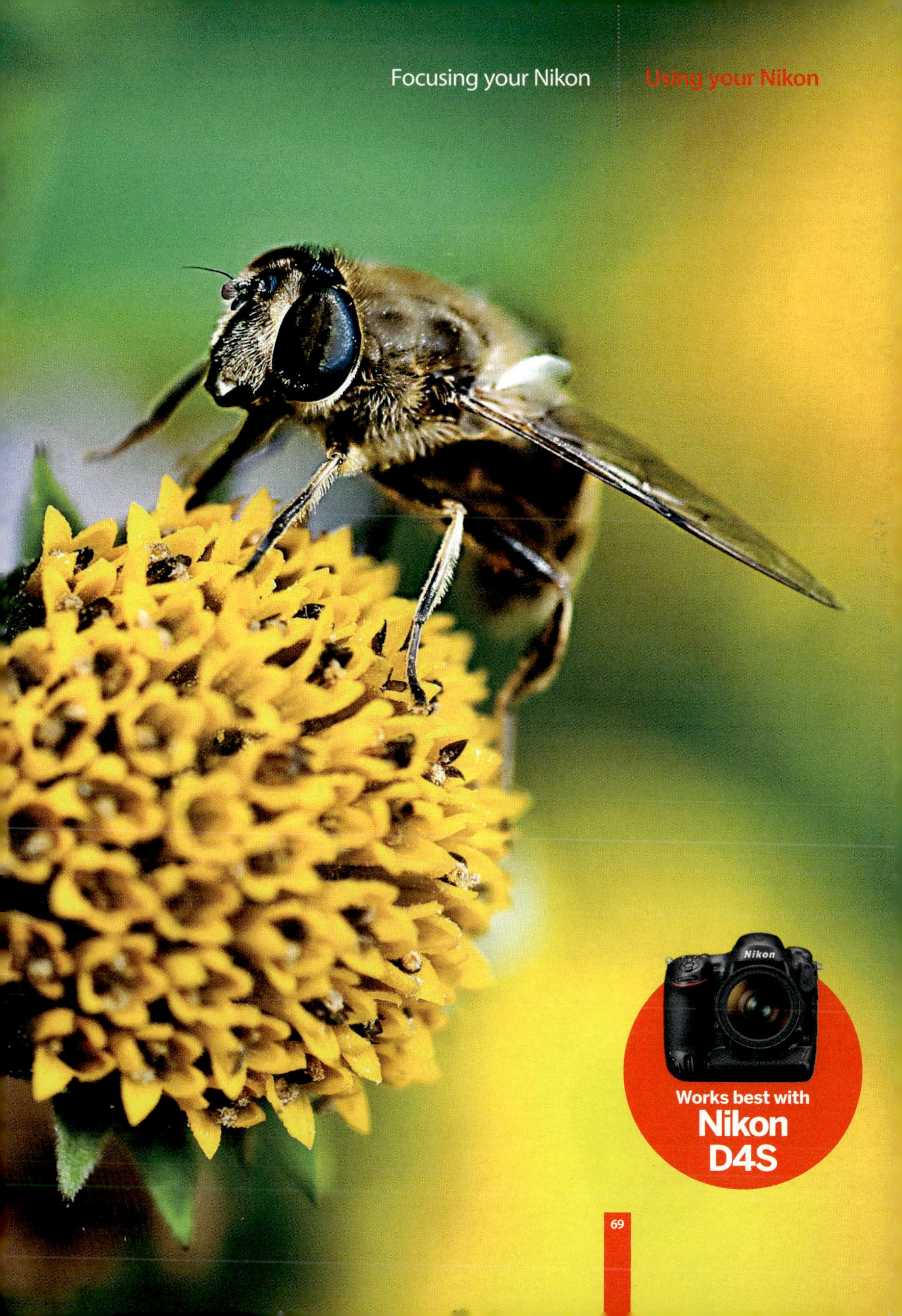

Works best with
Nikon D4S

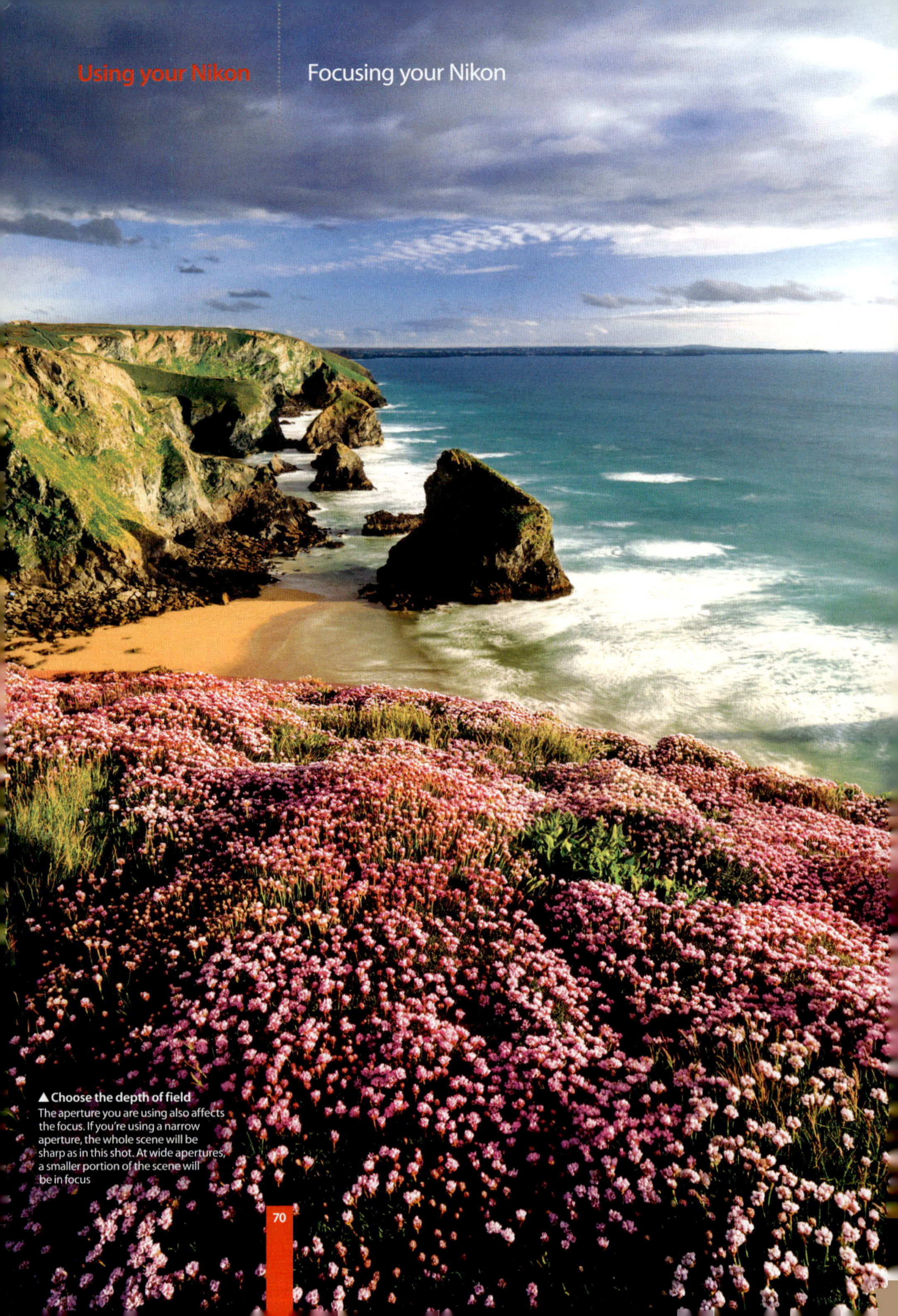

▲ Choose the depth of field
The aperture you are using also affects the focus. If you're using a narrow aperture, the whole scene will be sharp as in this shot. At wide apertures, a smaller portion of the scene will be in focus

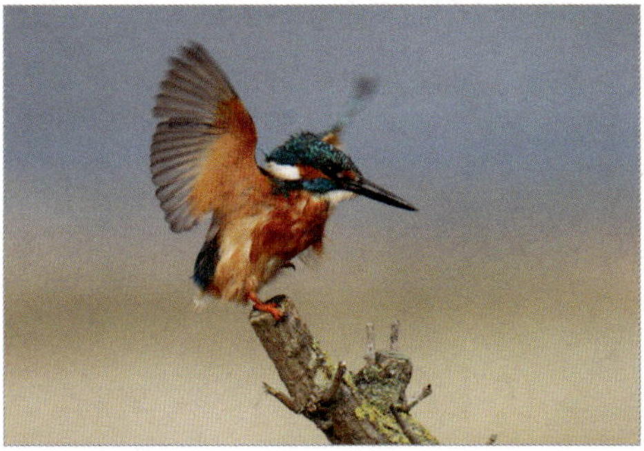

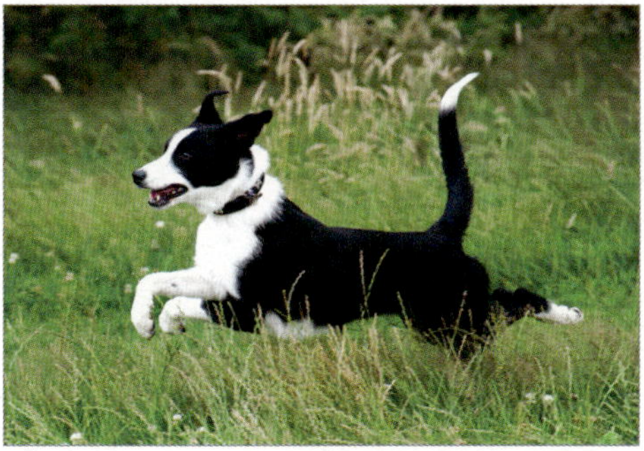

It's vital to learn the focusing modes. Nikon cameras come with the fundamental AF-S and AF-C modes. AF-S stands for Single-servo AF and it will lock focus when you half depress the shutter-release button. This is useful for static subjects like landscapes and still life. If your subject is moving, switch to Continuous-servo AF and your camera will continue to focus while the shutter-release button is halfway down – it will only lock focus when fully pressed, so is perfect for moving subjects like wildlife and sports.

Another focusing trick is to choose what part of the frame to focus on by moving the AF point to that area. Of course, the most accurate way is to focus manually, and this is often the chosen method for macro shots but you won't be quick enough for action. There is a useful method you can apply, though, whereby you choose a spot you know your subject is likely to move into, pre-focus on it, then press the shutter-release button when your subject moves into that spot.

Now you've learnt the vital settings and a few tricks, you're on your way to sharper shots, but don't forget the effect depth of field has on the outcome. Your camera focuses on a single point, but this may have a large area in front and behind it that's sharp, or a small area. At wide apertures this area is very small, so if you want more of your image sharp and in focus, you'll need to use a narrow aperture.

"The AF-S mode is useful for static subjects like landscapes. If your subject is moving, switch to AF-C mode"

▲ Continuous focus
If your subject is moving, it's important to switch over to the Continuous-servo AF mode so the camera keeps hunting for the right focus. Use a fast shutter speed to avoid motion blur, too

◀ Pre-focus shots
If there's an area you predict your subject will move into, manually pre-focus on this part of the frame and wait for your subject to appear! We focused on this branch, predicting it as an area the bird was likely to land on

Keep sharp and avoid shake

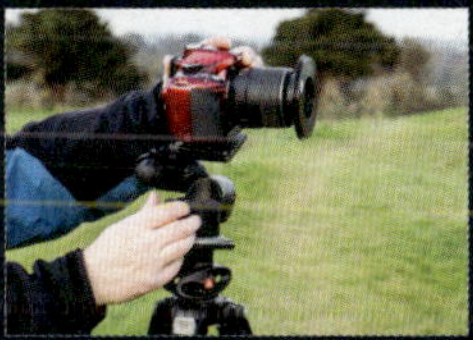

As well as mastering your focusing technique, you also need to consider camera shake. Small movements in the camera at slower shutter speeds can blur the image, but there are ways around this. Use a tripod or rest on a hard surface and use a self-timer to take the shot to avoid the movement of pressing the shutter release button.

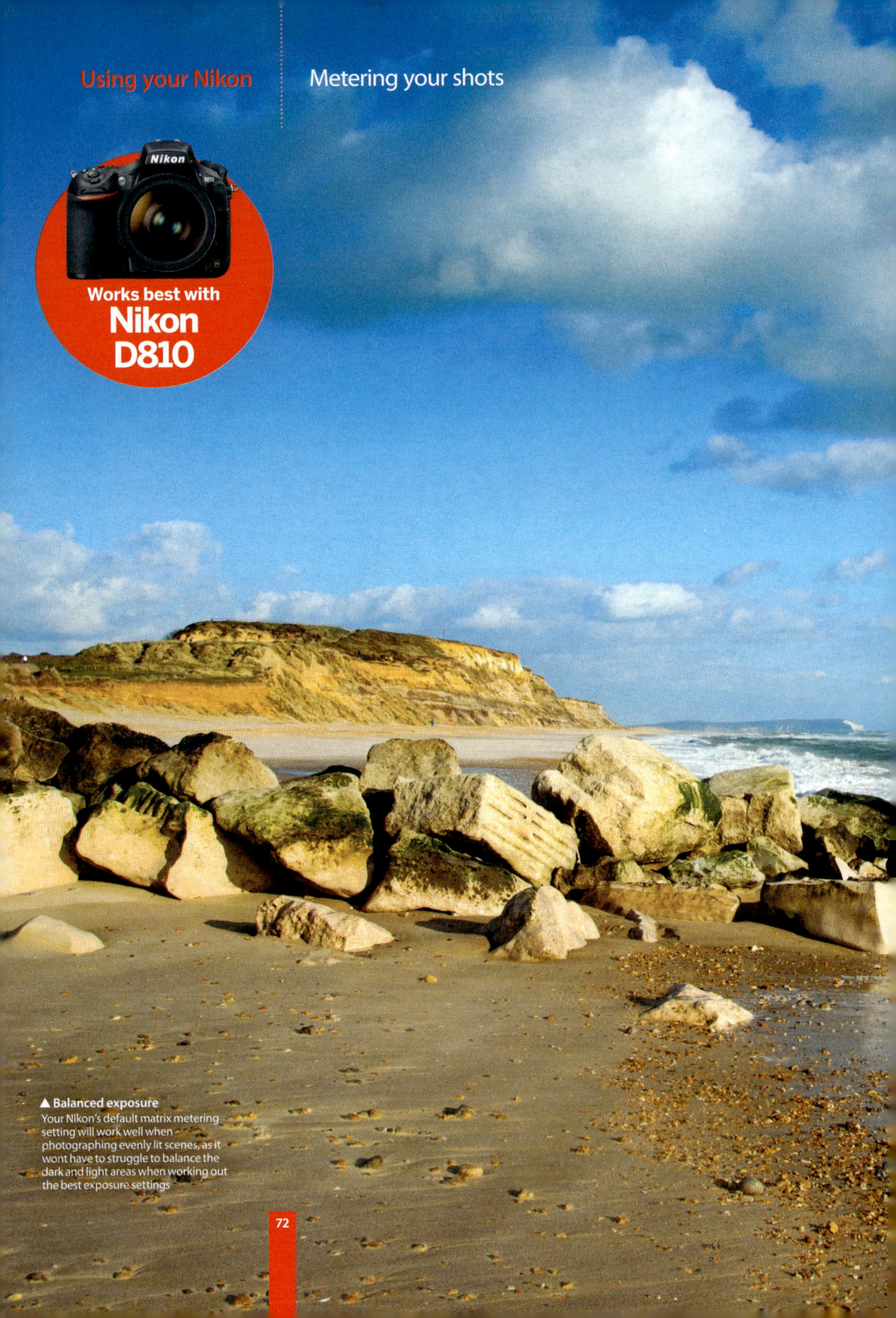

▲ **Balanced exposure**
Your Nikon's default matrix metering setting will work well when photographing evenly lit scenes, as it wont have to struggle to balance the dark and light areas when working out the best exposure settings

Metering your shots

Controlling how your camera reads the light will help you take well-exposed photos and uncover new creative techniques. Master the metering options of your Nikon for perfect shots every time

Just like our eyes, cameras record the available light in a scene in order to produce an image. However, a camera is not quite as sophisticated as the human eye and can sometimes struggle to record light accurately.

When we view a scene, our eyes automatically balance out the different level of light intensity so that we can see as much detail as possible. Cameras also try to do this, however due to their relatively limited dynamic range, areas of shadow can appear incredibly dark, whilst bright areas can appear excessively light. To avoid this problem, it helps to know how to control your camera's metering system.

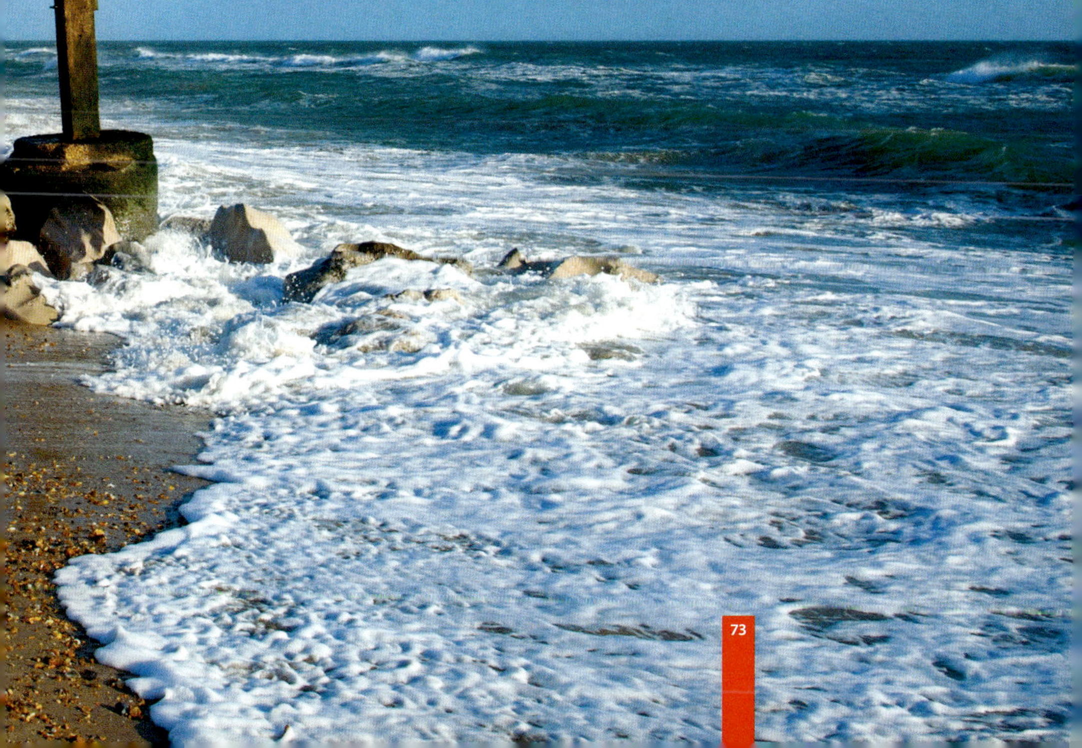

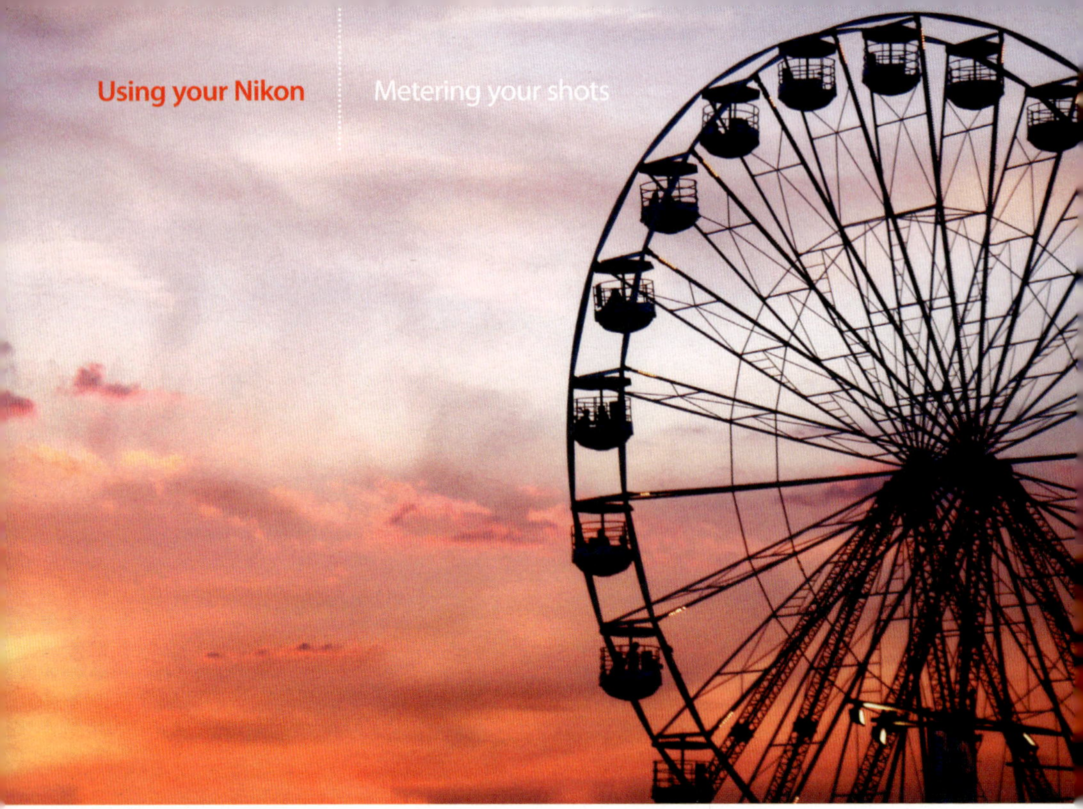

▲ **Create a silhouette**
To create a silhouette, use matrix metering and ensure the bright background takes up most of the frame, or switch to spot metering and focus on the bright backdrop

When it comes to digital photography, there are two main methods for measuring light. The first is to use an incidental light meter. This measures the amount of light hitting your subject and then tells you the best camera settings to use for a well-exposed shot. The second is reflected metering, which is the system found within all digital cameras. Reflected metering measures the amount of light reflected off everything in the scene, and then determines the correct exposure. If you're using auto or semi-auto modes, your camera will automatically select the settings. However, if you're in manual mode, it tell you if it thinks your shot will be over or underexposed by way of an exposure dial or preview of the image on the screen. Then it's up to you to adjust your settings accordingly.

The default metering setting on most digital cameras is matrix or evaluative metering, which measures the light for the entire scene and balances out the light and dark areas to work out an average exposure. However, you can also switch to one of two other metering options. Centre-weighted metering only measure the light for the middle section of the frame, whilst spot metering measures the light for the specific area that you choose to focus on.

Keep an image's whites white

When photographing bright white or deep black subjects, your camera's metering system can often struggle, as it will read the reflected light as either being too bright or too dark. This is why snow can often look grey in your shots, because your camera has read it as too bright and underexposed the shot. To fix this, adjust your exposure compensation to balance out your camera's mistake. Set it to +1 or +2 to brighten the shot, and -1 or -2 to darken it.

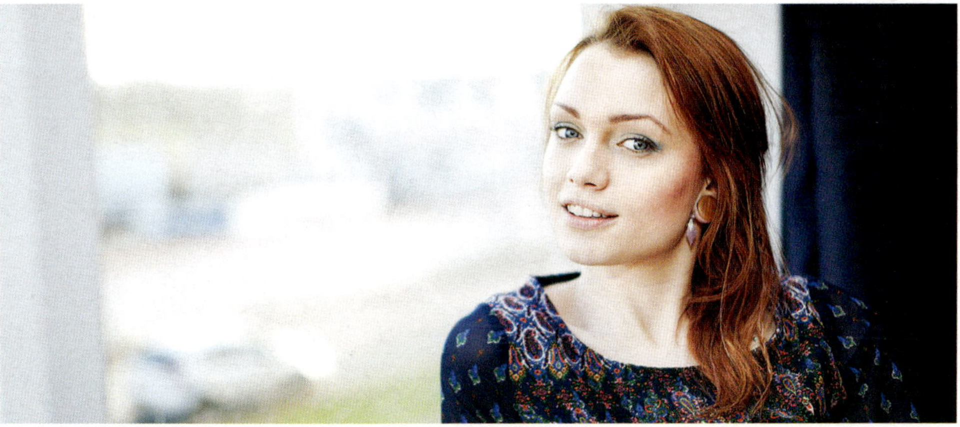

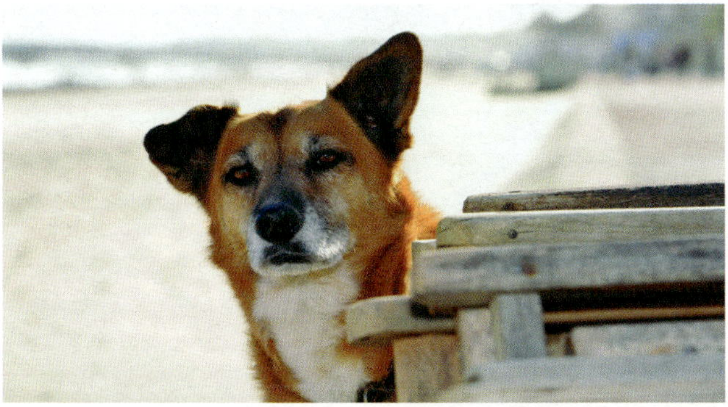

▲ Matrix metering
Your camera's matrix metering setting will measure the light for the majority of the frame, so if there is lots of contrast between bright and dark areas, it will struggle to know which bit to keep bright

◀ Spot metering
Spot metering will read the light for wherever you set your focus point, so is ideal for keeping portrait subjects well-exposed. Simply focus on their face or eye and they should appear bright

▼ Centre-weighted metering
If your subject is in the centre of the frame, it is best to use centre-weighted metering. This will ensure that your subject appears well exposed in your photo, even if the light is behind them

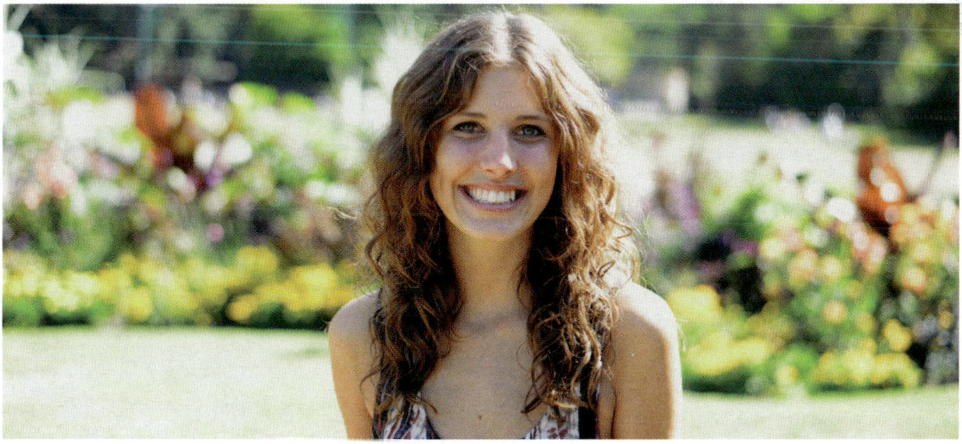

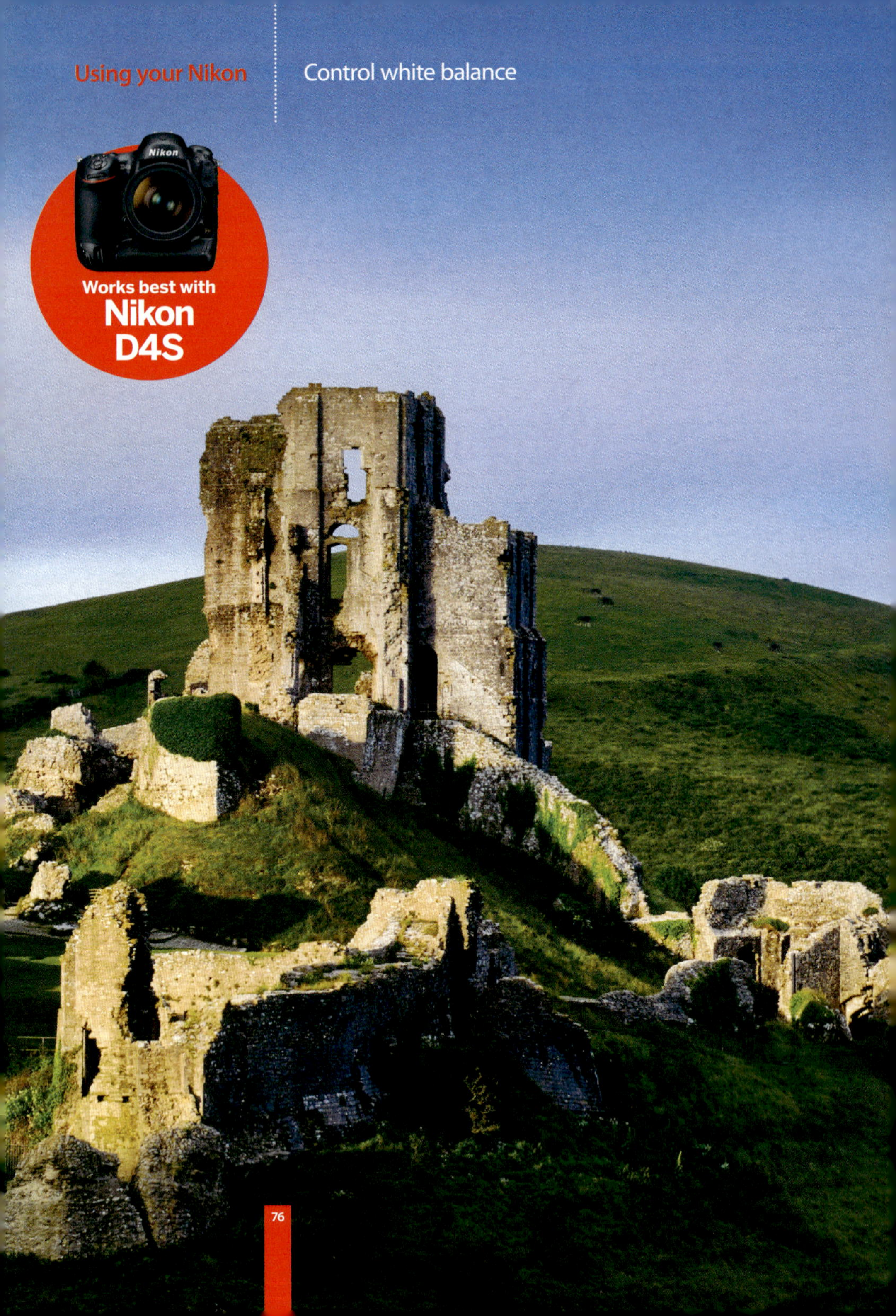
Nikon
Works best with
Nikon
D4S

Control white balance

Discover how your camera's white balance setting affects colour in your captures and learn how to use it

Your white balance setting plays an important role in how your camera captures colour but seeing as most auto white balance modes are so accurate these days, it is something that is often overlooked. In this guide, we'll explain how white balance really works and point out why it's worth getting out of Auto and exploring what this mode really has to offer.

Here you'll discover more about each white balance setting and find out how it can be used to help record colours accurately in your shots or even add creative effects to your photos.

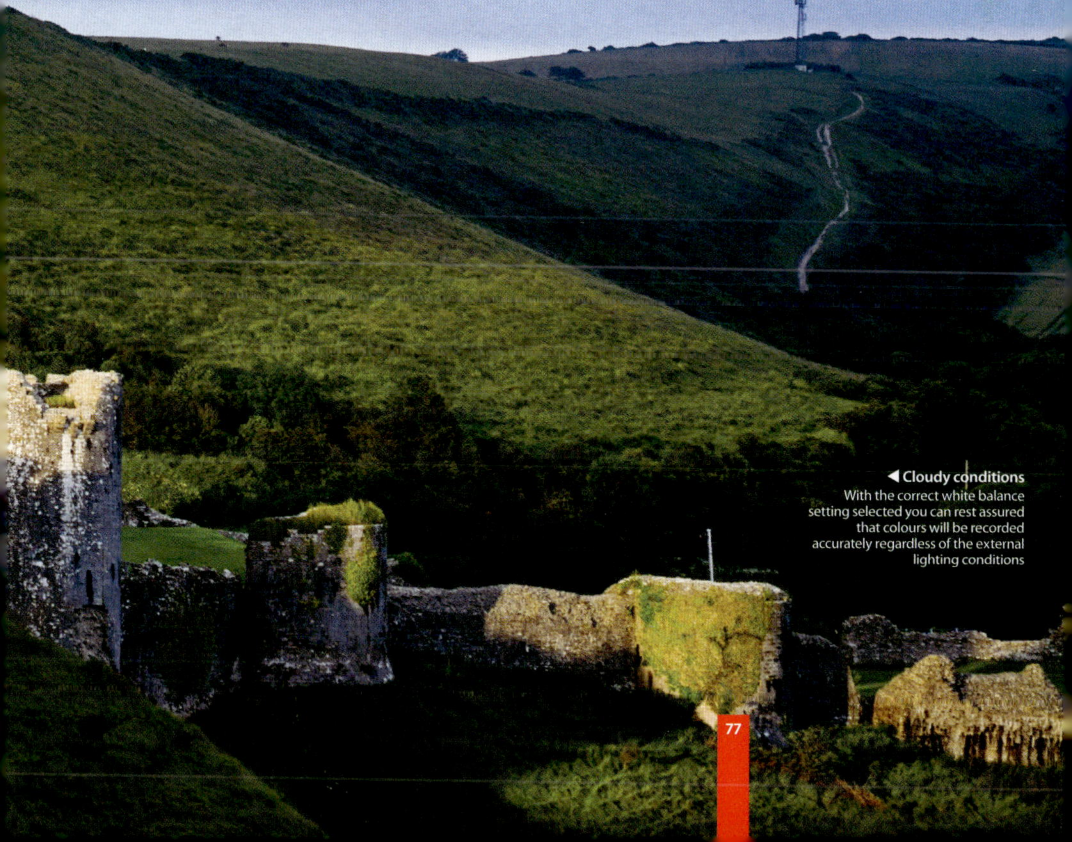

◀ Cloudy conditions
With the correct white balance setting selected you can rest assured that colours will be recorded accurately regardless of the external lighting conditions

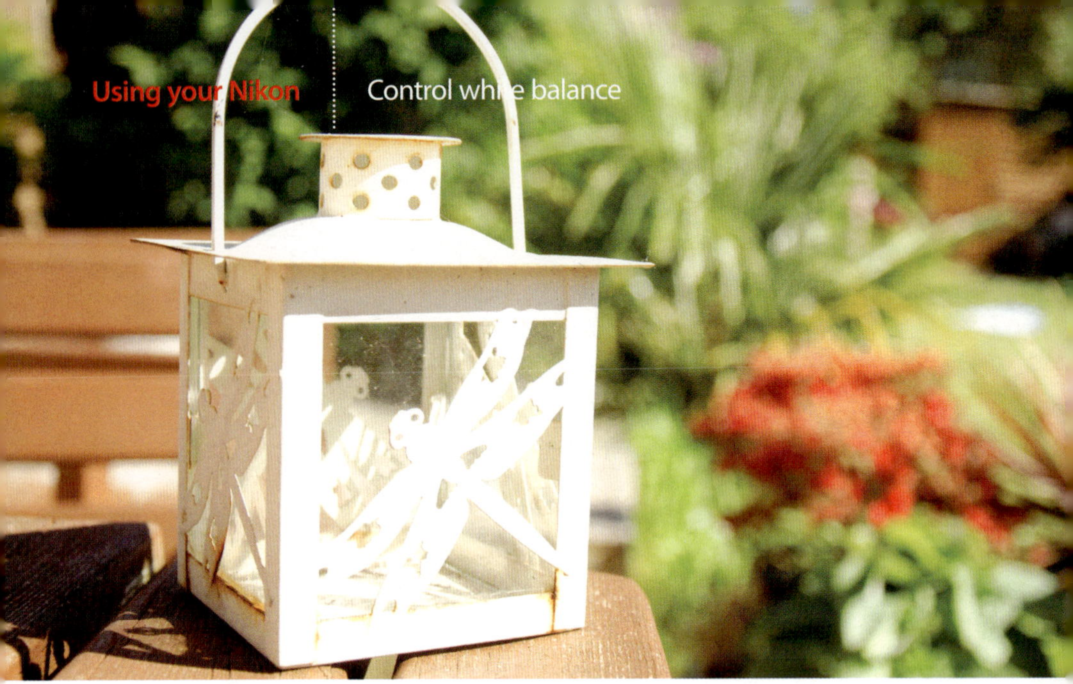

▲ **Flash**
Flash emits a much cooler temperature of light, which means images taken with flash can look a little cold. By selecting the flash white balance setting, the camera will help counter this effect by adding some warmth to your shots

White balance is used to help prevent colour casts as it's designed to ensure that white areas appear white. To do this, the camera takes into account the colour temperature of the light you're shooting in.

All light sources emit different colour temperatures. You'll notice this if you've taken a bad shot indoors under incandescent lighting, as the image will appear orange. Most modern cameras offer pretty accurate auto white balance settings, so it's unlikely you'll notice dramatic colour casts in your shots day-to-day.

However, it's good to alter your white balance setting so it accurately reflects the scene you're shooting. White balance can be changed in your camera menu and most even feature a shortcut button on the camera body. Simply hold down the button marked WB, and use your scroll wheel or arrow pad to select a setting.

Although white balance is commonly used to ensure accurate colour recording, some photographers use it to get creative colour cast effects. Selecting an incorrect white balance setting will result in an obvious colour cast; this works well if you want to enhance an atmosphere in your photos. For example, selecting the incandescent white balance setting when you're shooting in sunlight will add a cold blue cast.

Once you've gotten to grips with adjusting your white balance, experiment in-camera with some of the other effects you can achieve by using opposite settings to the scene.

JPEG vs RAW white balance

It's important to note that if you're shooting in JPEG and have set the wrong white balance it will be difficult, and sometime impossible, to correct it later when editing as JPEG files are compressed. If you want to experiment with adding colour casts using white balance, only do so if you're shooting in RAW. RAW files are uncompressed, which means you can get creative with white balance in-camera and adjust or correct it easily later on if you happen to change your mind.

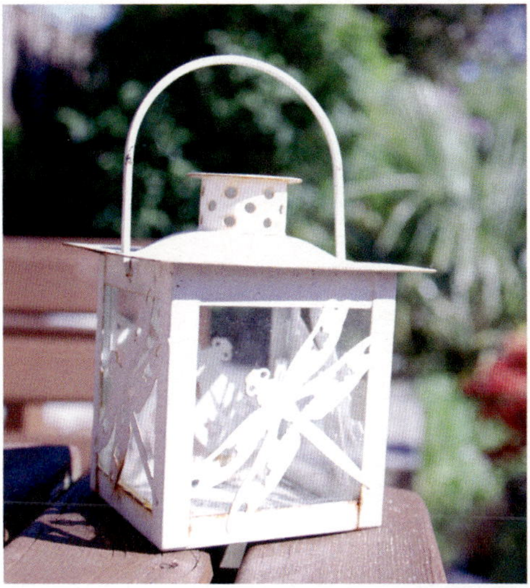

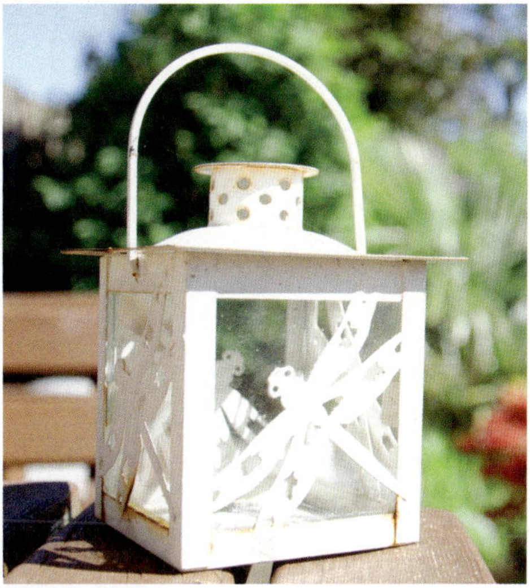

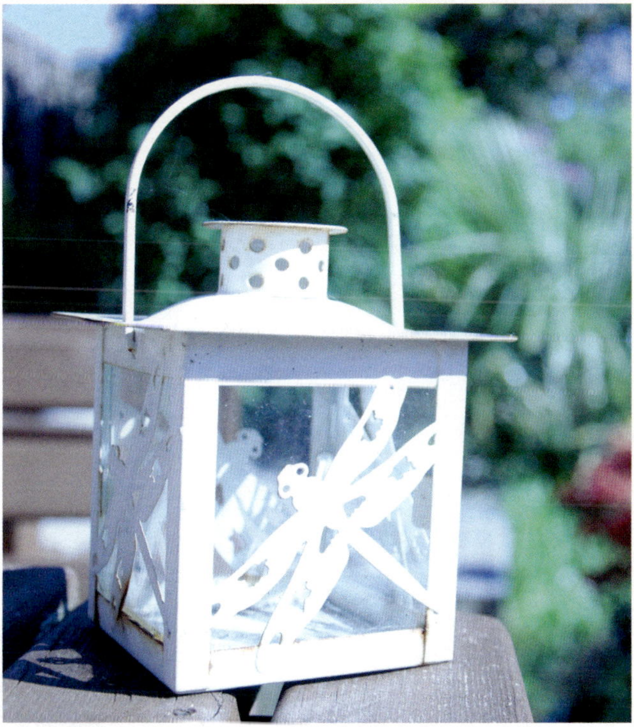

▲ Daylight
There are three types of white balance settings for outdoors, including daylight, shade and cloudy. Daylight will help reduce the warm glow of sunlight by cooling the image slightly whereas shade and cloudy, which can appear cool, will be warmed up to a degree

◤ Fluorescent
Fluorescent lighting can add magenta tones to your shots, which is much harder to correct in editing. Ensure you select the Fluorescent white balance setting when shooting under this light in order to reduce the magenta hue with green

◀ Incandescent
When you're shooting indoors under incandescent light, shots can take on a warm orange glow. To neutralise this effect, the camera will add cooling blue tones when you're shooting using the Incandescent white balance setting

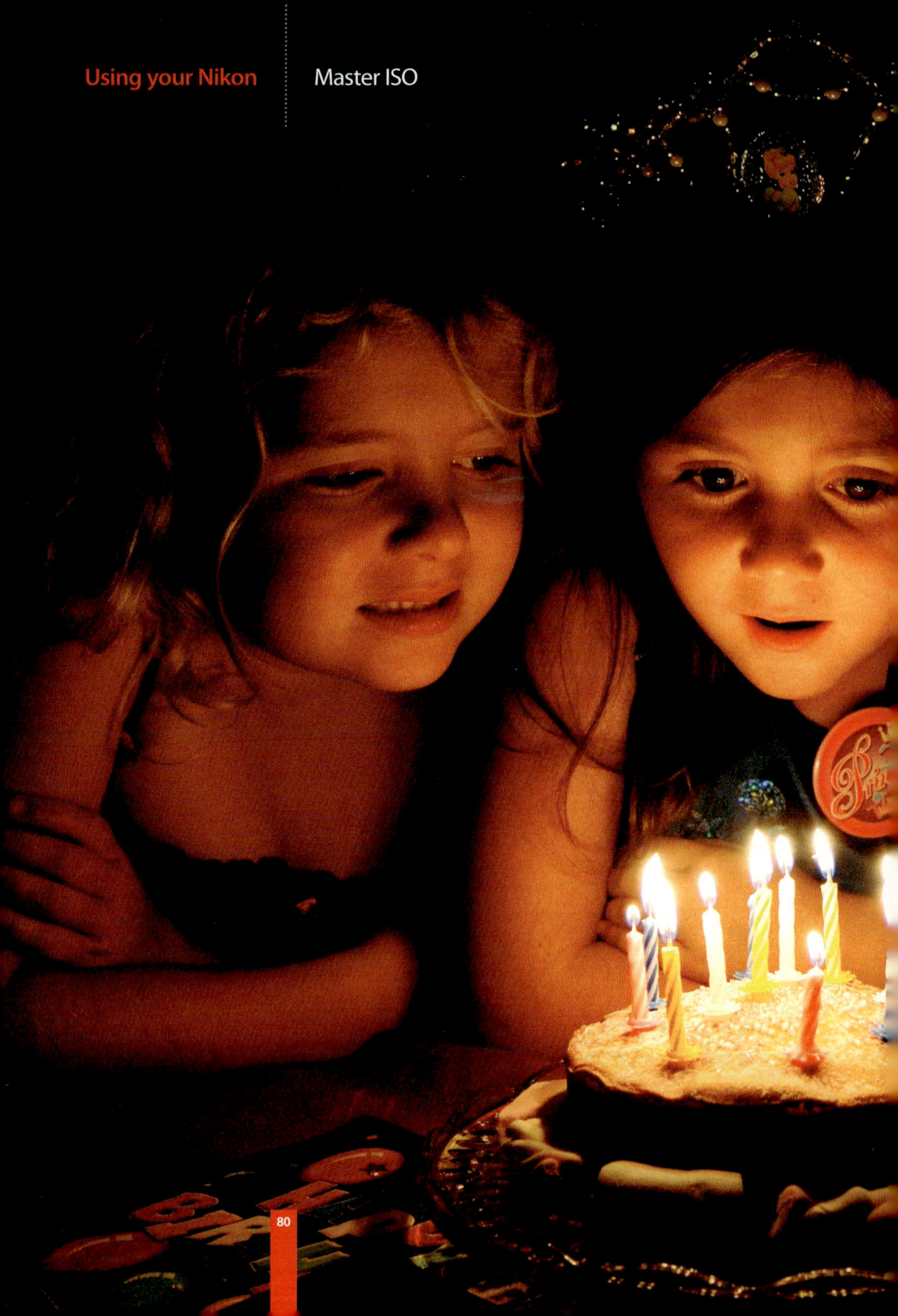

Master ISO

Discover this essential element in manual exposures and when the best time is to use it. Sometimes you're just going to have to crank up the noise!

ISO is the third part of the exposure triangle alongside aperture and shutter speed. Setting a higher ISO will increase how sensitive the sensor is to light, which brightens up exposures. Some modern cameras have a huge range – you can now shoot in incredibly dark environments and still get useable shots. The downside is that noise will surface at higher settings, resulting in specks appearing and you may notice the colours become desaturated and details are softer. It's a payoff you have to be aware of but it's an incredibly useful tool.

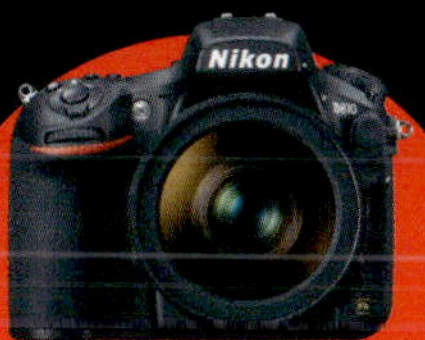

Works best with Nikon D810

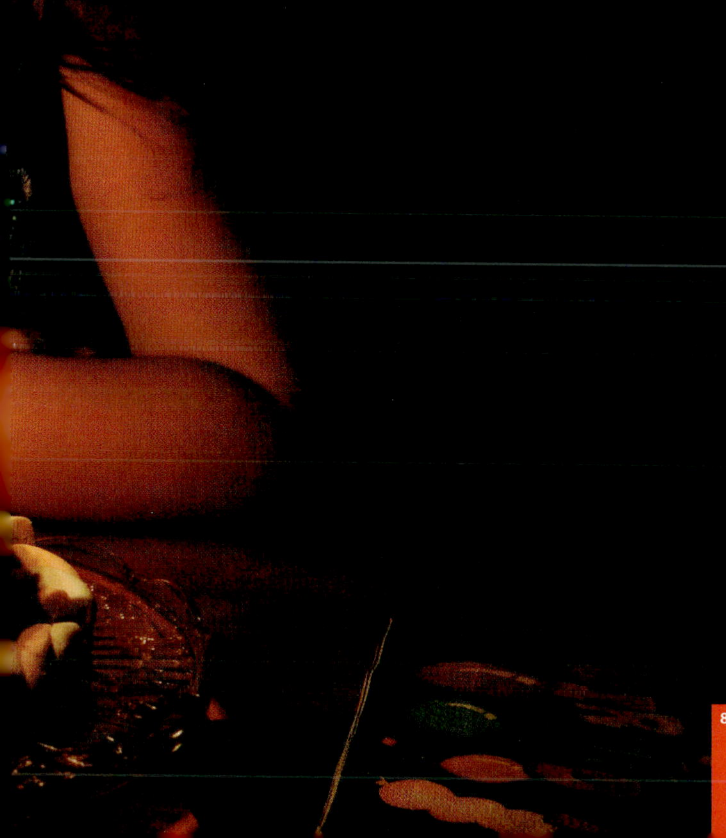

◀ Higher ISOs
ISO 1600 has been used here so that the shot could be well exposed. Modern cameras can handle quite high ISO settings before noise really becomes a problem

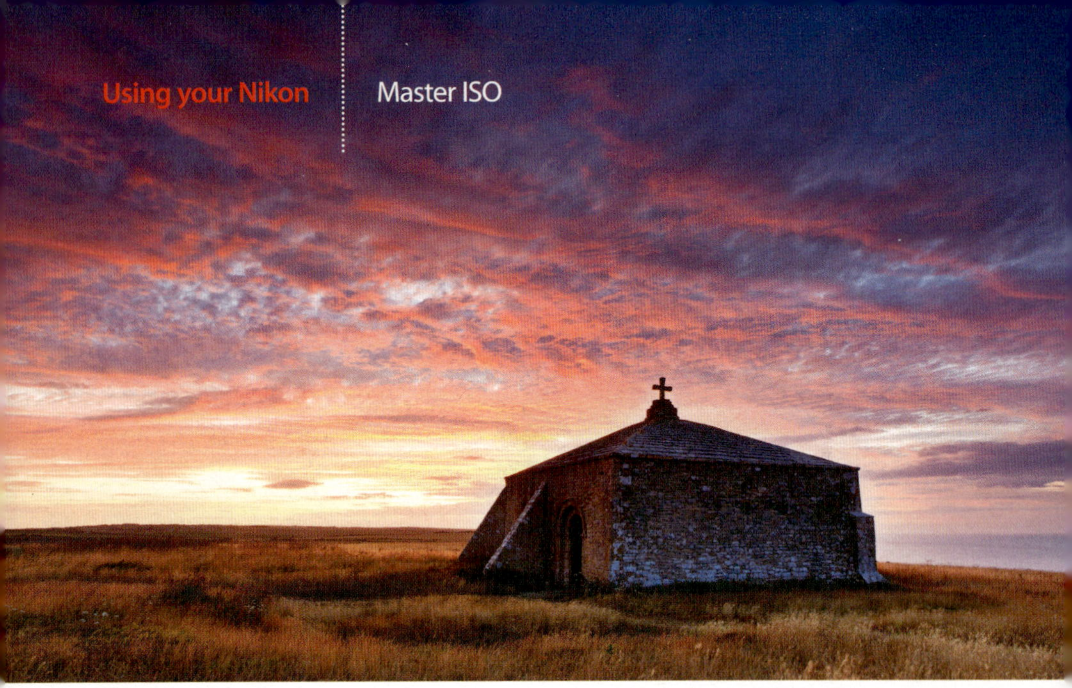

▲ **Low ISO landscapes**
In certain low-light situations where your subject isn't moving, it's better to keep your ISO low and use slow shutter speed and a tripod to get well exposed shots. This way you will keep noise out of your images

Edit out noise

Sometimes you just have to raise your ISO and accept that noise will appear, but there is a way to reduce its effects. Most editing suites will have a noise reduction feature – in Photoshop head to Filter>Noise>Reduce Noise. If you shoot in RAW you will have even more control (use the Detail tab in Adobe Camera RAW). This does have a softening effect, so try not to overdo it.

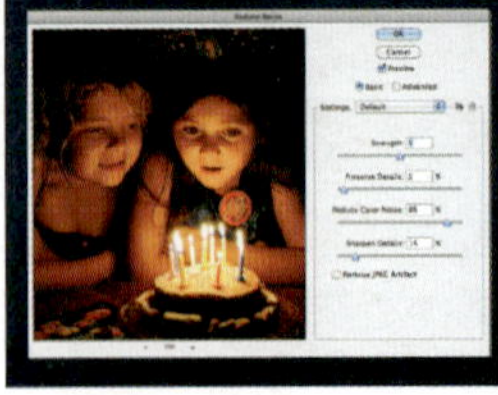

If higher ISOs can cause noise in your shot, why would you want to use them? The main reason is they allow you to use faster shutter speeds and narrower apertures while still getting correct exposure in low light. With static subjects like landscapes, most photographers keep ISO low and use a slow shutter speed to brighten the exposure, but you'll need a tripod to stop camera shake. If your subject is moving, however, you'll need to use a fast shutter speed to stop them appearing as a blur. You could use a wide aperture to let more light in but sometimes that's not enough and you'll be forced to raise your ISO. You also might not be able to use a tripod, in which case raising your ISO may again be the only option available to you.

You may question why you wouldn't just use flash? While flash is a good option in a lot of situations, there are times when this isn't feasible, such as in venues that ban flash or when it would drown out the pleasing tones created from ambient lighting, such as with gig lighting or candlelight. In this case, ISO is your best friend.

Modern cameras are becoming better and better at dealing with noise at higher ISOs, but one thing that's worth bearing in mind is that small sensor cameras will produce more noise than those with the high megapixel counts. That's something worth bearing in mind if low-light shooting is on your agenda when selecting a new camera upgrade.

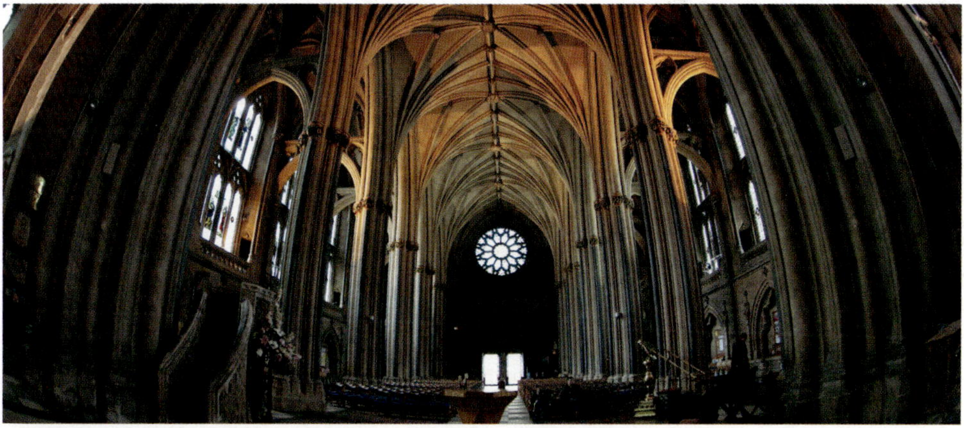

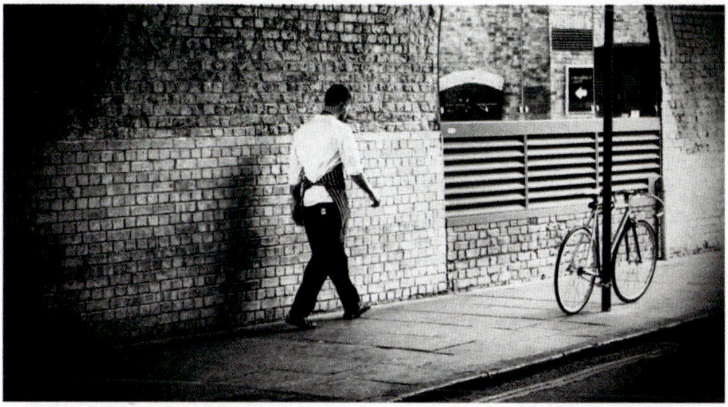

▲ When flash is banned
Certain buildings such as churches and museums ban the use of flash. In this instance a higher ISO will allow you to get correct exposures in dim lighting conditions

◀ Embrace grain
Noisy images are much more forgiving when converted to black and white, and grain can even add interest and texture in certain shots. It's often embraced by street photographers for its added gritty look

▼ Ambient is sometimes best
In certain low-light situations, using flash would drown out all the great tones created by ambient light, so in this case you'd need to raise your ISO

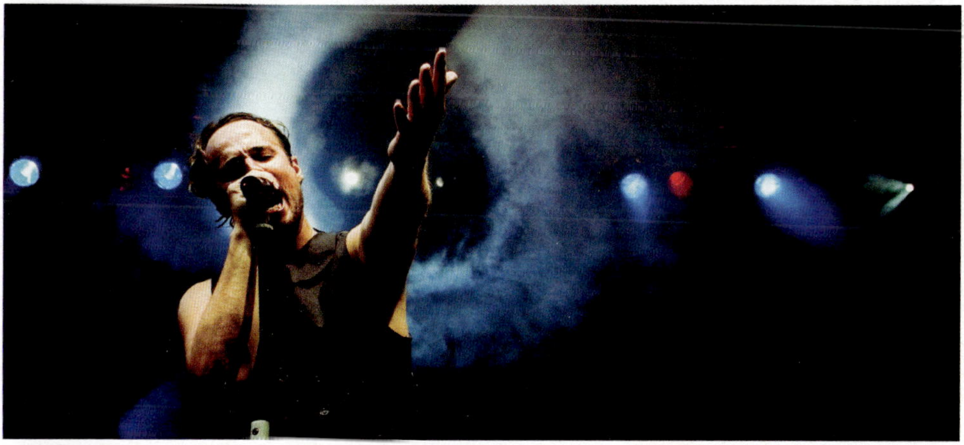

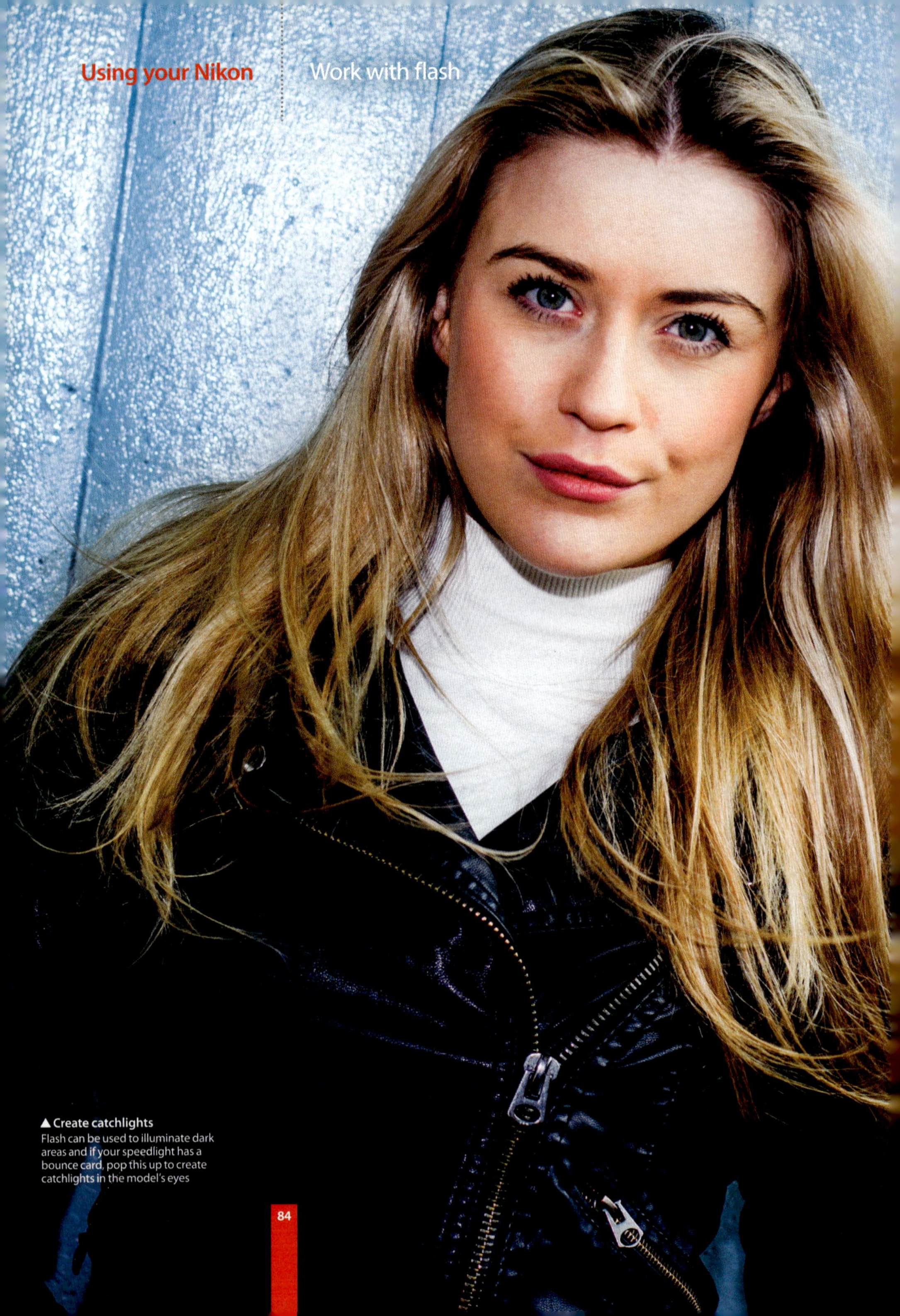

▲ **Create catchlights**
Flash can be used to illuminate dark areas and if your speedlight has a bounce card, pop this up to create catchlights in the model's eyes

Work with flash

Learn how to make the best use of flash to illuminate your subject and enjoy even more control with a speedlight unit

Flash can be the ultimate tool in your kit bag if it's used correctly. It can help to achieve correct exposures in dark environments such as parties or weddings, help with difficult lighting situations, or it can even freeze action due to the rapid burst of light. The problem is, most people start off using flash and end up unhappy with the results. Flash can be harsh if fired straight on, resulting in unpleasant shadows. Here we will teach you how to take control of your kit to avoid these pitfalls and get the best results.

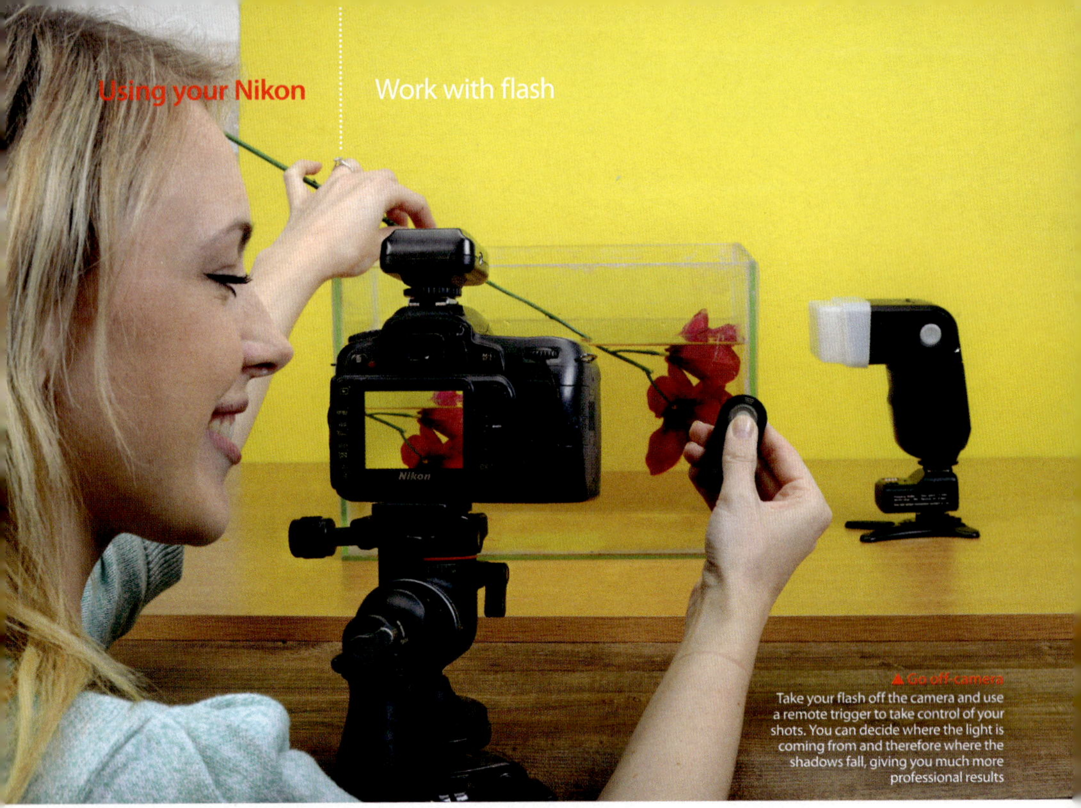

▲ Go off-camera
Take your flash off the camera and use a remote trigger to take control of your shots. You can decide where the light is coming from and therefore where the shadows fall, giving you much more professional results

Improve pop-up flash results

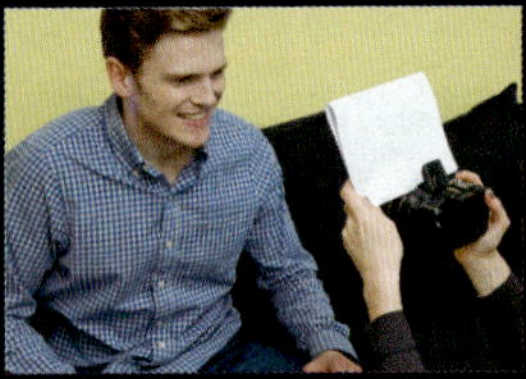

If you can't afford a speedlight right away, there are tricks you can apply to improve the results you get from your camera's fixed flash. Try placing a piece of white paper underneath it, angled towards the ceiling. This will bounce the light, creating softer, more even results. Also, you could place an old milk carton over your flash to diffuse it, or a piece of tracing paper in front can make a subtle but effective difference.

Flash is a powerful weapon; even your pop-up flash can improve your images. Try using fill-in flash on backlit subjects – where once a subject was in shadow you'll now see an even exposure. The problem with fixed flashes, however, is when fired straight on they can have harsh results, and this is where a flashgun can help.

Speedlights offer a greater level of control. Not only can you dictate how much light is fired, but you can also angle it to bounce off ceilings or walls, producing softer results. You can even place them off camera and use a remote trigger, to move it away from your subject or dictate the angle it hits the subject from.

Use TTL metering and the speedlight will communicate with the camera to select the correct level of flash, or take control with manual mode. The aim is to balance ambient light with flash. Start by setting your camera's maximum sync speed (1/200sec on most Nikons), ISO 100 or 200, f8 and around 1/8 flash power, then tweak the settings to see how they affect the outcome. A longer exposure will make the ambient light seem brighter but you can also use a narrower aperture and increase the flash power to make the ambient light darker.

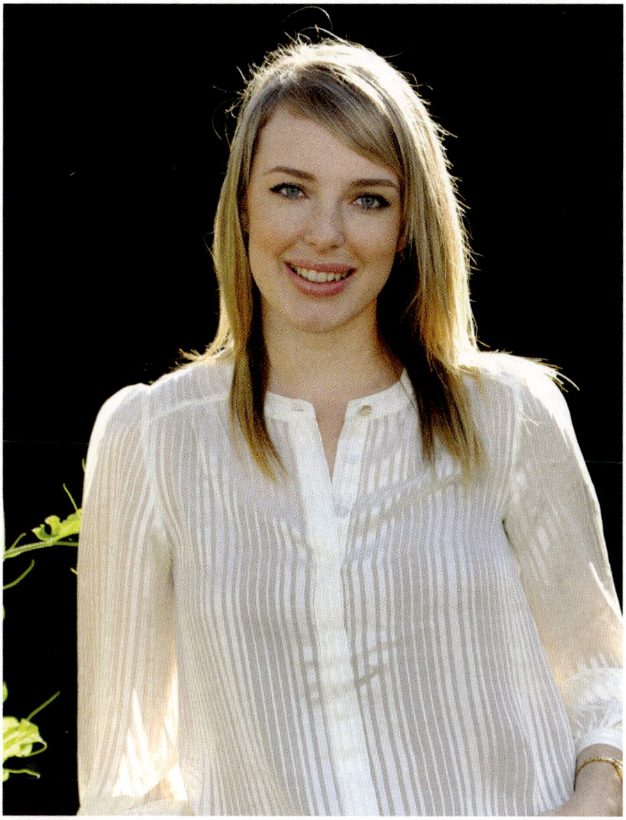

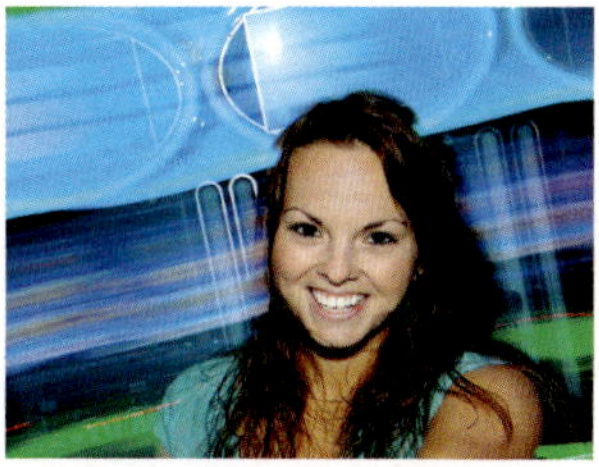

▲ Experiment with flash modes
Set your camera to slow-sync mode to produce creative blur in the ambient light but keep your main subject sharp. You might also want to try stroboscopic flash, which fires multiple times to capture different stages of motion

◀ Fill in backlit shots
When your subject is backlit and their face is in shadow, use your flash to fill in the light. Even a pop-up flash can make a big difference in this particular scenario

▼ Bounce the flash
When shooting indoors, direct the speedlight towards the ceiling to bounce it off there and then towards your subject. This create a more diffused light that has a much more flattering result

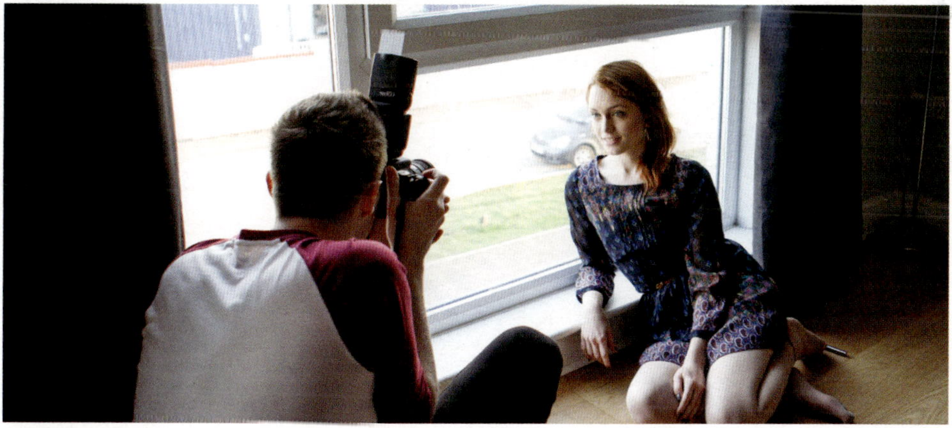

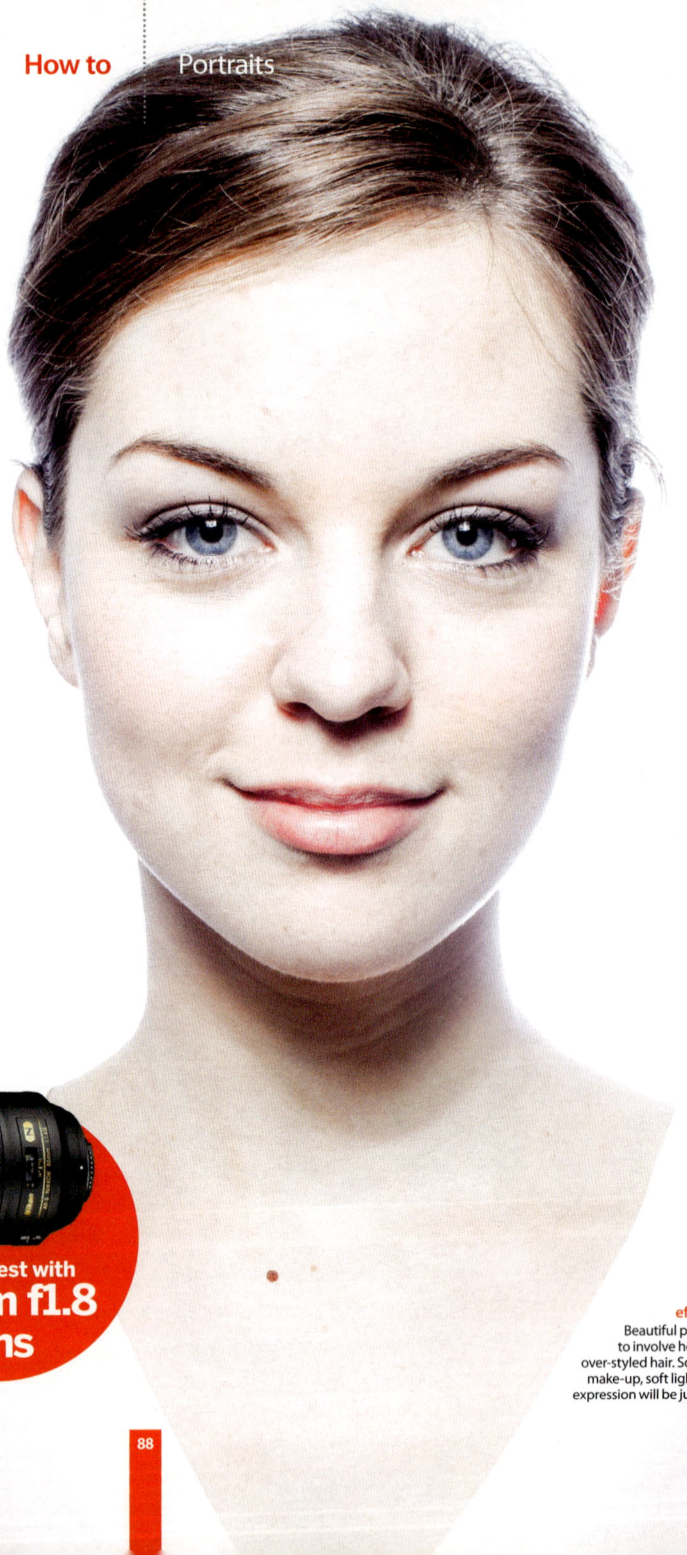

Works best with 85mm f1.8 lens

▲ Simple but effective portraits
Beautiful portraits don't have to involve heavy make-up and over-styled hair. Sometimes minimal make-up, soft lighting and the right expression will be just as eye-catching

Capture stunning portraits

Exercise your creativity to create simple, yet effective portraits without the need for big flashy setups

Portraits, head and shoulder shots, selfies, or even passport shots – no matter how you look at it, portrait photography is a massive part of our day-to-day life. So how can you ensure that you're capturing stunning portraits, even with basic equipment? After all, the art of taking a person's picture is a skill, and like all good skills, it's something you learn, so let's start with the basics.

The essential kit

For any photographer starting out, all you need are the three core materials: light, a camera, and your subject. Once you have acquired your model and your kit, it's time to look at the technicalities of both what and how you're going to photograph.

People come in different shapes and sizes, so it's easy to get carried away in the flow of taking images and forget what actually

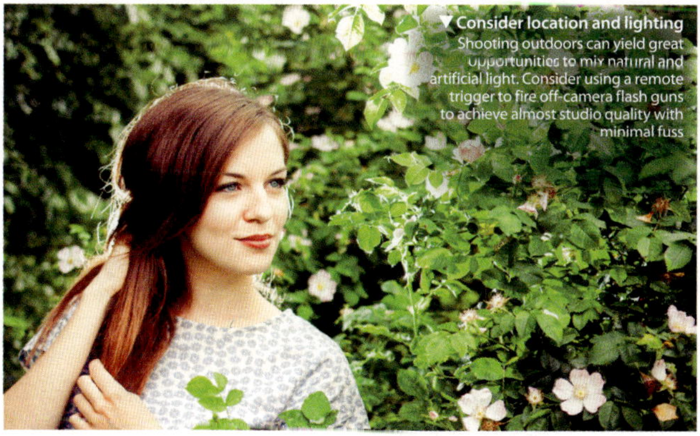

▼ **Consider location and lighting** Shooting outdoors can yield great opportunities to mix natural and artificial light. Consider using a remote trigger to fire off-camera flash guns to achieve almost studio quality with minimal fuss

Lighting styles

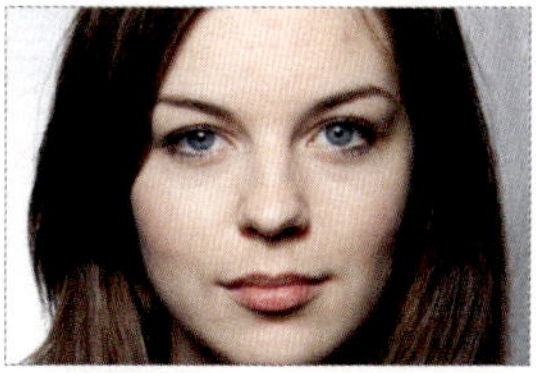

1 Flat lighting
Use even lighting to flatten shadows on your model's face and even out skin tones.

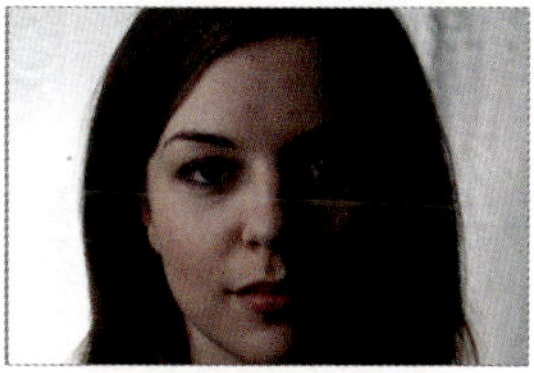

2 Rembrandt lighting
Create a deliberate shadow for a dramatic look by lighting predominantly from one side.

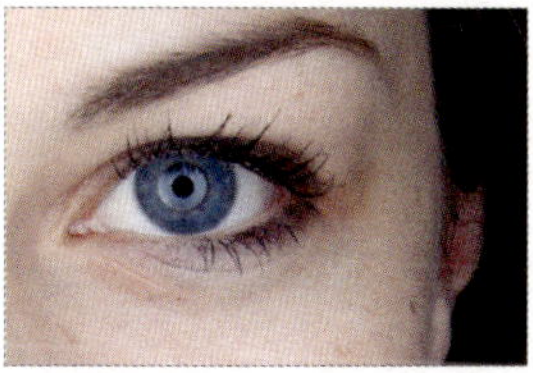

3 Ring flash
Designed to create hard edges and bleach out detail, ring flash is ideal for interesting portraits.

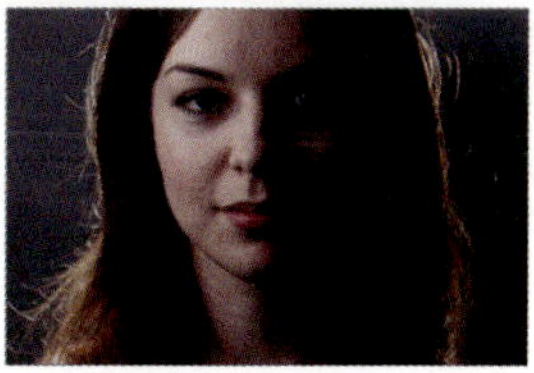

4 Rim lighting
Add rear lighting to create a rim of light around their body; great for adding drama and forcing focus.

Portraits

Lens and depth of field

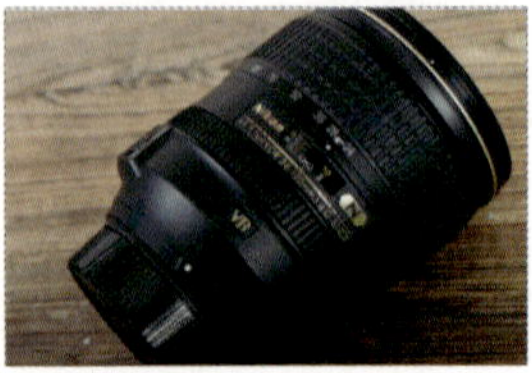

1 Zoom lens
A zoom lens has the lowest aperture on both the widest and the furthest telephoto option.

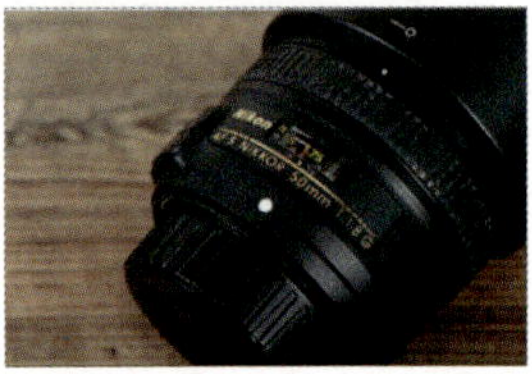

2 Prime lens
The prime lens has no zoom function, so the aperture is achievable constantly.

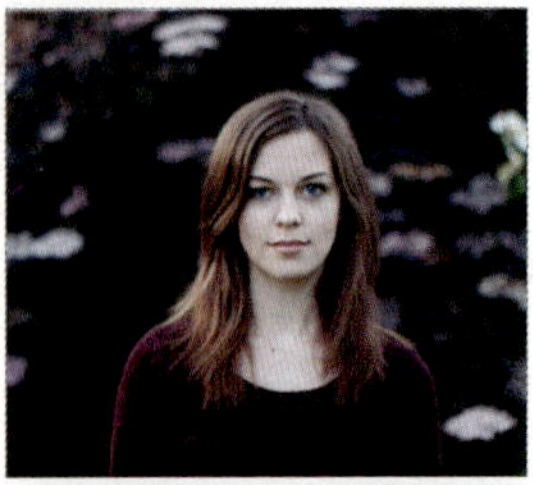

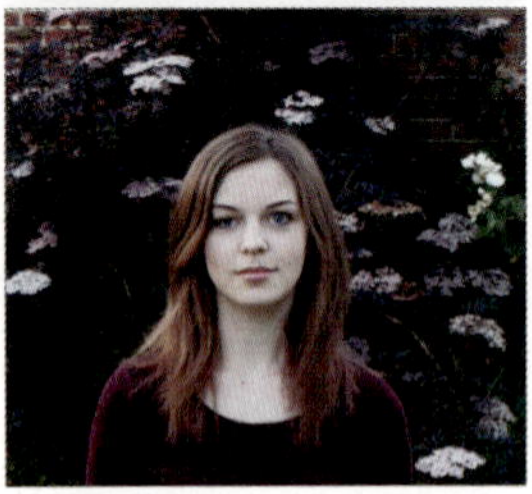

3 Depth of field
An aperture of f2.8 will soften foreground and background; f16 will give more overall focus.

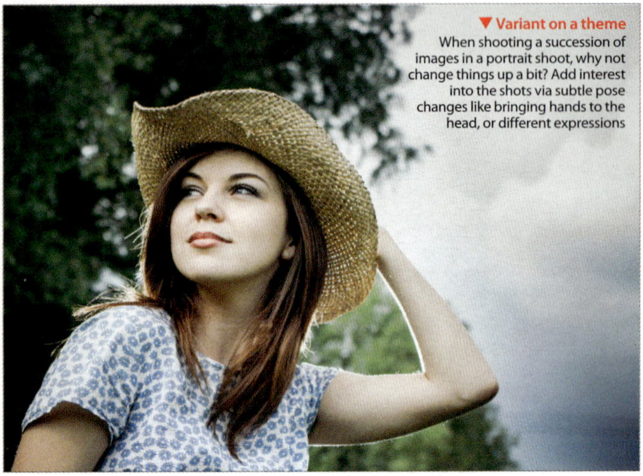

▼ Variant on a theme
When shooting a succession of images in a portrait shoot, why not change things up a bit? Add interest into the shots via subtle pose changes like bringing hands to the head, or different expressions

looks good and flattering to your subject. For instance, look at your choice of lens; every lens has its own set of distinct properties. If you are using a zoom lens then chances are it will start off at a wide-angle, somewhere in the region of 18mm and go to a narrower angle like 55mm or further. The point of the zoom system isn't solely so that you can get closer to a subject without moving, but also to alter the depth of the image and the perspective of the subject being shot. Of course there are other benefits from lens to lens, such as the minimum aperture range, which will be slightly different when you shift from one focal length to another.

Typical lenses used in portraiture are a fixed 50mm which will have a wide aperture, starting at around f1.8 at the lowest, allowing for a narrow depth of field, and a higher aperture around f16 giving a wider depth of field. The only negative of using a lens with such a wide aperture is that it can be prone to softer images, because your body movement, as well as the model's, at that aperture, will result in a shift in your depth of field making them soft.

Another lens commonly used is an 85mm prime. This shares a similar wide aperture to the 50mm, but the 85mm has a narrower angle to keep the distortion of the image to a minimum, which also helps keep ambient background detail limited when your subject is filling the frame.

Another tip for flattering shots is to take your own body positioning into account. This is as important, if not more so, than that of your model's when it comes to taking the shot. If you are

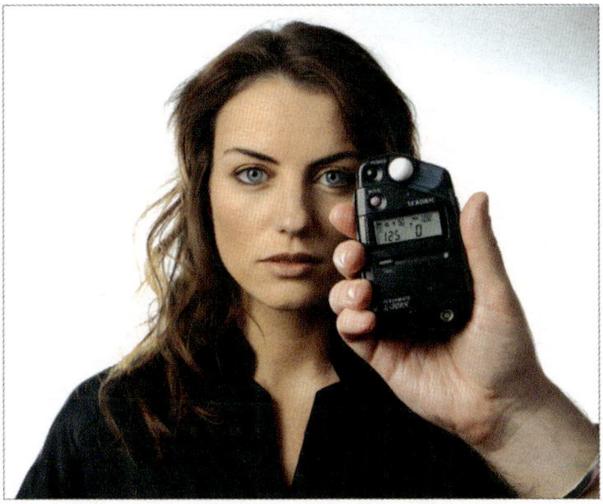

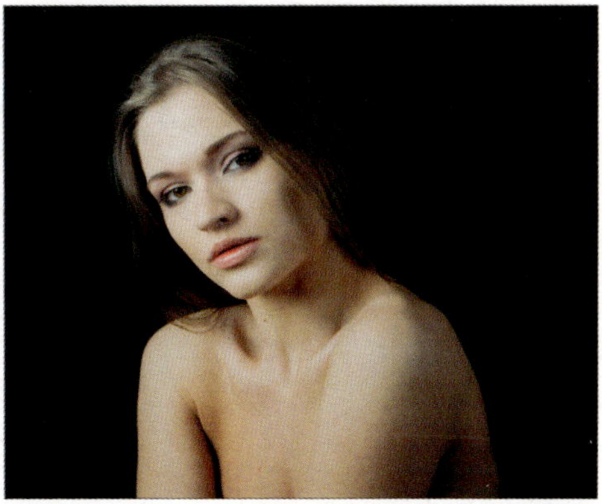

▲ Alter your lighting for big impact
In a studio environment, try turning off all your lights bar one. With the correct lighting modifier and power you will be able to create an atmospheric portrait quickly and easily. All your model will have to do is alter her pose

◀ Meter your light
Use a light meter to measure how powerful your light is. These handy little devices are relatively expensive but are a must-have if you are using studio lighting or creative lighting outside

looking up at your model, it can slightly distort their appearance in an image, making them look like they have a fat neck and a small head. For best results, have your eye line slightly above your model's – again, only slightly because you don't want to be looking too far down on them.

As a rule of thumb, looking too far down on a subject makes them look small and submissive, while looking up at makes them look big and dominant. Straight on with squared shoulders looks dominant and unflattering in body shape. This isn't to say that the only way to shoot a model is face-on, however. It's definitely worth experimenting with various angles to see exactly what works best for your model.

After all, once you know this basic rule, you can exploit it. One example is to get your model to stand facing you, then twist to the side slightly so their shoulder is facing more toward you and get them to look over the shoulder slightly, naturally lowering the eye line. Break the rigidity in their stance by getting them to bend the knee that is facing you a little and then add interest by moving hands to hips, hair or shoulders. These are basic posing tips that

"As a rule of thumb, looking too far down on a subject makes them look small and submissive, while looking up makes them look big and dominant"

Quick tip

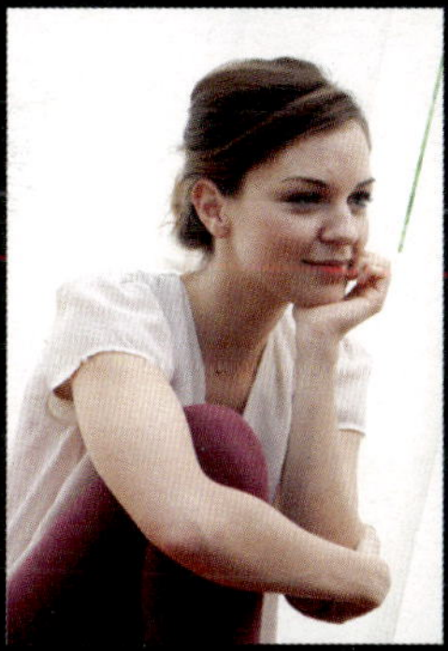

If shooting at home, try using white sheets as a backdrop, or in this instance, white blinds. The natural light will bleach out the sheet when you expose for the model in front.

Cropped sensors and focal lengths

There are two types of camera sensor: cropped and full-frame. The full-frame sensor is representative of 35mm film and gives you all of the focal length that your lens can offer. A cropped sensor can't give you that unless your lens is designed for a cropped sensor. What happens when you use a cropped sensor camera is your focal length is extended. This means, in short, that rather than having a 50mm lens, you instead have a lens operating in the range of a 75mm.

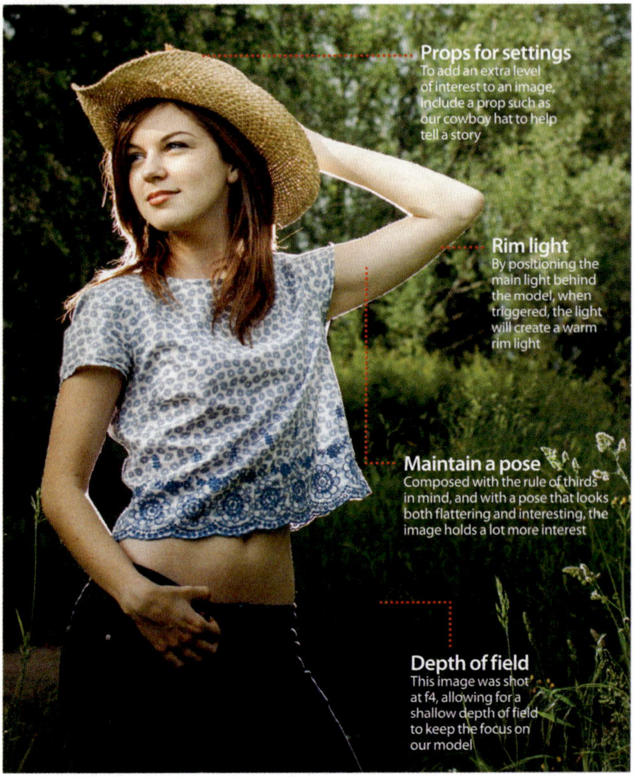

▶ **Shoot stunning portraits on location**
By using a remote trigger for your flash gun, create stunning location portraits that have an edge easily and seamlessly

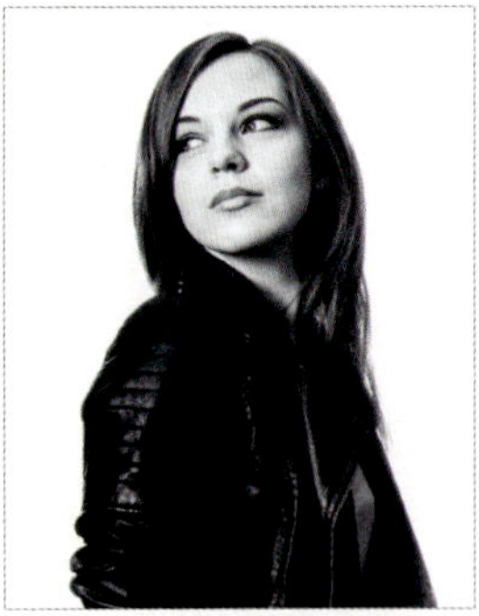

▲ **Strike a pose in black and white**
To add a dramatic edge to your shot, break the rules. By shooting low and striking a subtle 'hero pose' we add purpose to the stance, add in the leather jacket as a prop and convert the image into black and white and your image can become a whole lot more powerful

can be used in any setting, whether that happens to be in a studio setup or outdoors.

Lighting affects the impact of your shots, so really consider your location. Will you be using a reflector for natural light or will you be relying on flash or studio lighting?

With location shots, using a reflector to bounce sunlight back at your model will replicate the sunlight around you, enabling you to enhance your subject by controlling the way the lighting falls on your model. A flashgun will let out a direct blast of light that, if unadjusted, could easily bleach out your image entirely. However, if it is aimed correctly and powered accordingly, a flash gun will give smooth, accurate lighting.

As for studio lighting, you need to understand each light you use, how they interact and your choice of light modifier. Just one light with the wrong settings will unsettle the balance.

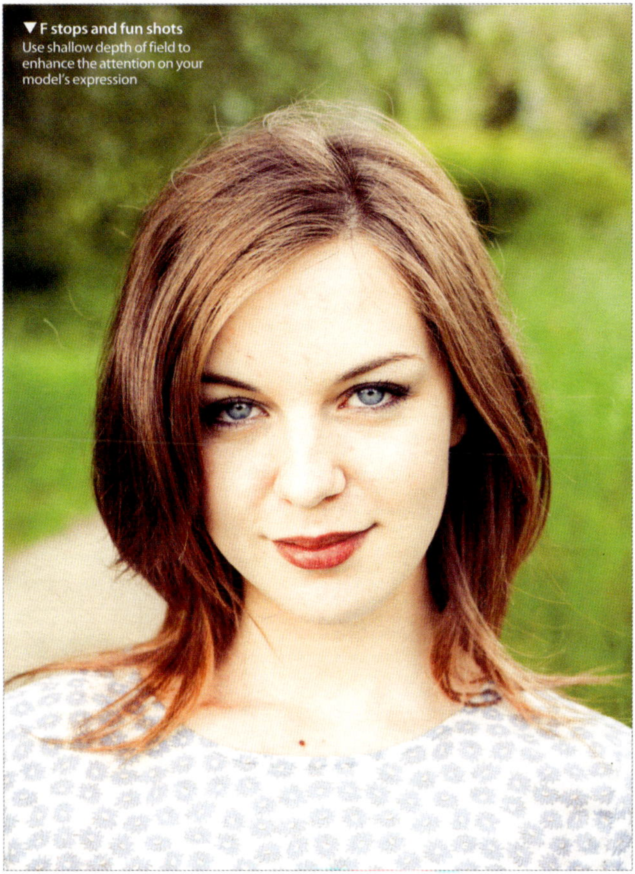

▼ F stops and fun shots
Use shallow depth of field to enhance the attention on your model's expression

It is simple to counteract these issues, though. When using a flash gun, bounce the flash light to minimise the risk of bleaching your subject. With regards to the studio lighting, use a light meter to measure each light's incident meter reading (the point where the light hits the subject) to gauge the strength of the light. Always review your shot and make sure that you are seeing the catch lights in your subject's eyes, as well as the shadow detail you want.

Stylistically, there is a lot you can achieve with the lighting and once you can repeat poses and lighting setups, you have a grasp of the basics. To add more impact, however, you can source low-cost studio backdrops or use a coloured drape sheet, a textured wall or even use a pop-up backdrop to really focus in on your subject.

Use an off board flash

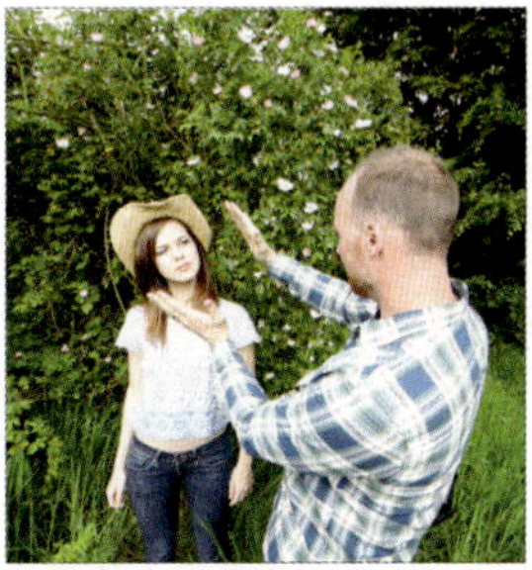

1 Position model
Ensure there is enough ambient light to expose without sacrificing aperture or shutter speed.

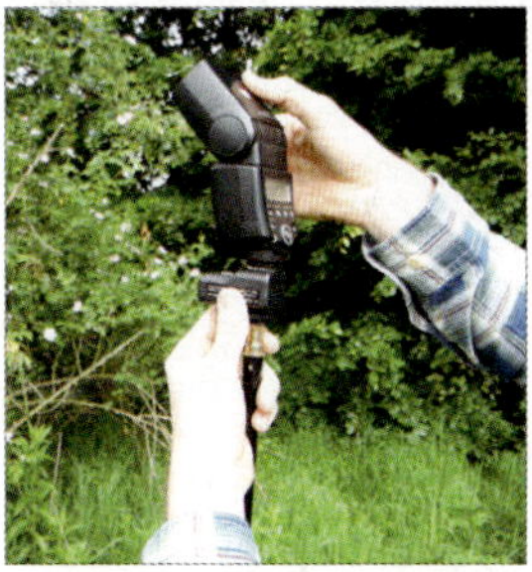

2 Use remote flash
Team a flash gun with a remote trigger and position behind your model for dynamic lighting.

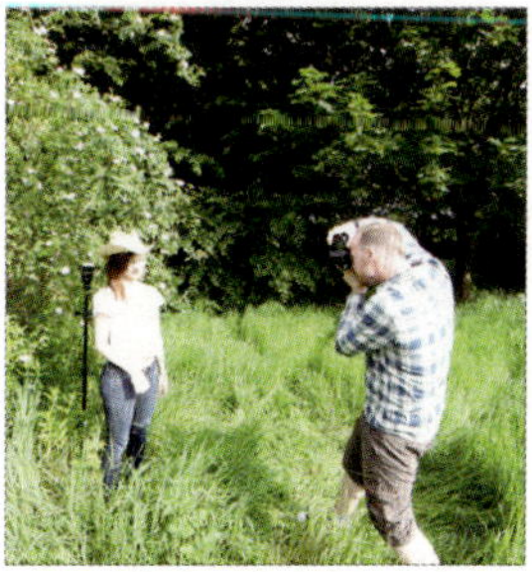

3 Achieve rim lighting
With the flash positioned and you metering for the face, overexpose their hair line for rim lighting.

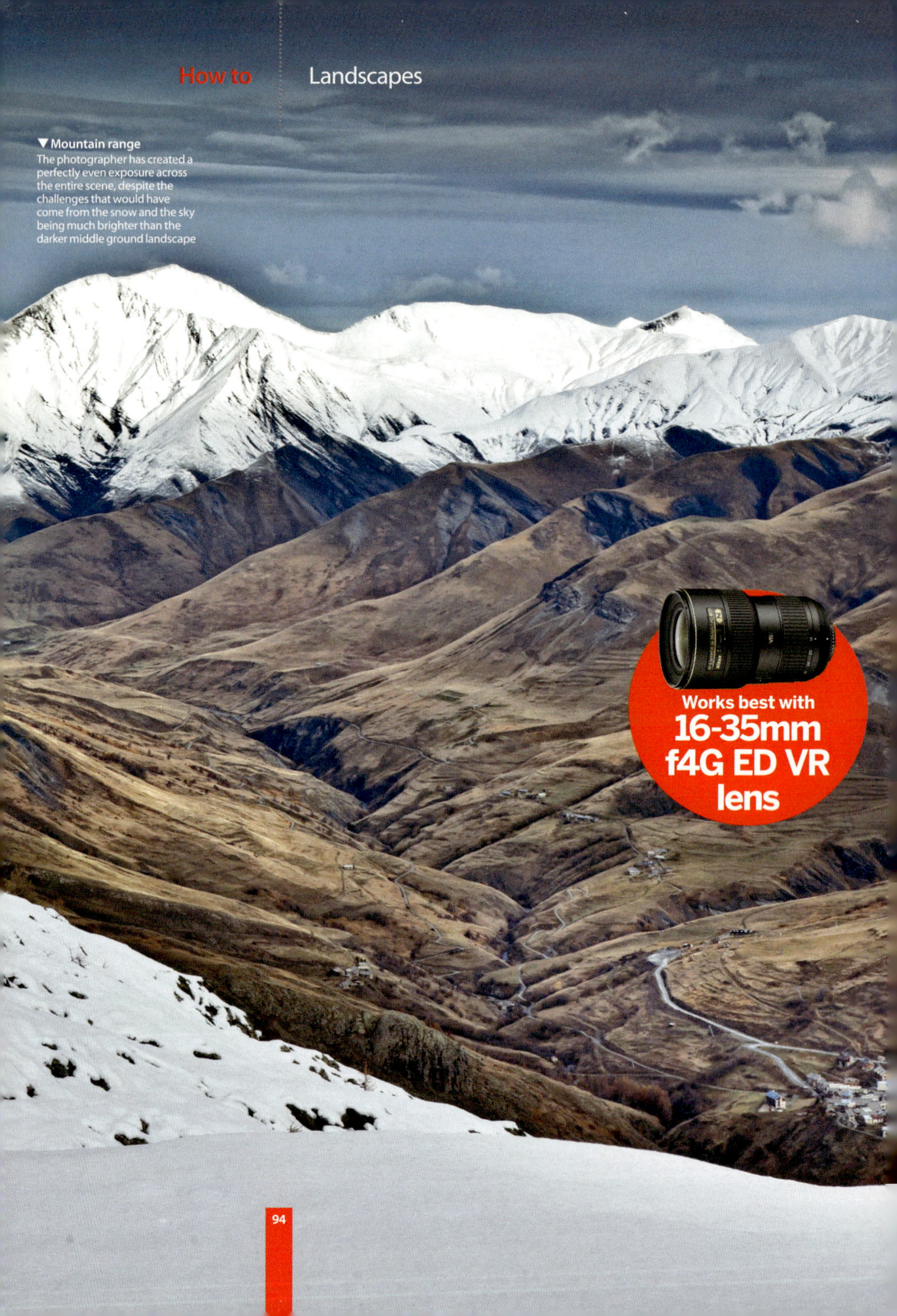

▼ **Mountain range**
The photographer has created a perfectly even exposure across the entire scene, despite the challenges that would have come from the snow and the sky being much brighter than the darker middle ground landscape

Shooting landscape photography

Capture the mood of dawn in the British countryside, the daunting magnificence of the French Alps or the quiet stillness of the great lakes of Canada with landscape photography

Landscape photography is one of the oldest and most widely appreciated forms of photography. Traditionally it has been used to explore the outstanding beauty of natural environments, whether it be dense forests, deserts or mountain ranges. Of course, landscape photography isn't limited to nature; it can be achieved anywhere and you'll find that urban landscape photography can be just as awe inspiring as that shot in the great outdoors. This amazingly diverse approach to photography has remained popular for centuries due to its ease of access. As long as you can find a space that inspires, you can shoot landscape photography. It's also an easy enough style to get into, as it doesn't require any specialist equipment; just a camera, a lens and a good eye for landscapes.

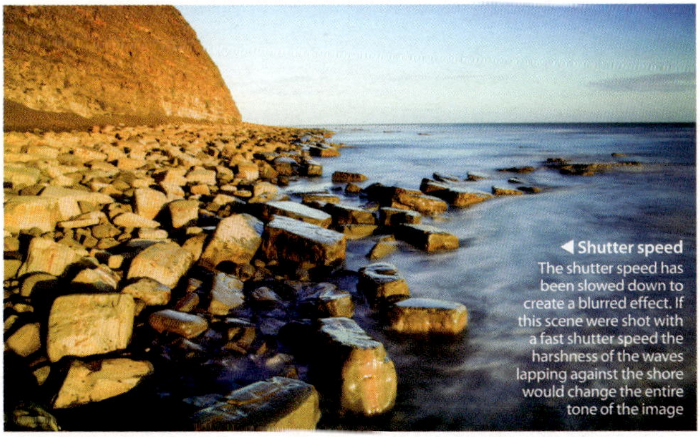

◀ Shutter speed The shutter speed has been slowed down to create a blurred effect. If this scene were shot with a fast shutter speed the harshness of the waves lapping against the shore would change the entire tone of the image

Top landscape edits

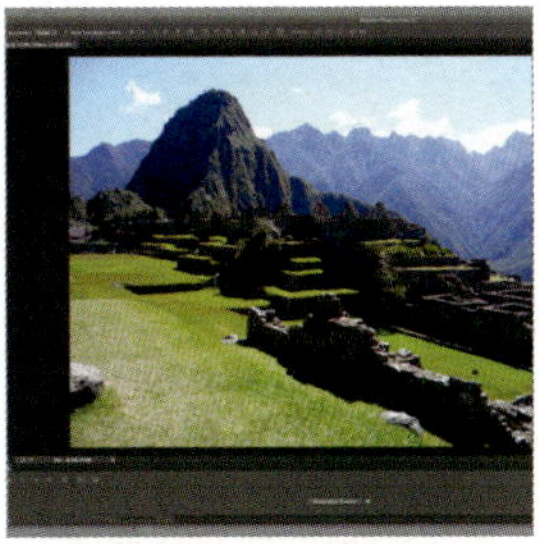

1 Post processing Although it's best to achieve your effects in-camera, there is room to improve and correct parts of your image with post processing using editing software such as Photoshop.

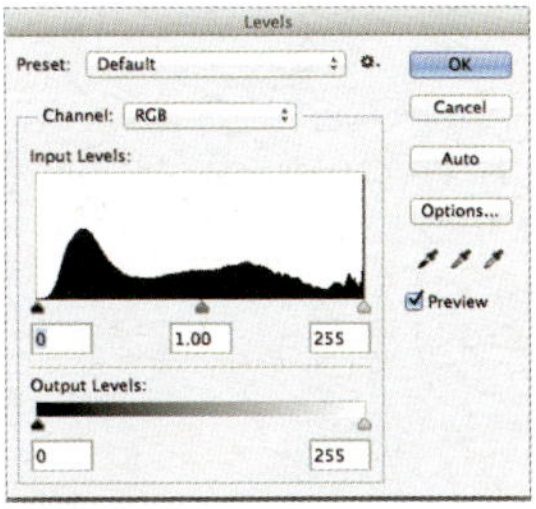

2 Levels The Levels tool can be used to reduce or increase the light levels of the shadows, midtones and highlights in an image, helping you to even out a shot's exposure.

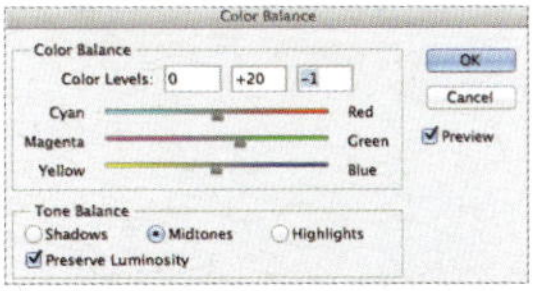

3 Color Balance Adjust the colour balance of a shot to make key colours pop out of the scene, most commonly these are the greens of the land and the blues of the sky.

Essential kit

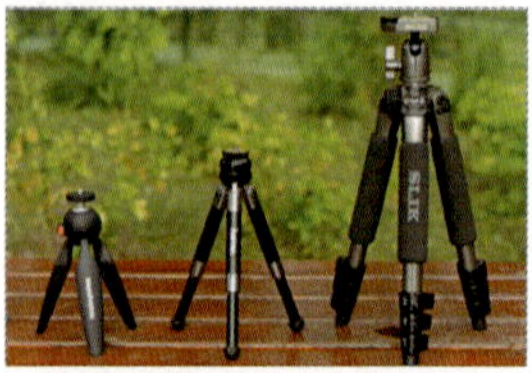

1 Travel tripod The ideal tripod should be lightweight but also durable with an inbuilt spirit level to straighten your shots.

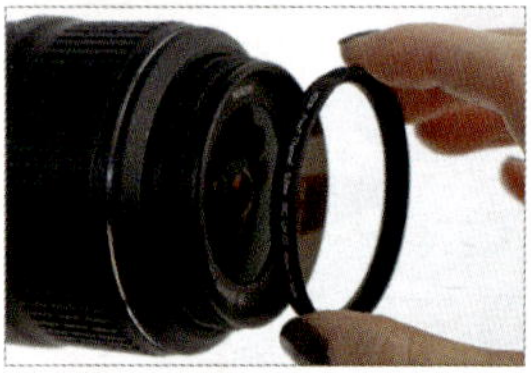

2 UV filter A good UV filter will protect your lens from UV light and grit without affecting the quality of your images.

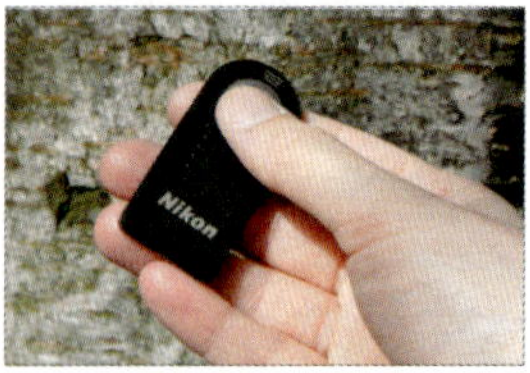

3 Remote shutter control Using a wired or wireless remote shutter reduces the risk of camera wobble.

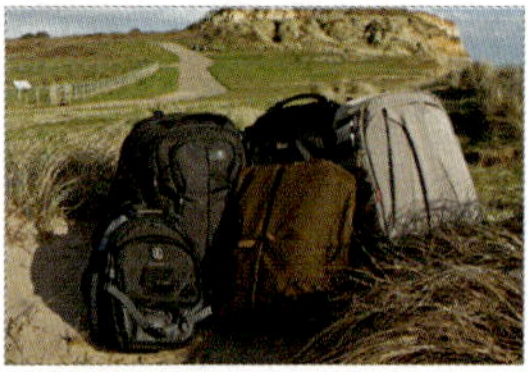

4 Camera bag A weather-proof camera bag is crucial to protecting your gear when out in the elements.

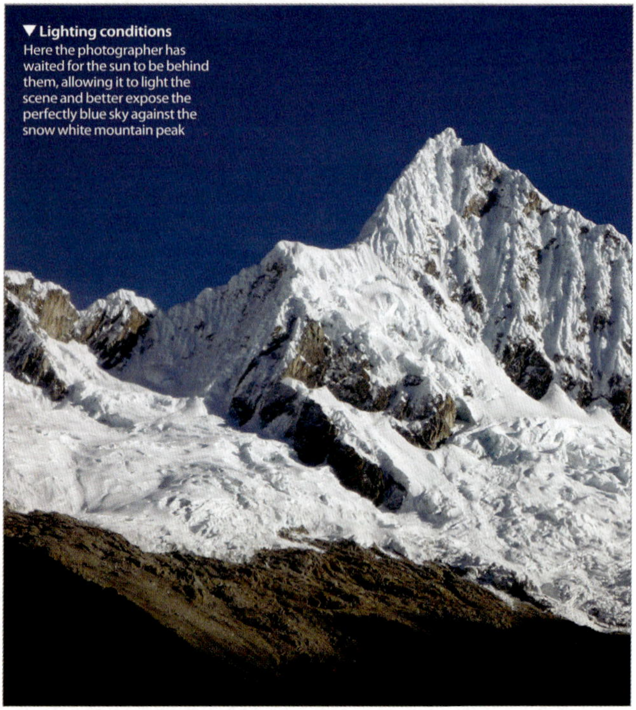

▼ Lighting conditions Here the photographer has waited for the sun to be behind them, allowing it to light the scene and better expose the perfectly blue sky against the snow white mountain peak

Picking a good lens

Although we said you don't have to buy special equipment, there is a benefit to building up the right kit when it comes to landscape photography. A suitable lens is worth its weight in gold. If you're looking for a lens specifically for landscape photography it's important that you consider your Nikon camera's format sensor. Nikon sensors come in two sizes; NX, which is a full frame and DX which has a 1.5x cropped sensor. So when shooting with a DX sensor there will be a magnification of 1.5x compared to an FX sensor. This means that you'll want to consider a slightly wider lens when shooting landscapes with a DX sensor compared to shooting with an FX sensor, to counterbalance the crop factor. An ideal lens for shooting full frame (FX) is the Nikon 24-70mm. If you're shooting with a cropped sensor (DX) consider the Nikon 16-85mm lens.

When shooting landscapes you want to aim to have the maximum depth of field possible, keeping everything in the scene as sharp as you can. This means that you are ideally shooting

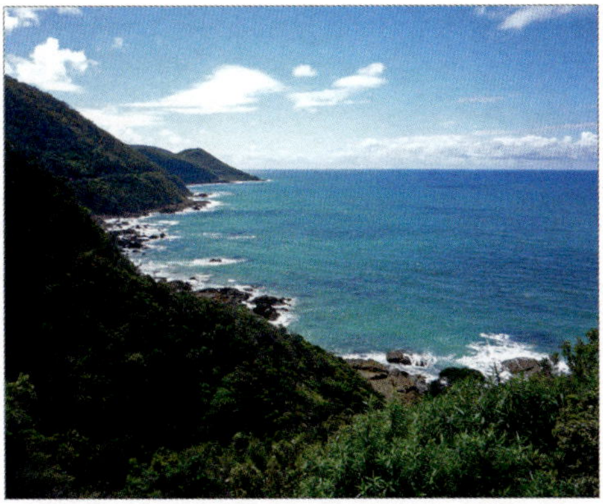

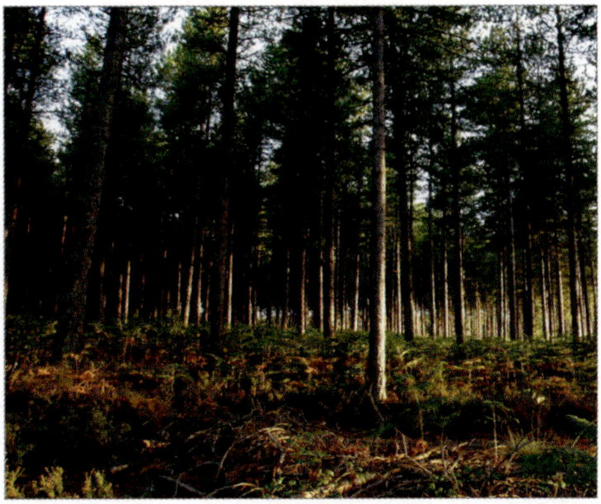

with a smaller aperture around f8 to f16. Because of this you don't necessarily need a lens with a high f-stop, the advantage being that this helps keep the cost of the lens down. Remember that when working with f-stops, the higher the number the larger the depth of field, meaning more of your shot will stay in focus. This is crucial when shooting the vast expanse of a landscape, because you capture the whole scene.

▲ **Depth of field**
A high f-stop has been used to give this shot the maximum amount of depth of field possible. The image stays sharp from the foreground right back to the trees in the far distance

◀ **Depth of shot**
Depth is a key feature of this shot. The foreground, midground and infinite background of the shot has determined the composition of the image

Extra equipment to consider

There are a few other pieces of kit worth investing in when shooting landscape photography. If you are interested in shooting with a slow shutter speed to created a blurred motion effect for different elements in the shot such as water or mist, then it's worth investing in a Neutral Density (ND) filter. ND filters effectively restrict the amount of light that goes through the lens, meaning you can slow down the shutter speed of your camera whilst still maintaining an even exposure.

A gradient ND filter can be used to restrict the amount of light coming from certain parts of the shot. You can use a gradient

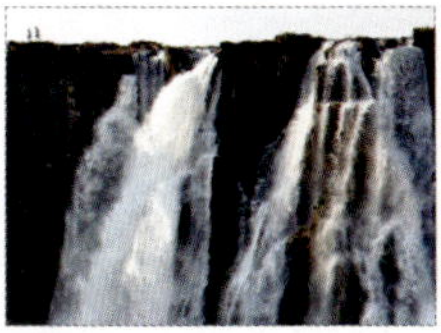

Bend the rules. This is flat with an overexposed sky, but these help make the photo stand out.

How not to shoot landscapes

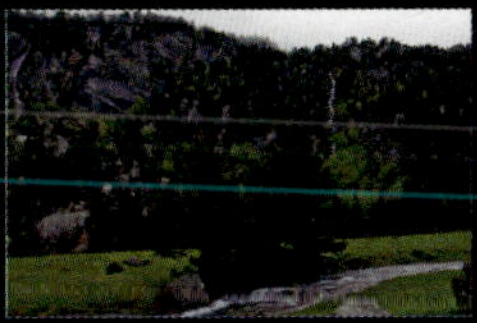

In this shot the point of interest (the two trees in the midground) has been placed dead centre in the shot, ignoring the rule of thirds. Also by shooting the hills in the background front-on, the shot has absolutely no depth. The sky is unevenly exposed and most importantly the shot isn't even, creating a disorienting effect.

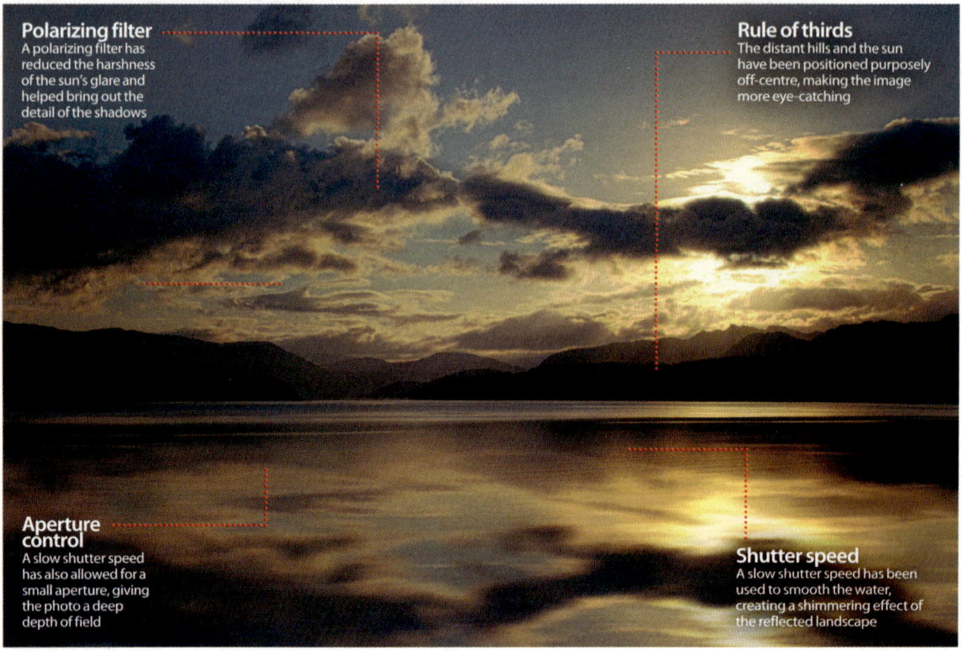

▲ Sunset
This is a perfectly simple and achievable landscape shot, incorporating several rules of photography as well as being shot in the golden hour just before sunset

ND filter to even out the exposure of the sky (which tends to overexpose) compared to the land. One more filter to look into is a polarising filter, which helps to reduce overly harsh glares from sources of light such as the sun or reflections, adding much better detail to highlighted areas of your shot and adding a general intensity of colour. A polarising filter also helps better protect your lens. Finally, a sturdy tripod is a key bit of kit for landscape photography. A tripod is crucial for steading your camera when shooting with a low shutter speed, as well as helping you to methodically set up your shot and wait for the perfect moment to start shooting.

Factors to consider

Weather is probably the biggest deciding factor when it comes to getting the shot you want, and getting the perfect light will make a big difference. A good time to shoot almost anywhere is just after sunrise, or just before sunset. The position of the sun at these times will exploit the shadows to better bring out the shapes of the surroundings. Breaking your shot up into a foreground, midground

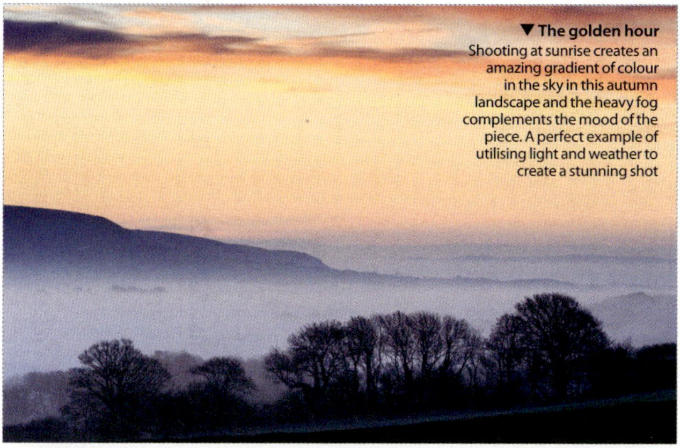

▼ **The golden hour**
Shooting at sunrise creates an amazing gradient of colour in the sky in this autumn landscape and the heavy fog complements the mood of the piece. A perfect example of utilising light and weather to create a stunning shot

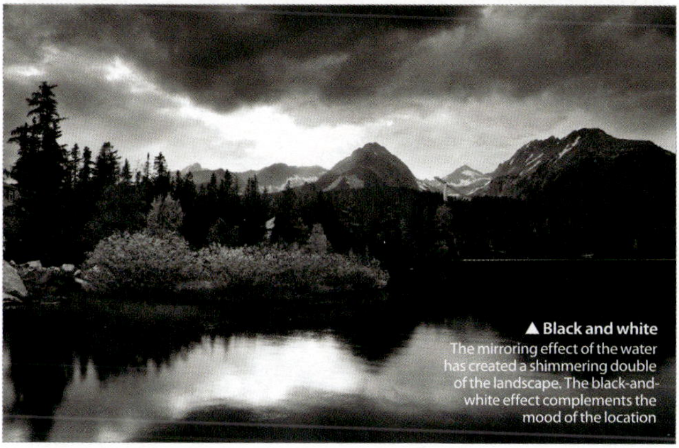

▲ **Black and white**
The mirroring effect of the water has created a shimmering double of the landscape. The black-and-white effect complements the mood of the location

and background is a useful way to compose your shot. The more layered the shot, the more stunning it becomes.

Try and avoid setting up a perfectly symmetrical shot by applying the rule of thirds. This requires you to break the shot up into three sections horizontally and vertically, then you can compose the most eye-catching parts along one of these invisible lines. Most Nikon DLSRs provide a grid overlay to help you shoot with this in mind. Also be mindful of when you take the shot. Look at some landscape photography and you'll see that the photographer has waited for the perfect moment, whether that be allowing for the haze of a morning fog to lift or for the sun to fall perfectly through the leaves of the trees. It takes patience but is worth it.

Composing a shot

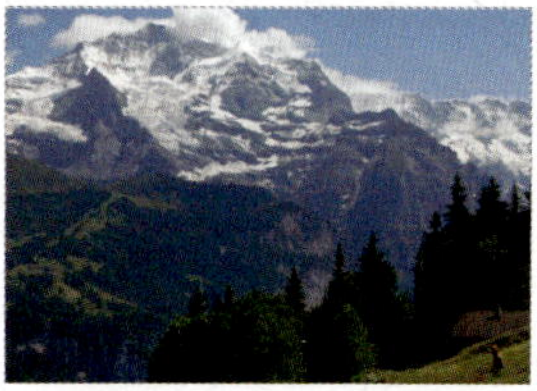

1 Layering a landscape In this image the foreground, mid-ground and background are perfectly composed. The rule of thirds has been utilised so the eye is drawn to the key points of interest in the shot.

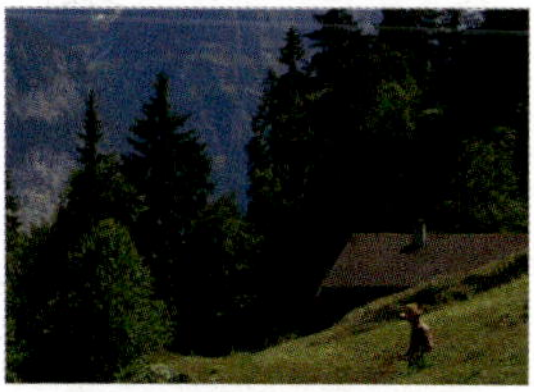

2 Foreground The foreground should stand out in a landscape photograph, but don't let it dominate the scene. In this case the house and worker do help to complement the distant mountain range.

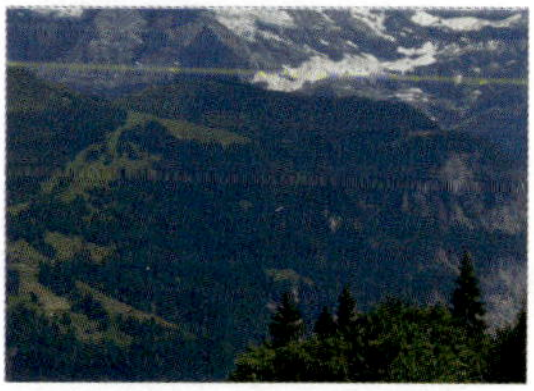

3 Midground to background By placing distance between the foreground and midground, then having the midground blend more seamlessly with the background, the shot feels as though it has a natural composition, without drawing too much attention to itself.

Shooting the finer details of life

Getting up close and personal with the incredibly small isn't just about bugs – everyday textures such as bubbles can seem alien through a macro lens

Macro photography is arguably one of the most abstract incarnations of the art, whether it's photographing tiny insects and making them look like behemoths or capturing textures and transforming them into abstract landscapes. Whatever your subject, it is sure to take on a completely different life once captured.

So what is macro photography? The simple answer is close-up, detail photography, like photographing details in a landscape through binoculars. How macro photography works is relatively straightforward as it's all about distance. Not just the physical distance a photographer has to their subject, but more a closeness inside your camera. The sensor within your camera, whether it's cropped or full-frame, sits static at the bottom of a lens once one is attached, and there it stays, capturing the light sent to it. All the lens

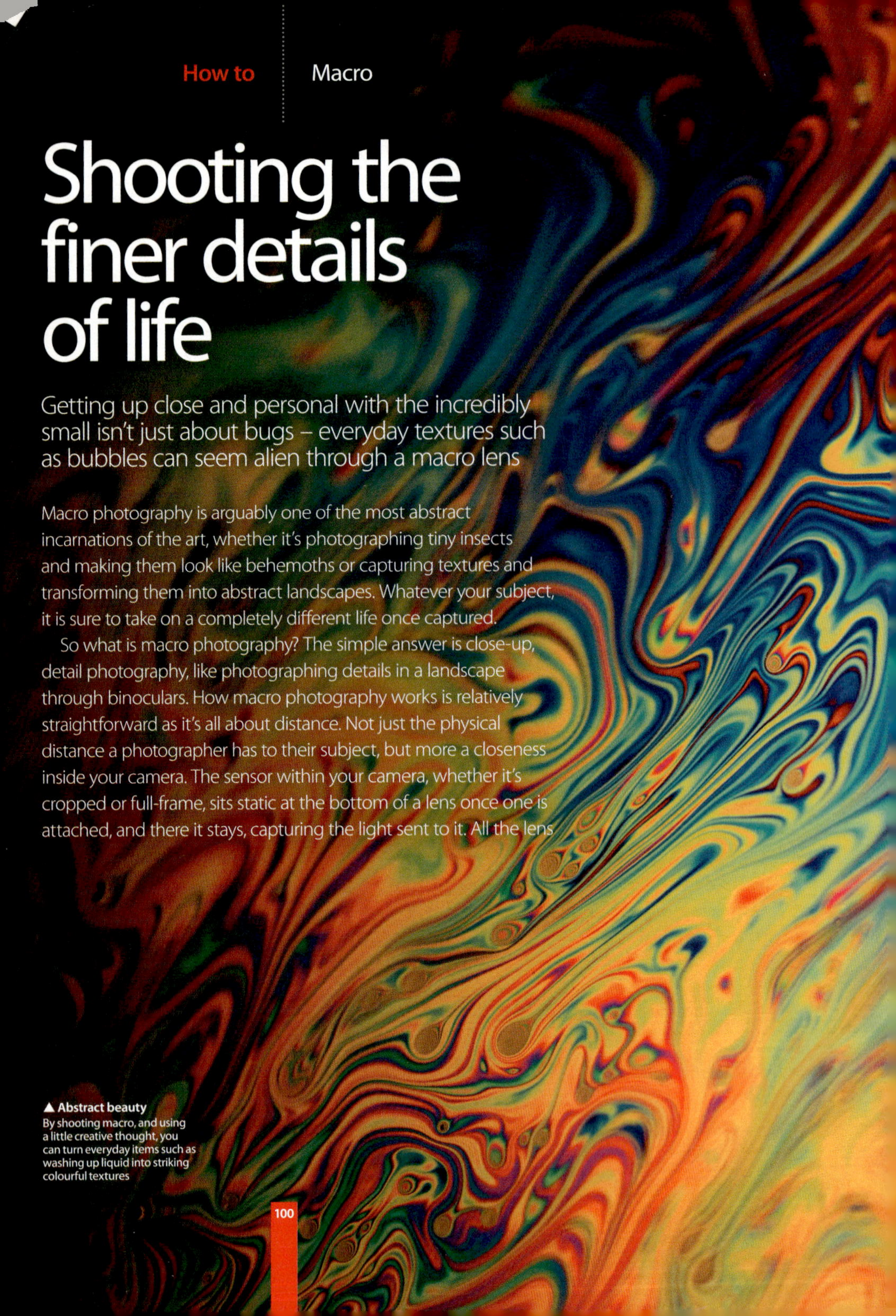

▲ Abstract beauty
By shooting macro, and using a little creative thought, you can turn everyday items such as washing up liquid into striking colourful textures

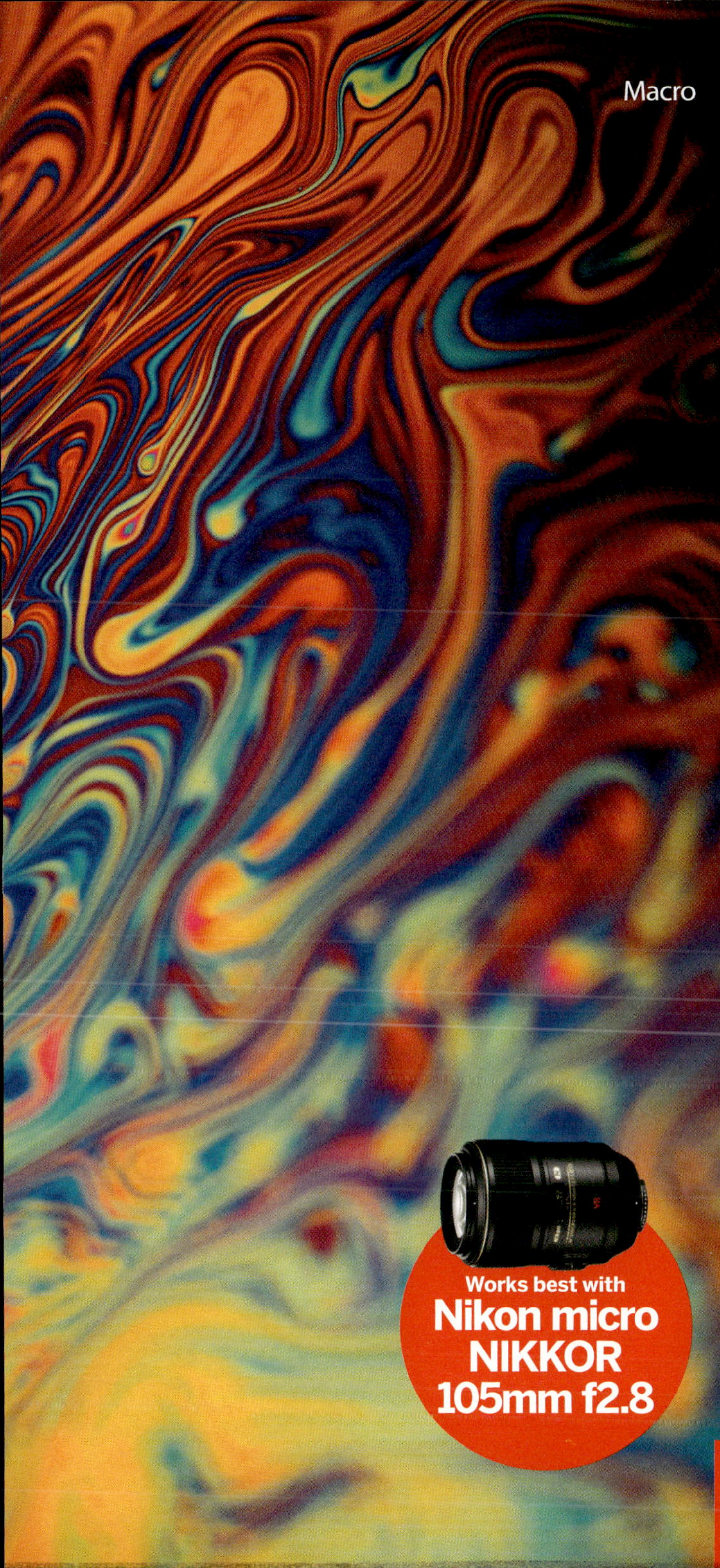

Works best with
Nikon micro NIKKOR 105mm f2.8

General macro tips

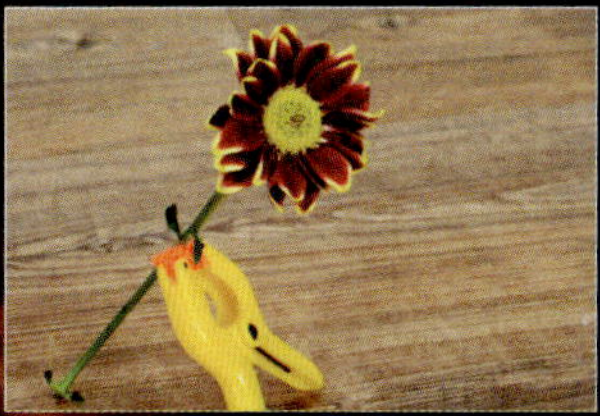

1 **Be supportive to your subject** With small objects, it can be helpful to support them via rigid clips or shield them from ambient wind if shooting outside.

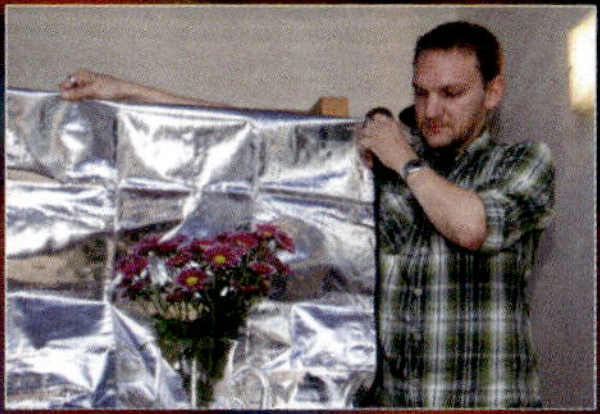

2 **Back ground checks** Just because you are shooting fine detail doesn't mean you can't use an interesting background. Try coloured sheets or something that creates bokeh.

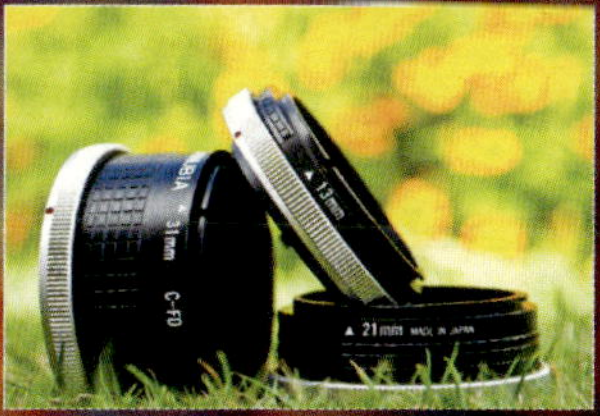

3 **Get closer with an extension tube** To get closely focused on such a tiny object is one thing, to fill the frame with detail is another. Increase your focal length with an extension tube.

Macro

Tips for macro success

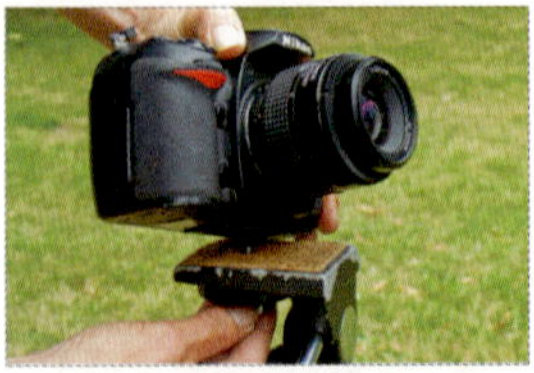

1 Use a sturdy tripod You will be micro focusing on an already tiny object so any movement could shift your focal point.

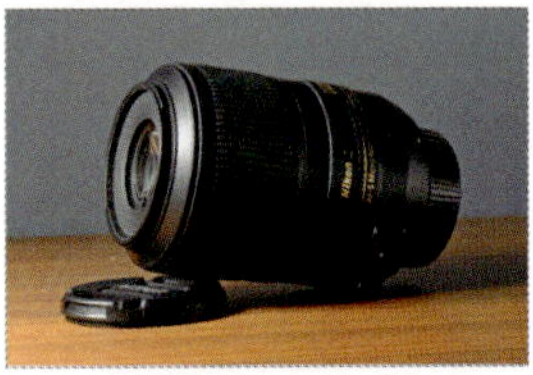

2 Use the right lens Depending on your subject, and the level of macro shooting you want to achieve, select the correct lens.

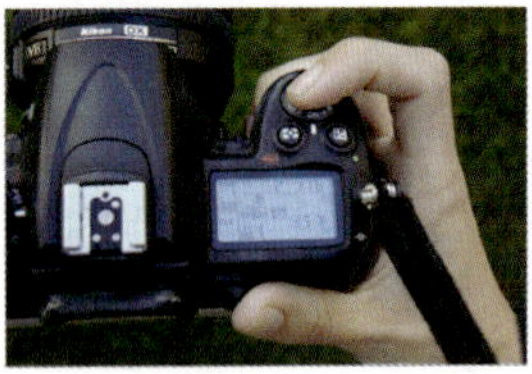

3 Set aperture If you are looking to focus on a specific area, or focus on the whole item, set the aperture accordingly.

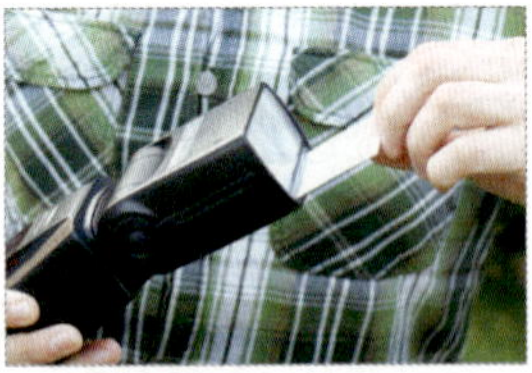

4 Use flash for extra detail Try bounced flash light. It's perfect for specular highlights and enhancing colour.

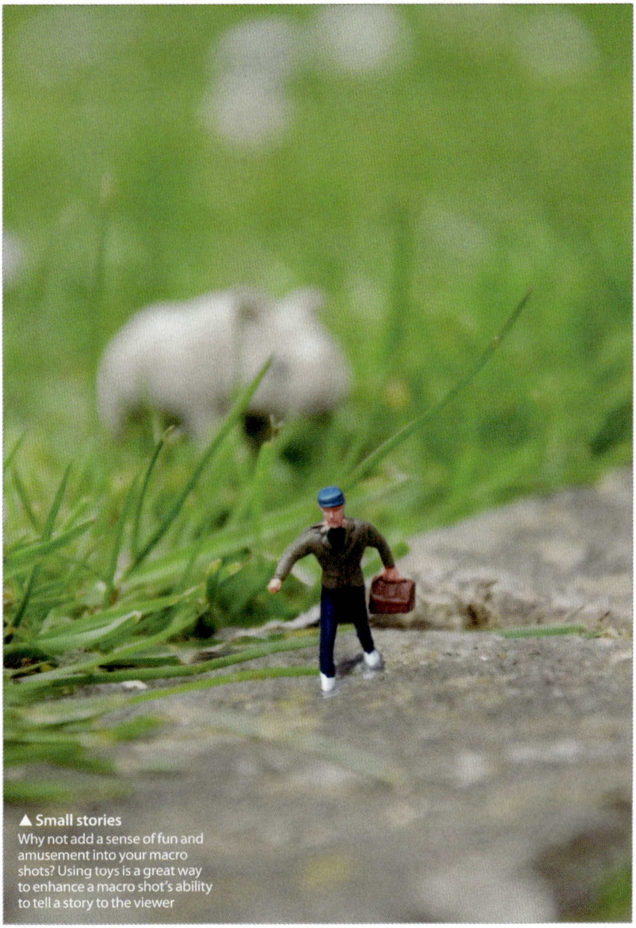

▲ **Small stories**
Why not add a sense of fun and amusement into your macro shots? Using toys is a great way to enhance a macro shot's ability to tell a story to the viewer

has to do is move glass closer or farther away from the sensor to send a focused or zoomed-in image.

The difference between macro lenses and standard lenses is lens construction. The internal glass element in a macro is further away from the sensor, and will usually be a prime lens. A prime lens is a fixed lens with no zoom. It stays at one focal length. The light passing through the lens has farther to travel, and the speed of which the light can travel is relevant to the f-stop listed on the lens.

The more glass there is in the construction of a lens, the higher the f-stop as there will be multiple pieces of glass for the light to

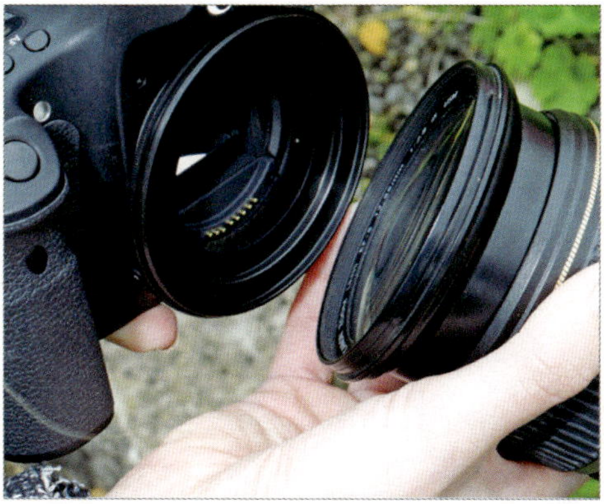

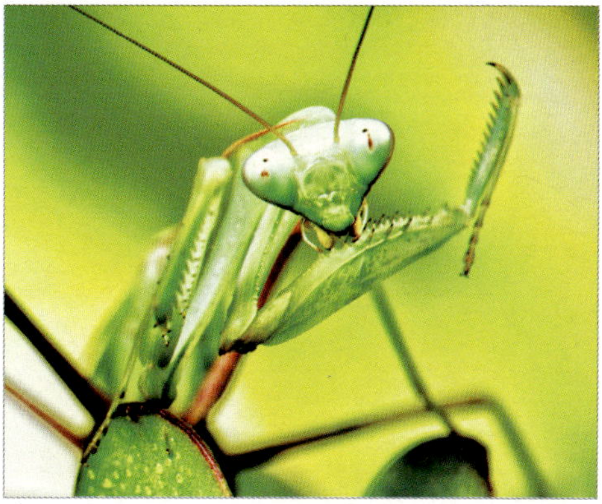

pass through, slowing the strength of the light. With a dedicated macro lens you will have minimal glass, meaning a faster f-stop, usually somewhere around f2.8. To shoot effectively in macro, what you will need is an idea of the subject you want to shoot, a lens that will enable you to get close enough to achieve the desired result and more than likely a tripod to keep things steady.

Which lens to use

If you are looking to photograph insects and flowers from a casual distance and are looking to dabble, then a prime lens in the region of 90mm to 105mm will be perfect, as you will be able to get in close enough to fill the frame and experiment with your depth of field. For the more seasoned macro enthusiast, who is wanting to get that bit closer and isn't afraid to step back and add some distance between them and the subject, a prime lens ranging in the ballpark of 150mm-200mm would be adequate. Again, this choice would enable you to completely fill the frame, using the aperture selection available within the lens to affect the depth of field of the image, forcing the attention on the subject.

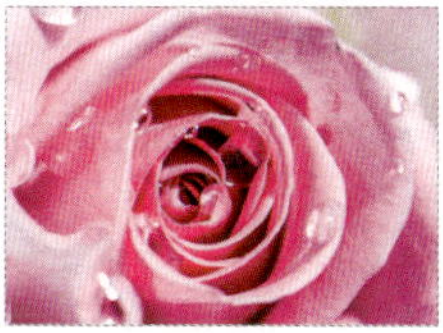

For macro flower shots, use glycerine to recreate water drops. Simply drip it into place.

▲ Ugly bugs
Shooting macro can not only allow you to get close to an otherwise unreachable subject, but also add a sense of personality to it. Take insects such as the preying mantis, who are far from human but we can still relate to simply due to their pose

◀ Reversal trick
Additional tools such as the reverser ring can be used as effective alternatives to dedicated lenses when shooting macro. By reversing the focal qualities of your lens, they bring the subject closer

Macro ring flash

Ring flash has become associated with high fashion and creative portraiture of late, however it was originally a lighting practice most commonly used in dental, medical and even forensic photography. Employed as a way to evenly light a subject with minimal shadows but still with maximum detail, it is the perfect lighting choice for macro photographers as the light sits in front of the lens itself.

Macro ring flashes are a lot smaller then the now more familiar portrait ring flashes as they need to direct the light into much smaller areas.

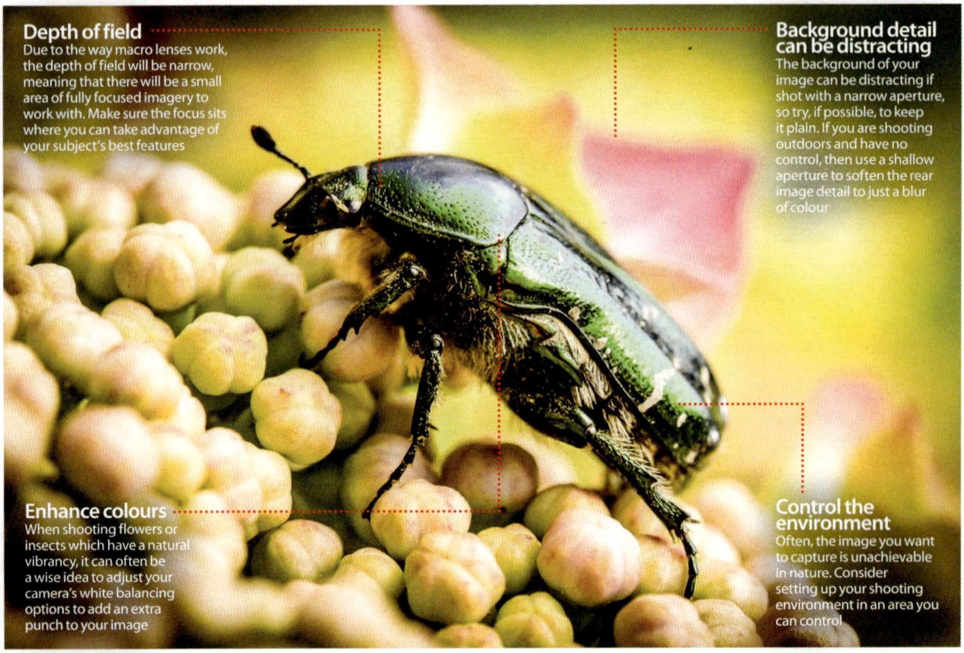

▲ A bug's life in full glory
As macro photography is a great way to shoot insects and flowers, let's look at what makes a great macro shot. Looking at the subject matter, as well as the composition, there is more at play than just finding the subject to shoot

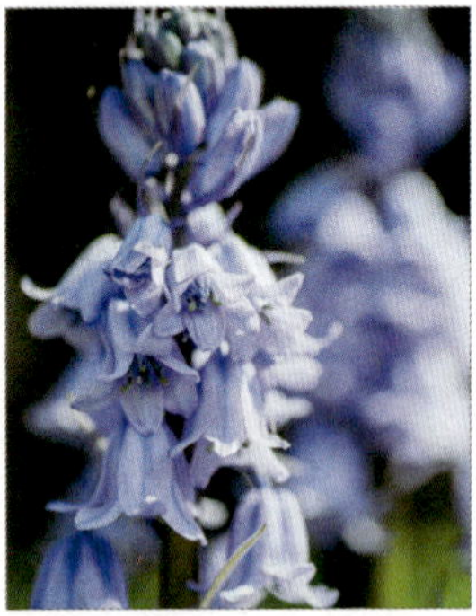

▲ Adding focus from macro shots
Shooting flowers is a great way to show off the depth of field capabilities available to you. By keeping the foreground in focus and softening the background detail, the subject of your affection is kept sharp

This is the main draw to macro photography – the sheer detail you can gather from a subject. Of course there are other alternatives available than dedicated lenses, such as a reverser ring, which reverses your current lens' focal distance by reversing the traditional attachment of your camera body and inverting your lens. Although initially a great and cost-effective measure, it does leave the most fragile part of your lens open to damage.

Filters and tubes

Another alternative is using macro filters that can be attached to your lens. Through a combination of glass screw-threaded filters, they bend the light through convex and concave glass.

If the focal length of your lens is unsatisfactory, the solution is to further the distance of the lens' main glass element from the camera sensor. The way to do this, with minimal lens distortion is through the use of extension tubes.

Extension tubes are exactly as the name implies – an extension tube to further the distance between the glass and the sensor, allowing for a closer shot. What you get in extra closeness though,

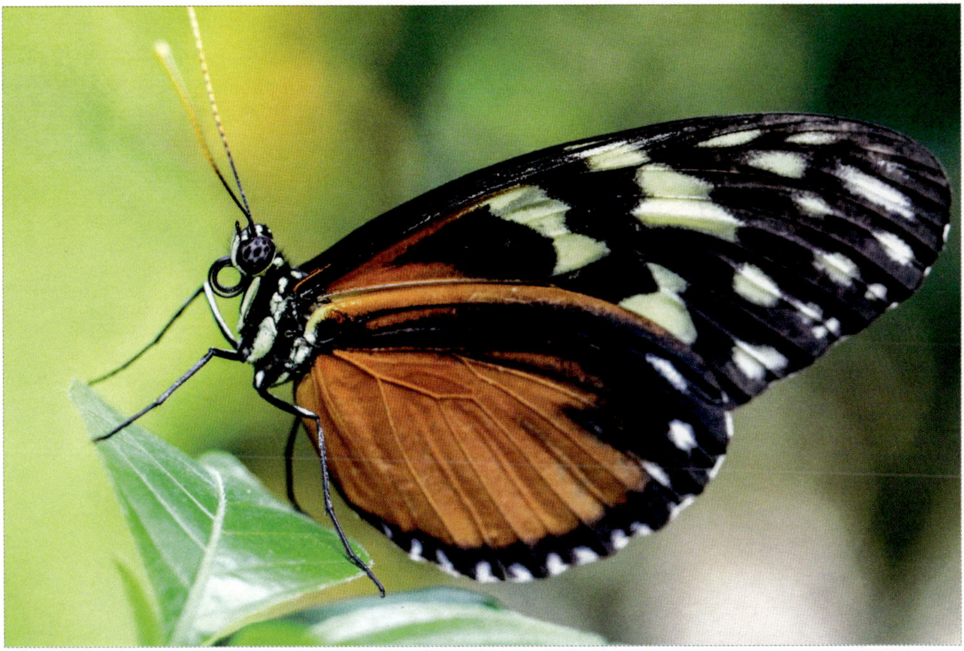

you lose slightly from your aperture, as the light is travelling further than intended, so it may be an option to consider your ISO or even a flash gun when shooting macro.

So, in short, these are interesting, budget-friendly solutions for acceptable results on a shoestring budget, but for true macro shots, you need to use a dedicated macro lens.

▲ **Spread your wings**
Butterflies are everywhere in summer, but we don't often take the time to look at them. Using macro techniques, they are all the more impressive up close.

Shooting macro textures

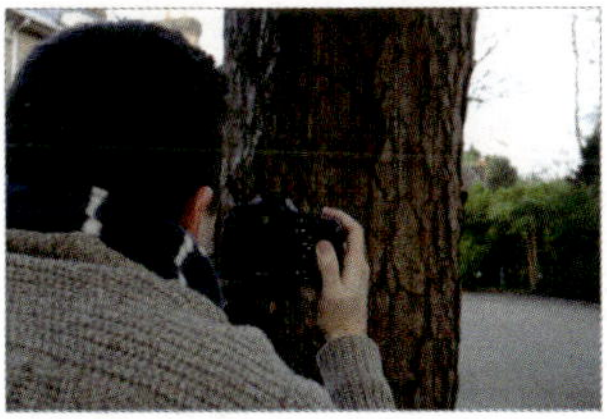

1 Create textures Why not create a textured landscape? Find a wooden texture, tree bark is ideal, and set up your camera on a tripod in front of it.

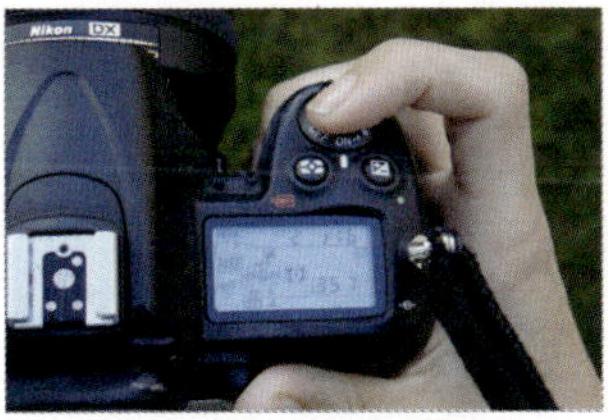

2 Work with a high aperture Set your aperture to f16 so you have a lot in focus. You may need to drop your shutter speed or alter your ISO.

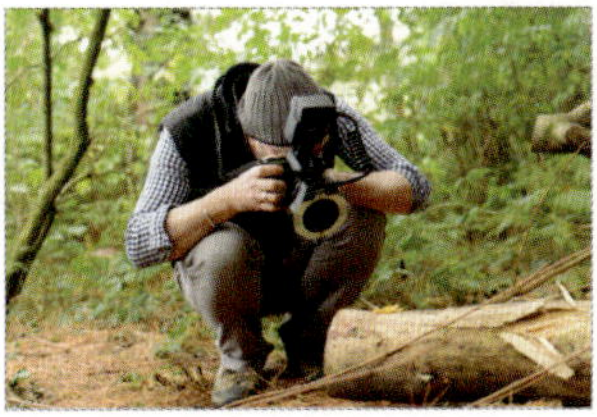

3 Add some extra light Use a small hand-held reflector to bounce light into the wood or alternatively use an angled flash gun or macro ring flash.

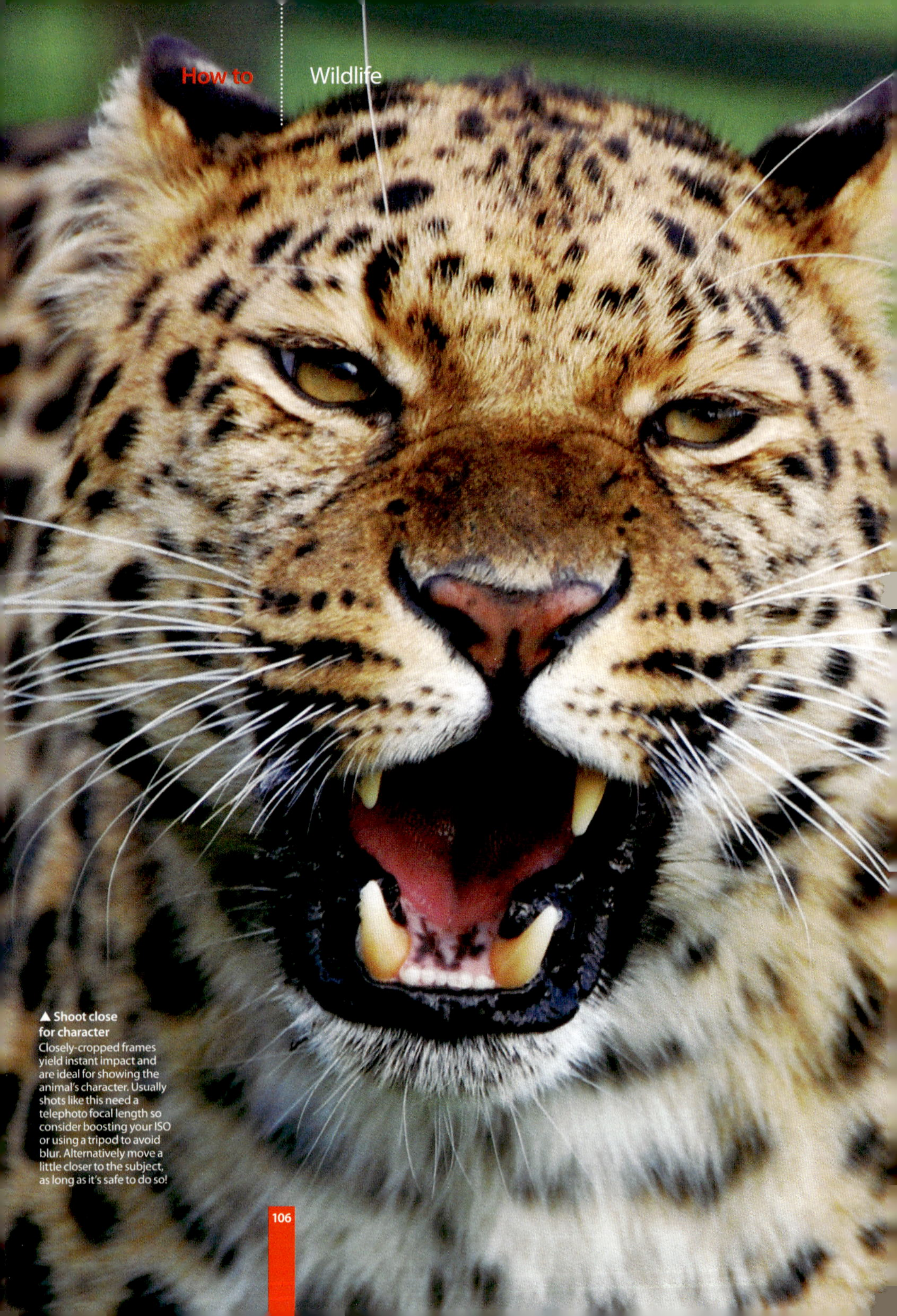

▲ Shoot close for character
Closely-cropped frames yield instant impact and are ideal for showing the animal's character. Usually shots like this need a telephoto focal length so consider boosting your ISO or using a tripod to avoid blur. Alternatively move a little closer to the subject, as long as it's safe to do so!

How to capture wildlife shots

Whether you're planning on photographing in your local woods or snapping away on the plains of the Serengeti, discover ways of improving how you shoot wildlife pictures

The greatest asset, other than a Nikon camera, that every wildlife photography enthusiast should have, is patience. If you're not a patient person this genre may be a struggle, as typically to get the most natural, awe-inspiring images you'll need to conceal yourself, keep quiet and wait, sometimes for very long periods of time, before your subject even emerges. What's more, when the animal does appear its presence may be fleeting, especially if it senses you, so it's important to know your camera inside and out, allowing you to work quickly and efficiently in the few moments that you have. Over the next few pages we'll cover everything you need to know from embracing the right settings to carrying the best kit.

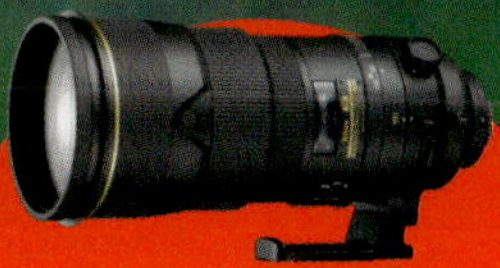

Works best with
AF-S NIKKOR 300mm F/2.8G ED VR II

Useful wildlife kit

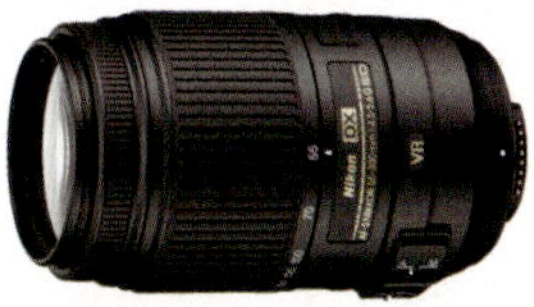

Telephoto zoom lens

Price: £200/$342+ **Tel:** +44 02 8541 4440
Web: www.europe-nikon.com

You don't want to scare the animals away, so a zoom lens is a must for every serious wildlife photographer, for getting close to the action.

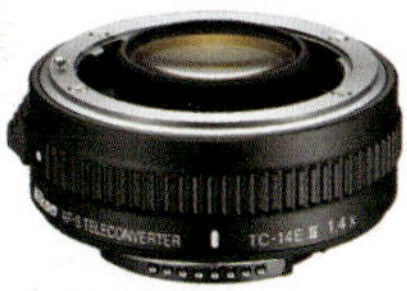

Teleconverter

Price: £100/$171+ **Tel:** +44 02 8541 4440
Web: www.europe-nikon.com

Teleconverters are a much cheaper, far more portable solution to the large telephoto lenses, available in various degrees of magnification.

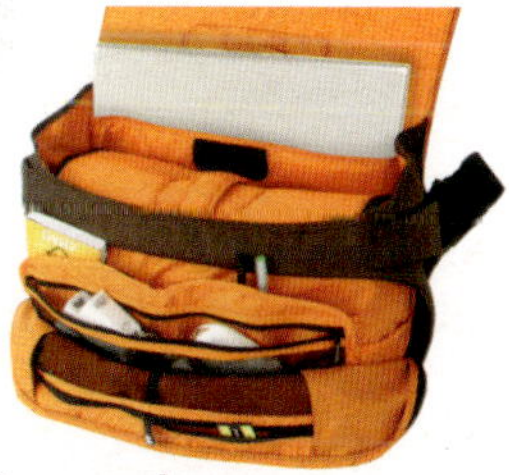

Camera bag

Price: £50/$85+ **Tel:** +49 221 949954-60
Web: www.crumpler.eu

Travel is often associated with this genre so use a waterproof, rugged and comfortable pack that can double as support for your large lenses.

Composition tricks

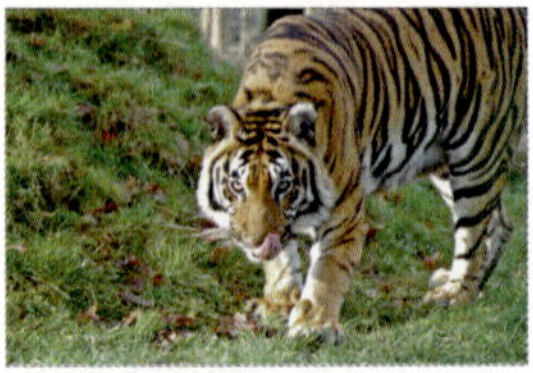

1 Rule of thirds Ensure the main point of interest lies on one of the intersecting lines or points. This suits telephoto and wildlife focal lengths.

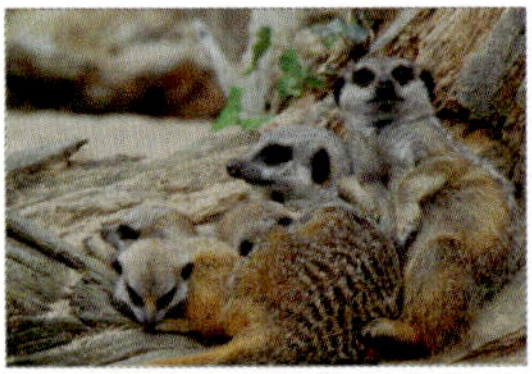

2 The eye dance Compose an image so the viewer's eyes 'dance' over the image. Frame the shot with interesting elements placed all over.

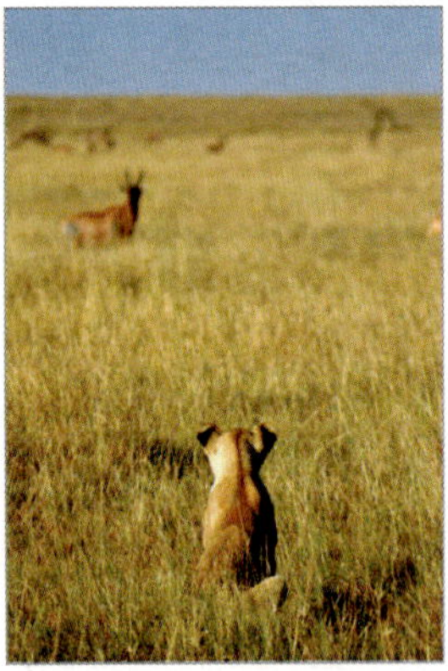

3 Break the rules Break the rules when the occasion calls for it, as not every photo needs a compositional trick to enhance it. Simply use them as a guide to help you get started.

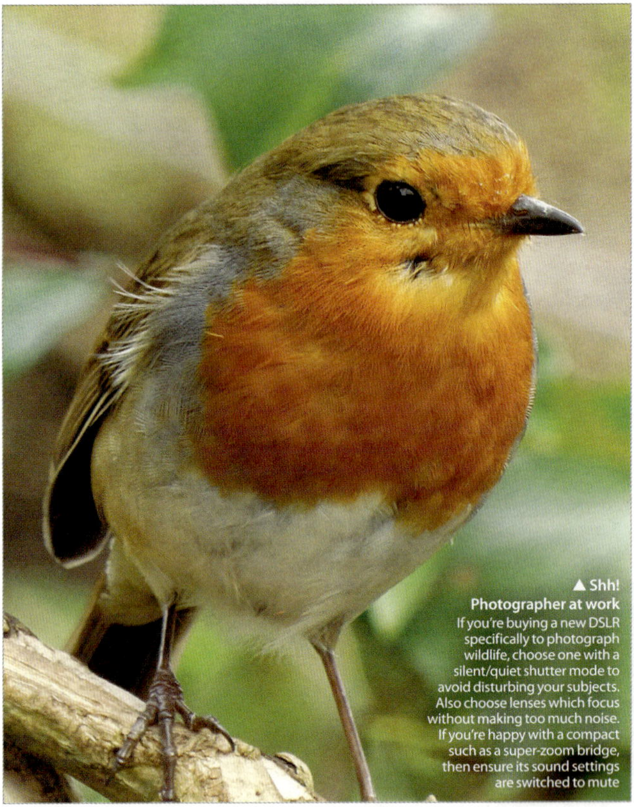

▲ **Shh! Photographer at work** If you're buying a new DSLR specifically to photograph wildlife, choose one with a silent/quiet shutter mode to avoid disturbing your subjects. Also choose lenses which focus without making too much noise. If you're happy with a compact such as a super-zoom bridge, then ensure its sound settings are switched to mute

Set up to shoot

Making sure your camera is ready for action before any wildlife appears will make the difference between getting the shot and not. As wildlife photography is all about speed, your exposures will need to be as fast as the subjects you are attempting to capture. What's more, as you'll often want to use far-reaching focal lengths you need to consider either raising the ISO or supporting the camera to ensure your frames are as crisp as possible.

So the first thing you'll need to know, if you're planning on shooting handheld, is how high you can push your camera's ISO without the negative effects of noise ruining the quality of your imagery. Test this at home before setting off and closely inspect the results on your computer. Once you know its limits, avoid going beyond this in the field, but don't be scared to go as close as you

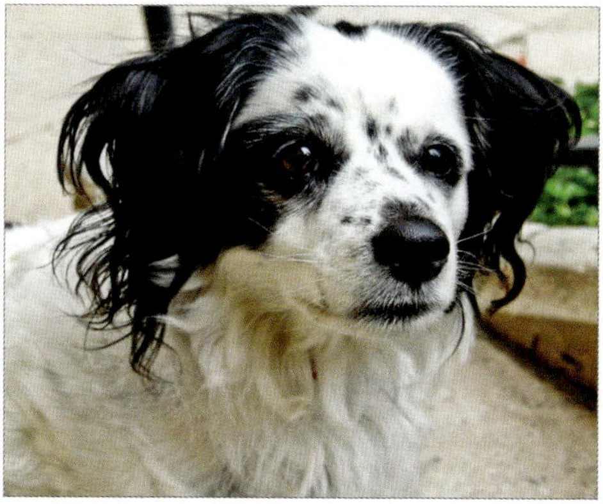

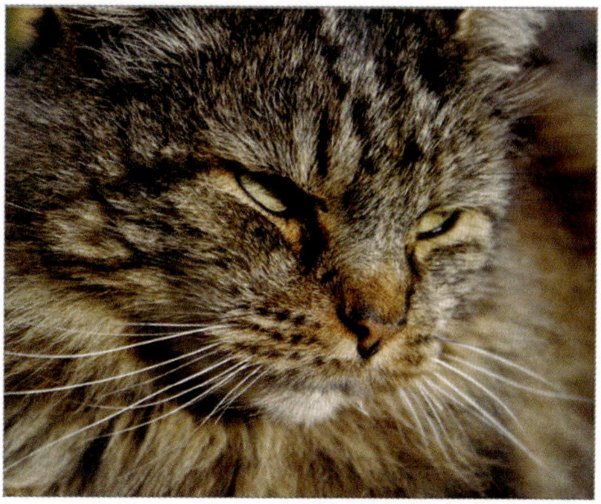

can to this limit as higher ISOs will allow you to gain faster shutter speeds, which is essential for this breed of photography. If you are able to erect a tripod covertly, low to the ground or alternatively lie on the ground and shoot with your camera supported on something like a solid backpack, your frames are less likely to suffer with blur. That said if you are shooting handheld, support the camera underneath with your spare hand and either support your shooting elbow on the ground or on your knee for added stability.

Picking a lens

Lens choice can be tricky. You should choose which lens you will use wisely as you'll want to avoid making any noise, such as that caused by changing lenses, in the beasty's habitat. A better idea is to bring along a couple of cameras with lenses sporting varying focal lengths already attached, so you can simply 'switch' lenses by swapping cameras. Whilst prime lenses provide undeniably sharper results, especially in low light, it's perhaps more advisable to use zoom lenses in this field unless you know your subject will stay in one place or if they are like to move very slowly. Zoom lenses are

When shooting handheld, place your elbow on the ground or on your knee, and place your spare hand under the camera for extra support.

▲ Practice makes perfect
A good way for any wildlife photographer to begin is by photographing pets and domestic animals. They are likely to be more willing than the real thing but you can start to see how speed is one of the most important factors here

Focal length versus speed

While most contemporary lenses host vibration reduction technology, it's a good idea if you're shooting handheld to know what the minimum shutter speed of the camera and lens is for ensuring your images are sharp and not blurred. The general rule of thumb for this is to not exceed an exposure time longer than the focal length, so for example if you're shooting at a 250mm focal length, so it's advisable to use a shutter speed faster than 1/250sec.

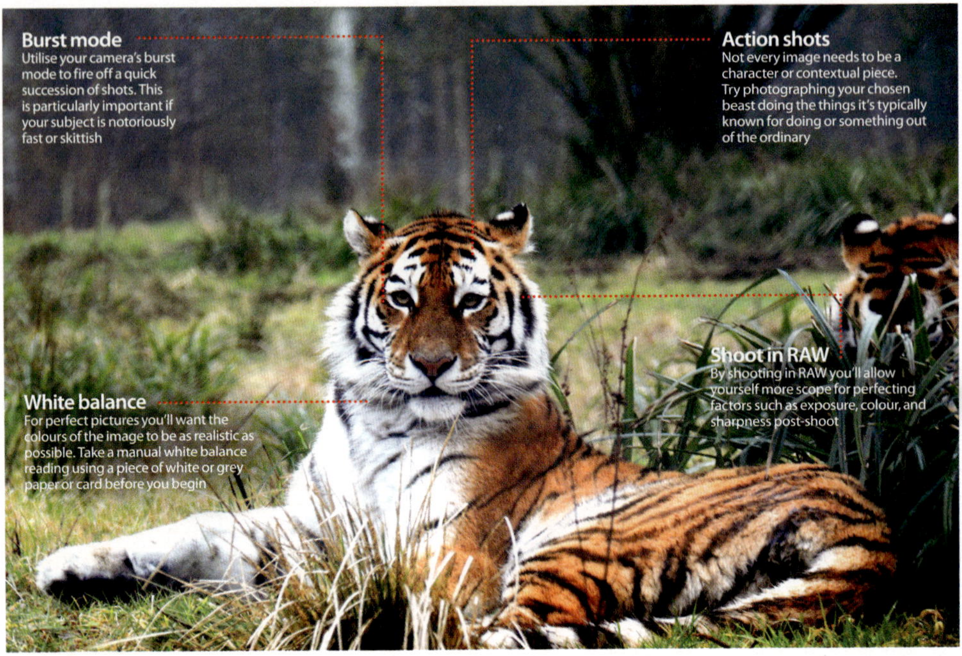

▲ **Work with the light**
Where possible, position yourself so that the light illuminates the subject, ie so that sun is behind you, shining onto the animal. If the sun is at its peak or too harsh, wait for them to sit under a shaded canopy, and work this lovely softened light

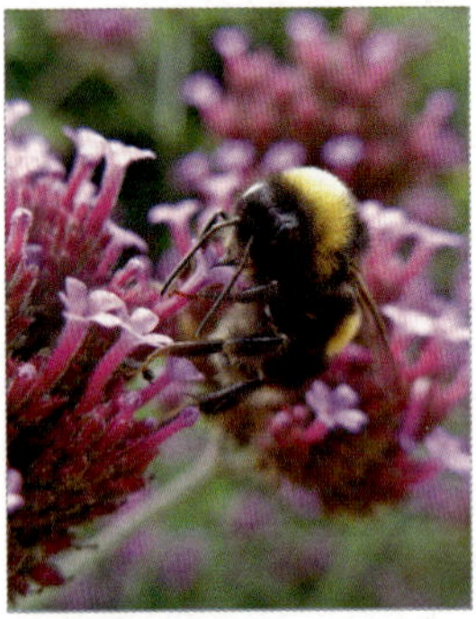

▲ **Advanced shooters**
When it comes to settings, you'll probably find it easier to shoot in manual or Shutter Priority, to ensure that the images are well exposed, with nice crisp details and accurate colours

better for faster-paced or less predictable animals, as they will offer greater compositional scope.

Know your animal facts

Knowledge is power; the more you know about the animal you wish to photograph, the more likely you are to capture stunning imagery. A little research will go a long way here, and you don't even need to know that much, as simple things like what hours of the day it's active will tell you when to get into position, plus discovering what it eats will give you a tip off as to where to lie in wait. The more you know, the more confident you will be to guess what it will do next, thus you can better follow the subject, anticipate its movements and get as many usable frames as possible. This is particularly crucial if you want to shoot character portraits that really show the personality of the animal. Get as close as you can and aim to frame with eye contact. Also consider cropping in closer to shoot the animal's textured skin and sometimes, eye-catching geometric patterns, as this can make for some really inspiring shots.

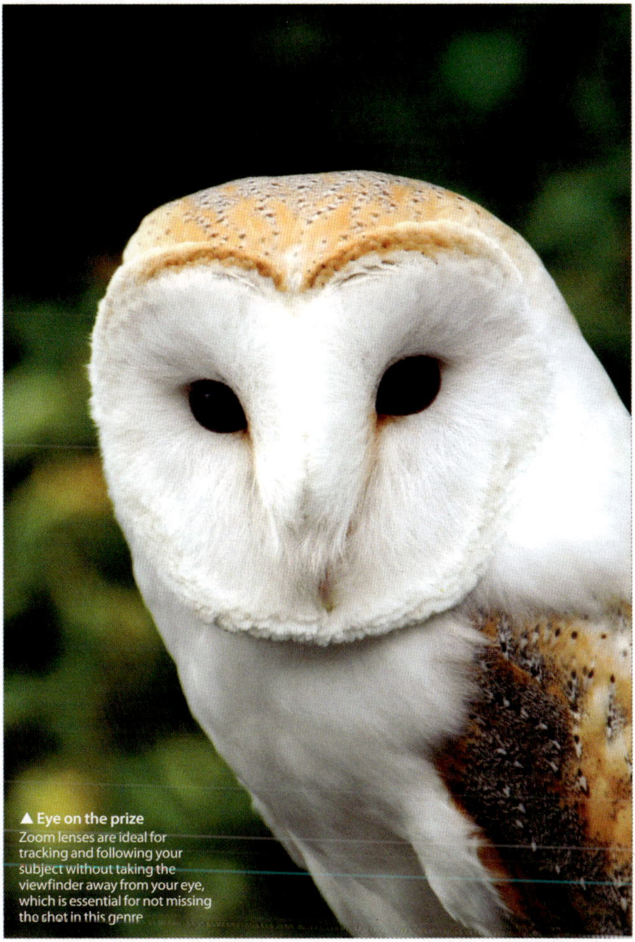

▲ **Eye on the prize**
Zoom lenses are ideal for tracking and following your subject without taking the viewfinder away from your eye, which is essential for not missing the shot in this genre

Other composition techniques that pay off in this genre are the rule of thirds and the golden ratio, which work regardless of focal length. Either ensures you have the focal interest off-centre with exciting elements spiralling out, or use your camera's grid to place the animal or part of the animal on one of the interesting points or lines. If you're using a wide-angle focal length these two techniques work nicely in capturing the animal in its environment; using the backdrop to add context to empower the image beyond a simple picture of an animal. Whatever you do, just have fun with it and enjoy what you're shooting, after all that's the whole point.

Get that perfect shot

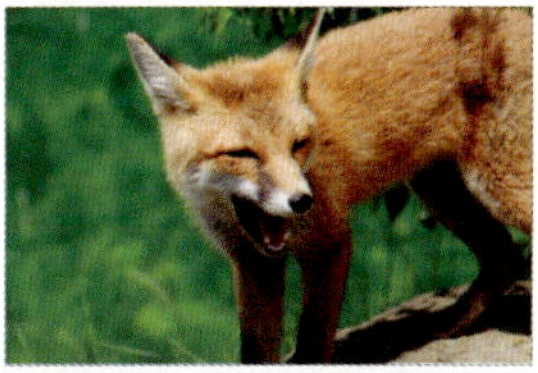

1 Patience is a virtue The more you know about an animal the better. Use this to narrow down the time and place of the shoot. Then wait for it to appear.

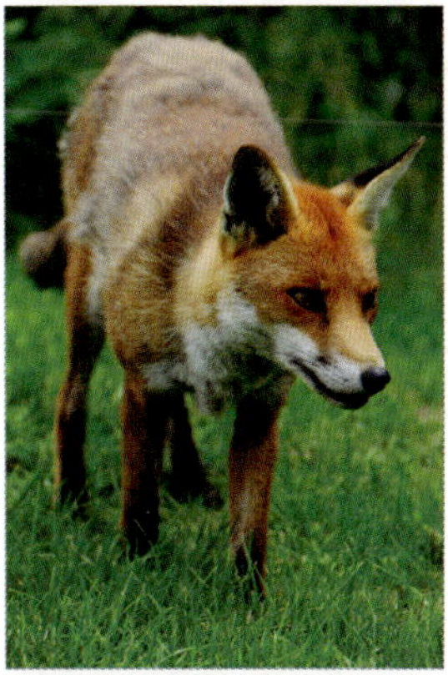

2 Settings in motion Before the animal appears, have your settings already dialled in. Aim for a fast shutter speed and know your ISO limit.

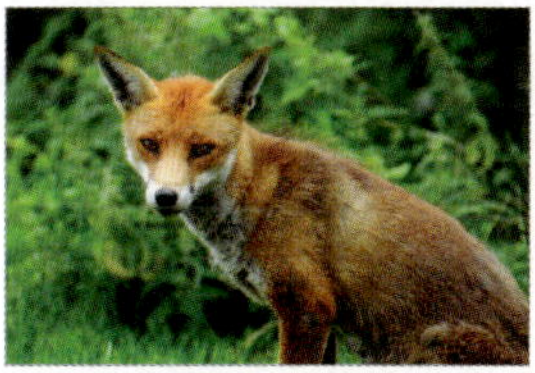

3 Killer capture Choose an orientation that best suits the animal, lock the focus and exposure then fire the shutter when the animal looks at you.

▼ Dramatic portraits
Use black and white in the studio to deliver stylish results. As you can see in this image, just a simple pose and delicate lighting add to the impact of the overall image

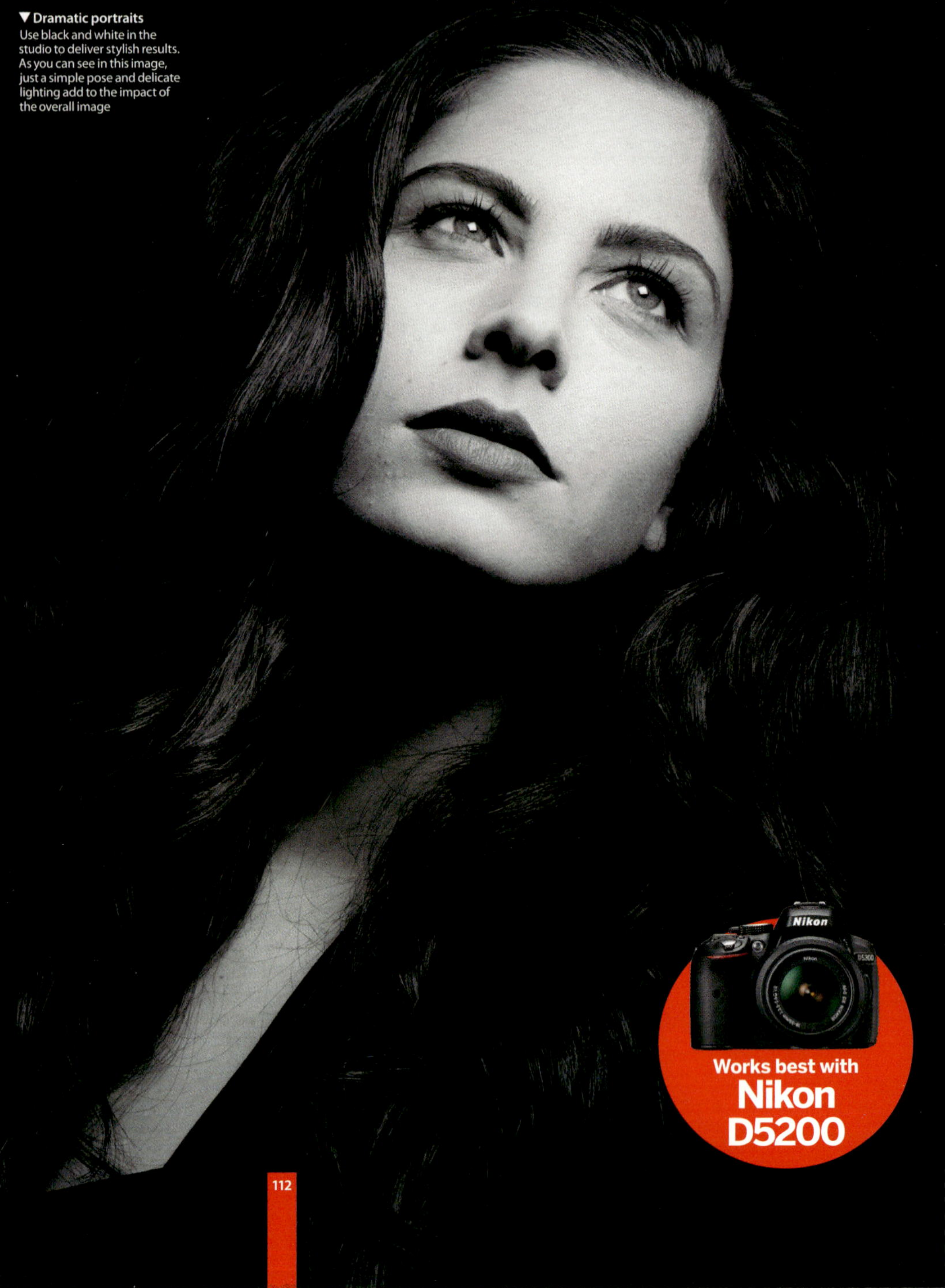

Black and white elegance

Add drama, intrigue and atmosphere to your images by using some of our tips on how to achieve flawless black and white shots

It's often said; keeping things simple will add to the image. Nowhere is this more true than when applied to the colour spectrum. Black and white images are timeless in their appeal and the good news is that the whole procedure can be simple. Because cameras have default style options for colour toning and advanced white balance controls, shooting in black and white is relatively easy. Select your shooting mode, set it to black and white and away you go. But if you are serious about the style, you will need to put in a little more effort for the results you want.

The rebirth of black and white

The *Sin City* film was an explosion of style that captured people's imagination. Shot on green screen, lit to replicate the classic film noir look and mainly black and white, it paid both homage to its source material, and also made black and white new and accessible again as a creative method. Whereas black and white had been typically

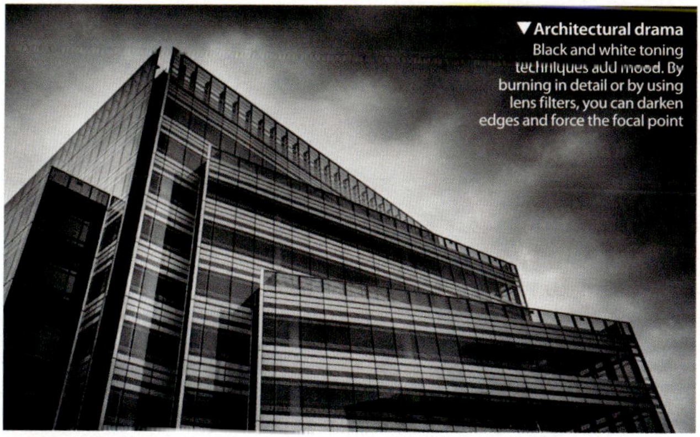

▼**Architectural drama** Black and white toning techniques add mood. By burning in detail or by using lens filters, you can darken edges and force the focal point

How to

Edit in Raw

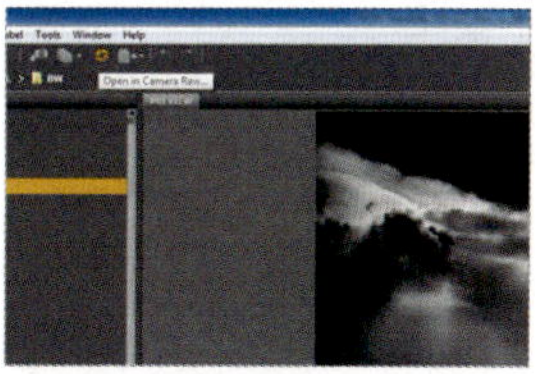

1 Open your image Open up your JPG or RAW file into Adobe Camera Raw by clicking the RAW edit button in Bridge.

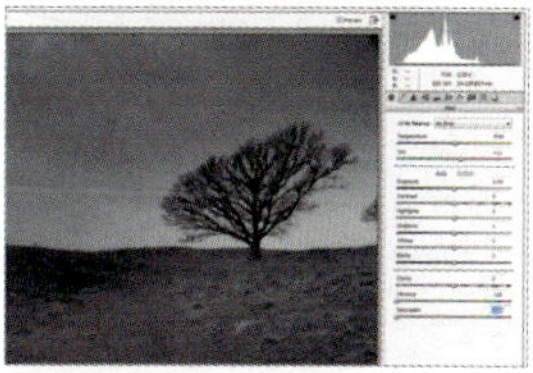

2 Reduce the colour Reduce the vibrancy and saturation of your image by sliding the colour adjustment controls to 0.

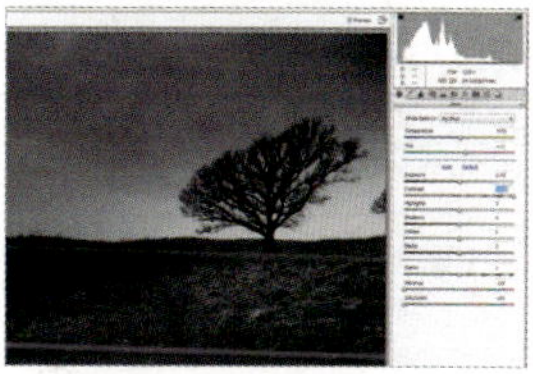

3 Add contrast Boost contrast by using the Contrast slider options. Use the other sliders to add more depth in the tones.

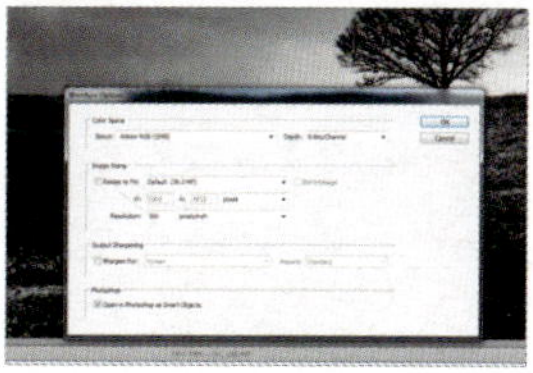

4 Convert to Smart Object Click the image detail option at the bottom of ACR and select the open as Smart Object option.

Photoshop edits

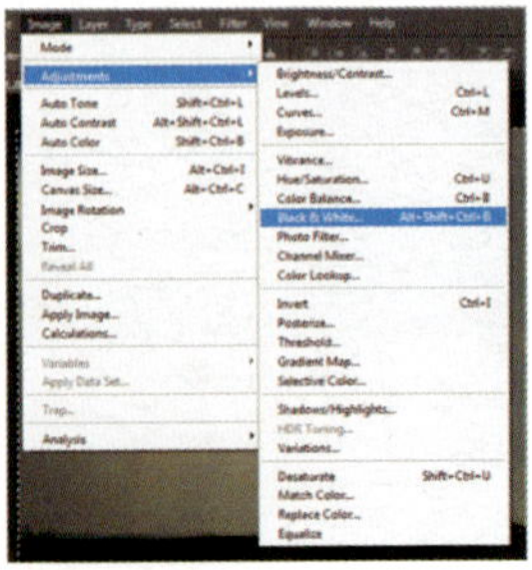

1 Edit for B&W To perfect in Photoshop, open your image and go to Image> Adjustments>Black & White.

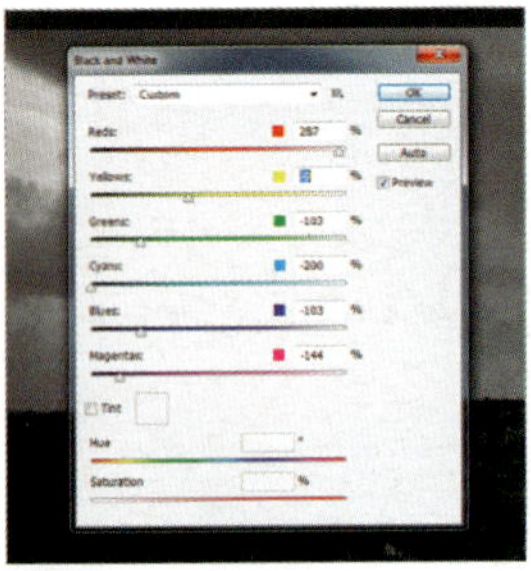

2 Slide the sliders Even though the image is B&W, you can use the sliders to adjust each colour's presence in the image.

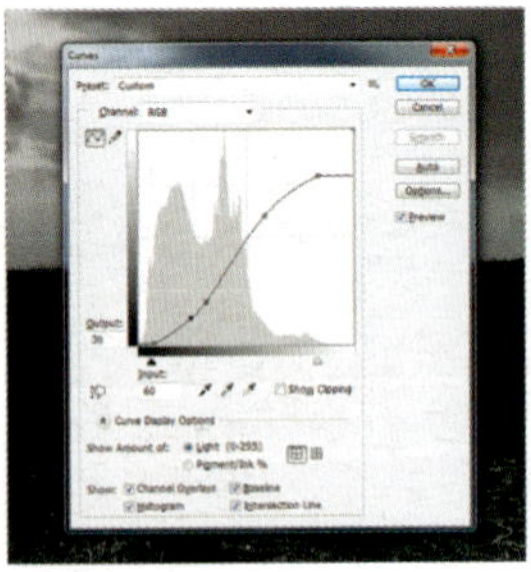

3 Add a little contrast By using Image>Adjustments>Curves you can enhance the overall contrast of the image.

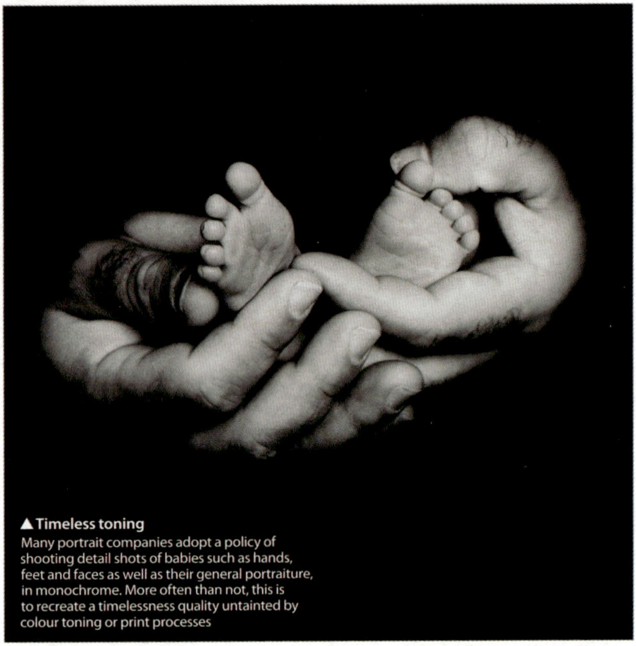

▲ **Timeless toning**
Many portrait companies adopt a policy of shooting detail shots of babies such as hands, feet and faces as well as their general portraiture, in monochrome. More often than not, this is to recreate a timelessness quality untainted by colour toning or print processes

employed as a reportage or fine art option for many years, suddenly billboards were saturated in timeless, modernised, monochromatic images designed to be edgy, cool, and dramatic. Brands adopted the style to sell products, and portraiture companies busied themselves to sell to the public.

Obviously black and white existed way before digital and way before colour, but since it's in vogue again, and with all the advantages of modern digital techniques for capturing and editing images, mastering the art is now an essential.

The kit determines the result

As you are in effect changing the colour tone of your image, lens choice and depth of field will be guided by your intended final image. For example, if you are looking to achieve an interesting architectural shot, you may want to be using a wide angle lens. If you are looking to photograph people, use a portrait lens around 50mm or 85mm.

Become familiar with the technical operations of your camera, such as your lighting setup if shooting in studio, or the colour

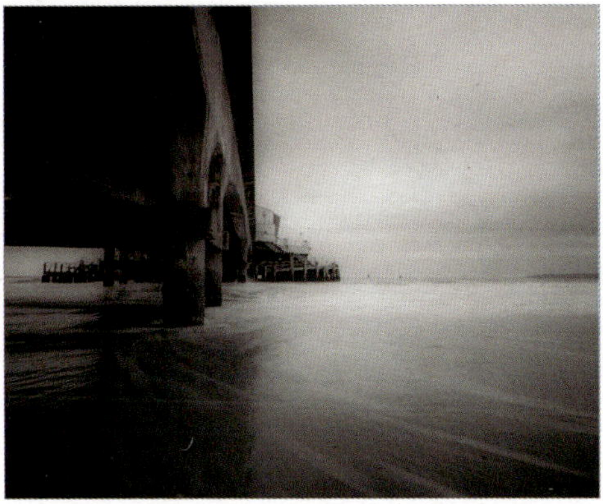

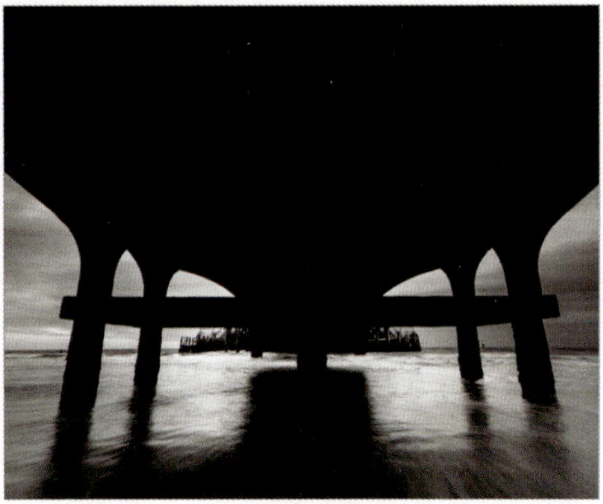

▲ Aim for symmetry
This image uses compositional tricks and a balancing of positive and negative space to draw the viewer into the shot

◄ Slow shutter speed
Using an ND 8 filter to block light from the lens, as well as a slow shutter speed and tripod, you can capture soft images

spectrum of the scene you wish to capture. Knowing how to manipulate/enhance these for black and white is half the battle.

If you are shooting in a studio environment, you are spoilt for choice given the dynamic results delivered by both constant and flash lighting. Add drama and emphasise the qualities of your subject by adhering to lighting ratios and techniques like rim lighting. Use simple patterns and silhouettes such as a fan or the line detail of blinds to tell a story by simply lighting them, creating shadow. Consider harsh lighting to strip colour detail away and introduce the natural contrast of a subject.

Understand how colour channels behave

When editing in a program such as Photoshop, you will have access to the colour channels in your image. These have a variety of retouching uses, but look at them as a means to view the impact of choosing one channel to dominate the conversion and you will see your image's potential.

The red channel will lighten the reds, yellows and oranges to a soft and subtle grey tone. The green channel will lighten greens,

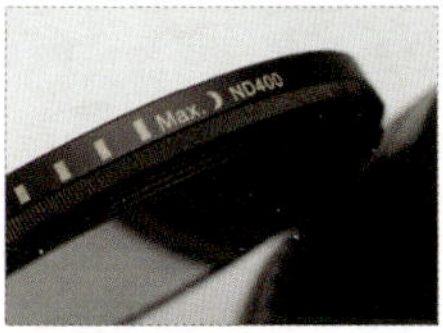

Big stopper filters create dramatic slow exposures, which look stunning in black and white.

Filter selection

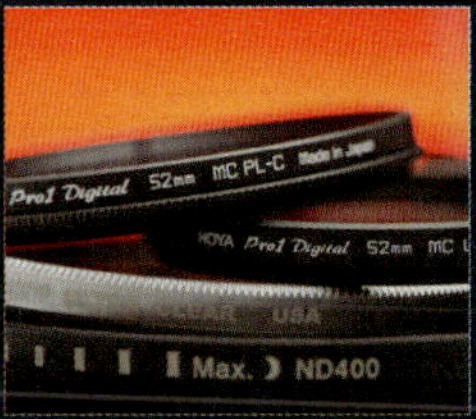

Filters are a great way to enhance black and white images. There are numerous options, such as gradient filters, which are essential in landscape photography for much the same reason as they are for black and white photography; they enhance the contrast of skylines.

Others such as full colour filters will adjust the contrast of specific tones in the image, so a red filter will react totally differently to a blue filter when used on the same image.

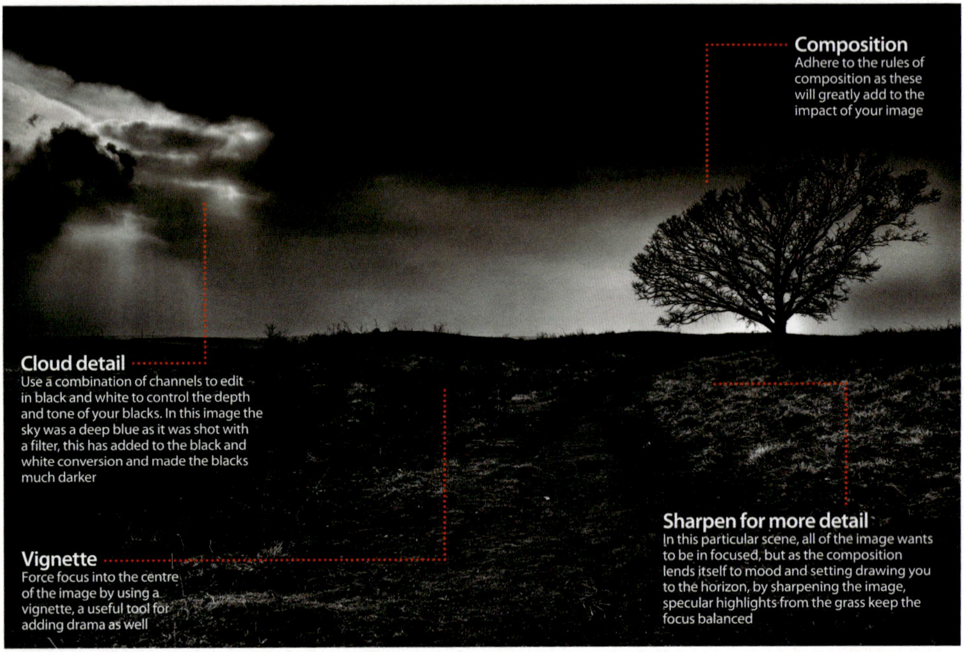

▲ Black and white landscapes
Dramatic landscapes in black and white are an artform. Taking into account every aspect available to you, ranging from the composition, the light and your kit, you can create some truly emotive scenes

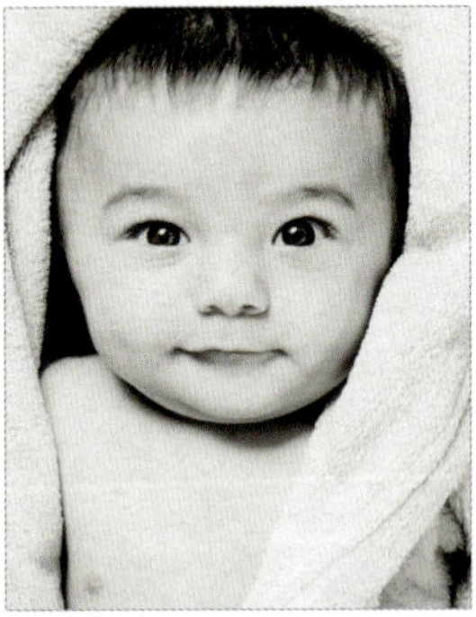

▲ Perfect skin tones
By using channel mixing techniques, you can smooth out specific colours. Subjects such as babies have skin that can sometimes be blotchy. By working with the red channel, you can eliminate this

cyans and yellows and the blue channel will lighten the blues. So if you are shooting a person on a grassy bank in the middle of summer, you will have a large degree of blue in the sky, green on the floor and a small amount of red in the person's skin tones. To keep the person's skin tones smooth and soft and keep the rest of the image a darker shade, you would edit your image into black and white via the red channel. Of course Photoshop has numerous ways to create monochrome imagery; using channels is just a straightforward edit process. To get deeper with tonal adjustments you will need to delve into the Channel Mixer.

This adjustment tool yields greater control over each colour in the spectrum, rather than just the three channels listed earlier. It will also allow you to push the lightness and darkness of the selected colour and not just be governed by one blanket adjustment.

Manual adjustments

Considering your subject, assess what is the main draw of the image. Take architectural photography as an example; do you want the building or the atmosphere and mood to be the dominant

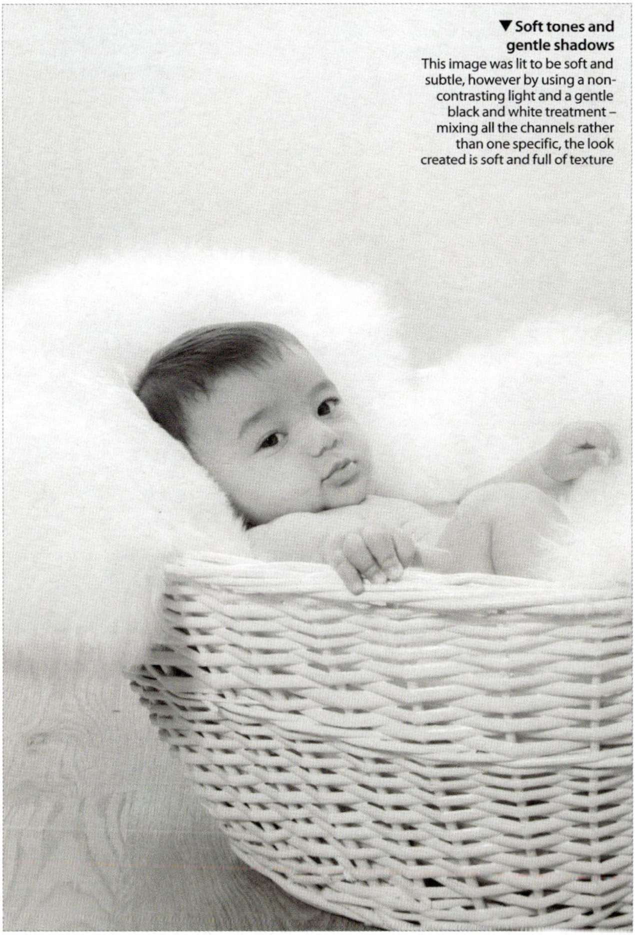

▼ Soft tones and gentle shadows
This image was lit to be soft and subtle, however by using a non-contrasting light and a gentle black and white treatment – mixing all the channels rather than one specific, the look created is soft and full of texture

feature? This is where filters step in. Circular polariser filters affix to the lens via a screwthread attachment. They consist of two polarised sheets of glass that when twisted, create a darker skyline and enhance the colours of your image. Gradient filters will affect only half of your shot and are perfect for darkening, adding mood and toning cloudy skylines.

Use a slow shutter speed on your camera as well as a stop down filter on your lens to capture the movement in clouds, again, when used in architectural photography, this is a great technique to add drama to a static object.

Darken skylines

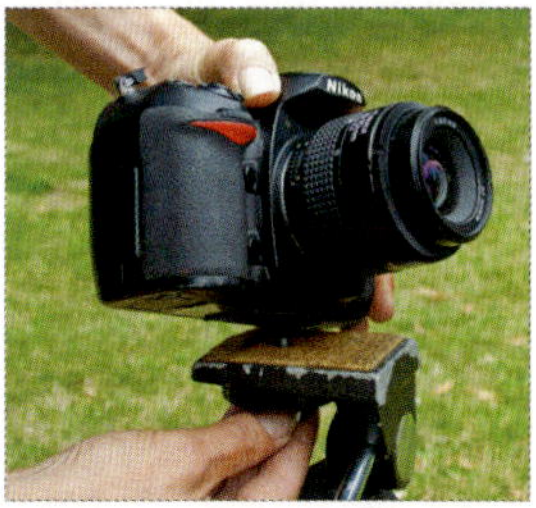

1 Set up a tripod Fix your camera up on a tripod and set it to Live View mode if available. Get the horizon level and the composition sorted.

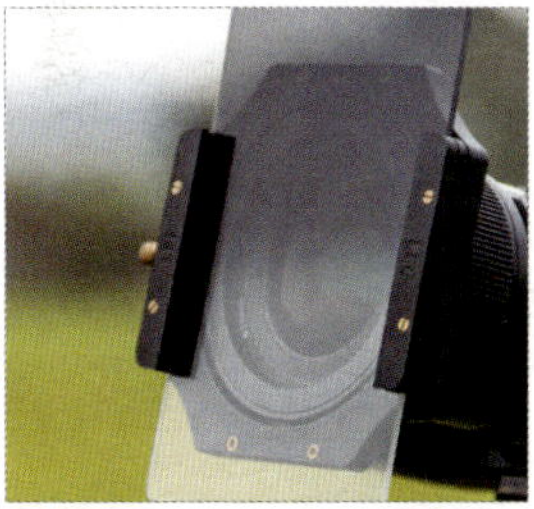

2 Filter magic By using a gradient filter you can darken skies, which will add drama to the scene. Attach the filter and line up the gradient with the skyline.

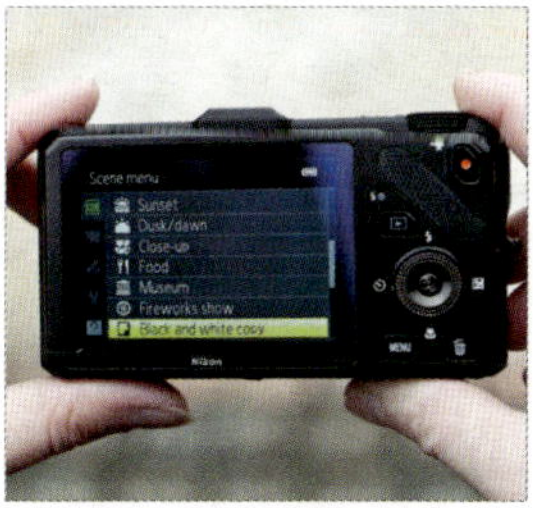

3 Set your shooting mode to B&W In your camera's shooting modes, you will find the black and white option. Select it to give an instant view of what your final image will look like.

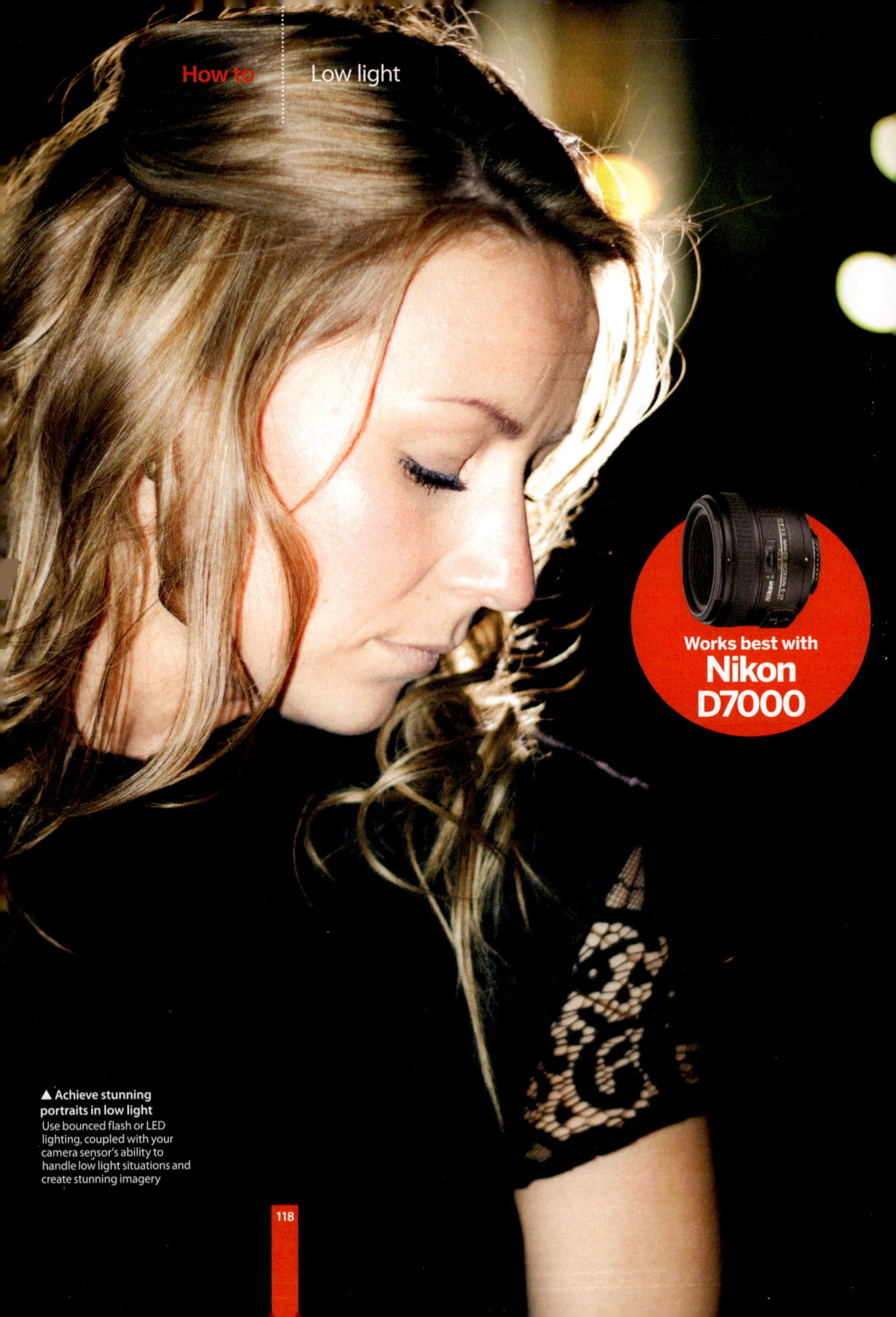

Works best with
Nikon D7000

▲ **Achieve stunning portraits in low light**
Use bounced flash or LED lighting, coupled with your camera sensor's ability to handle low light situations and create stunning imagery

Master low light photography

You don't need to have daylight or studio lighting to capture stunning images; experiment with low light and uncover a new world of possibilities

Shooting in daylight is something we all take for granted, after all it's when the majority of our shots are taken, but when it comes to mood and setting, low light is hard to beat.

Shooting in low light is a skill that utilises your camera's sensor capabilities for noise reduction and ISO sensitivity, as well as your lens' aperture range. When you set the ISO on your camera, you are adjusting its sensitivity to light. On a standard DSLR your typical ISO range would be 100 to 1600, and on higher-end DSLRs the range would be from LO 1.0, lower than 100, to HI 1.0, higher than 6400.

Know your ISO

A general guide to understanding ISO is that 100 is suitable for the brightest sunny day or studio lighting; 400 is for a typical day – slightly overcast, but still bright. ISO 800 would be for indoor use and anything higher, 1600 or upward, would be used in darker conditions such as night time or music photography. The interesting

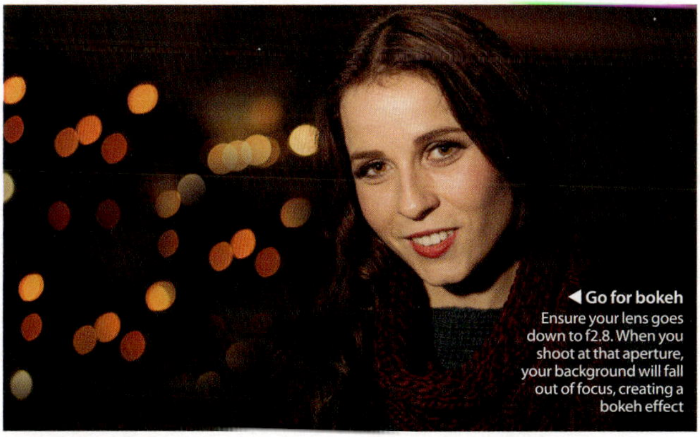

◀ **Go for bokeh** Ensure your lens goes down to f2.8. When you shoot at that aperture, your background will fall out of focus, creating a bokeh effect

Low light shooting

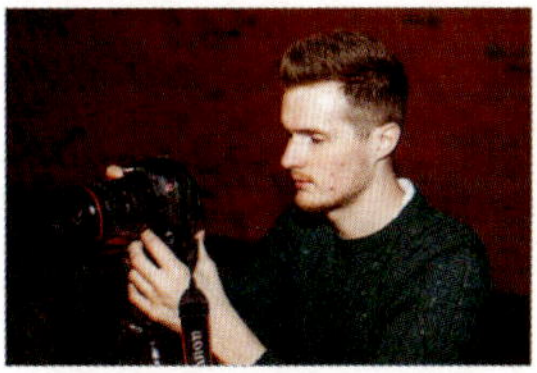

1 Pose your model Set your camera on a tripod in a suitable location with ambient light behind your model.

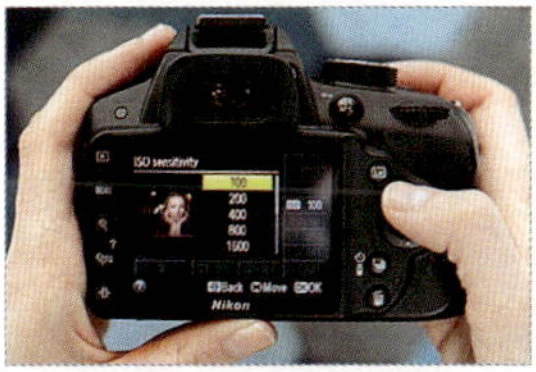

2 Adjust your settings Tweak settings for low light shooting, so a wide aperture, a high ISO and a slower shutter speed.

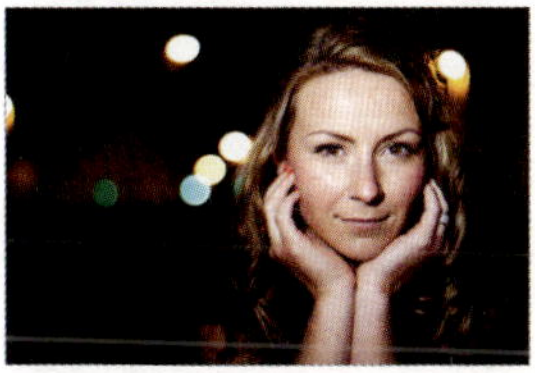

3 Shoot for bokeh With your camera's aperture at its lowest, the aim is to have a bokeh effect dominate your background.

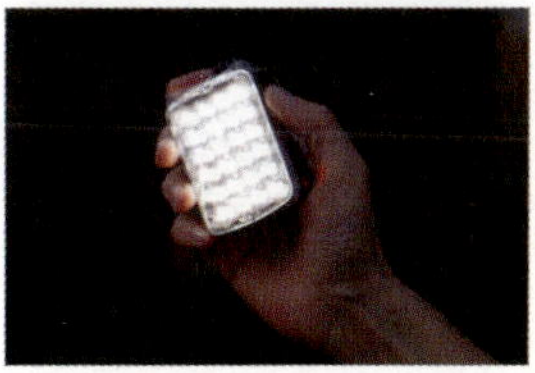

4 Use a torch for lighting As your flash could be too harsh for low light, why not use a simple torch to create soft lighting?

Three steps to remove colour casts

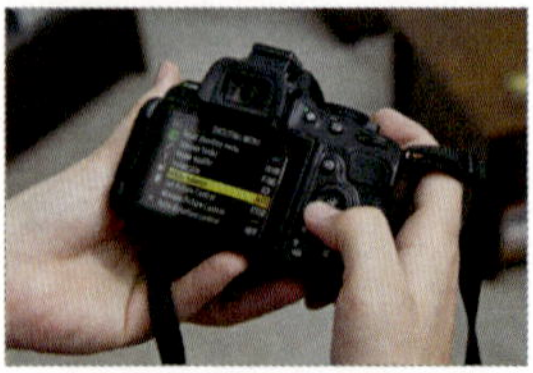

1 Set camera to tungsten Most low light location shoots will have an orange glow, so set your camera's white balance to tungsten, or if you can customise your Kelvin scale use somewhere in the 4000k range.

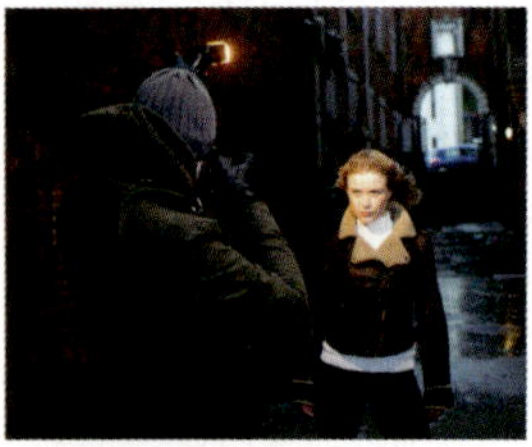

2 Use a cooling and warming filter Alternatively, most flash guns will have cooling and warming filters with them. These are designed to alter the colour temperature of an image by slotting on the flash head and tinting the image manually.

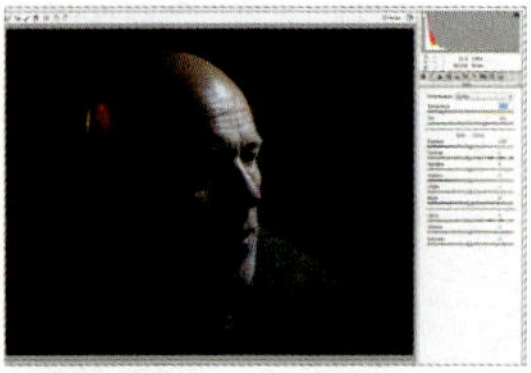

3 Edit in Raw Use the colour temperature slider controls in Raw to reduce and alter the colour tone manually. When combined with the split toning panel also in Raw shadow and highlights can be toned, removing casts easily.

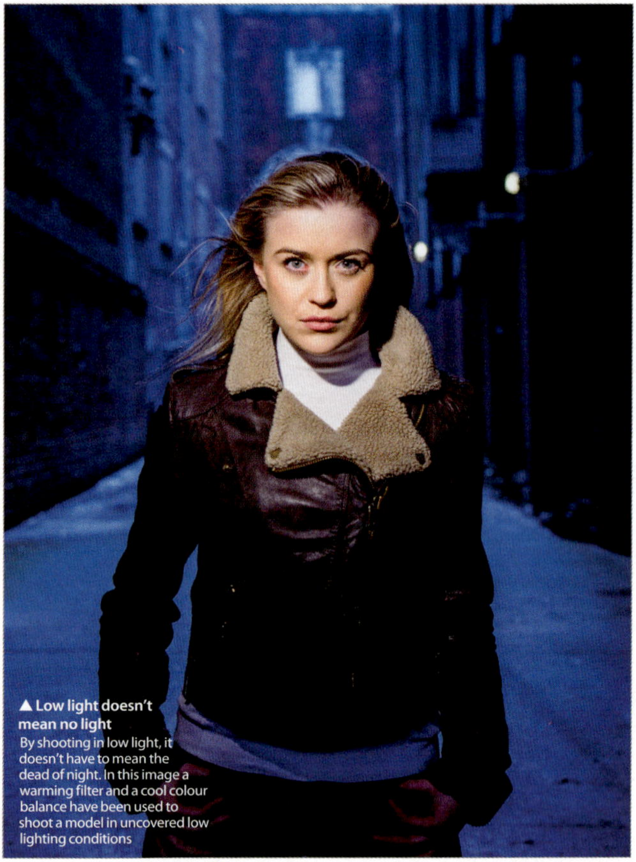

▲ Low light doesn't mean no light
By shooting in low light, it doesn't have to mean the dead of night. In this image a warming filter and a cool colour balance have been used to shoot a model in uncovered low lighting conditions

thing with ISO is that when you increase it, you can actually get better results from some of the other values such as shutter speed and aperture. This will allow you to shoot at a faster frame rate; a massive boost for wildlife and sports photographers, or if you wanted a much narrower aperture for an extensive depth of field.

However, there is a downside with using high ISO and that is that it will create digital noise in your image. This digital noise is the same as the grain you would have received from your film choice back in the day as all it is, is individual pixels of the sensor reading data. Having said that, with camera sensors now having a higher megapixel rating and their construction becoming more and more advanced, digital noise is fast becoming a moot point.

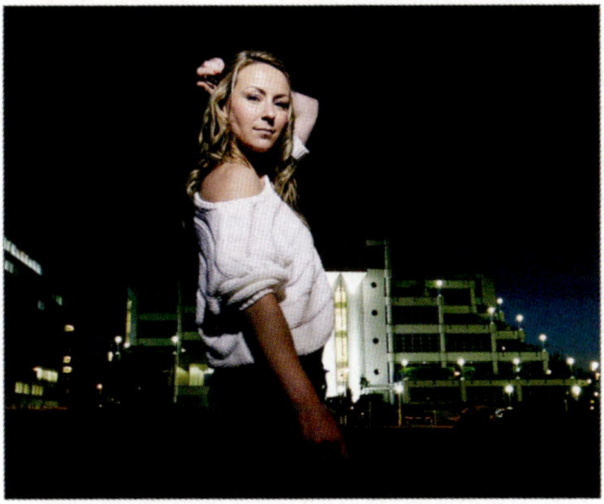

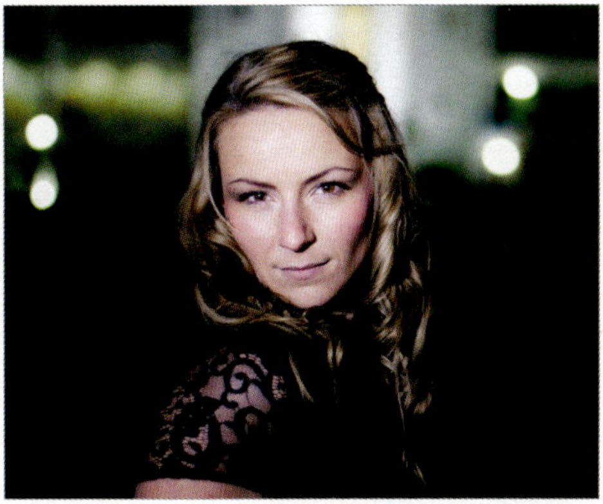

▲ Torchlight
By using torchlight to light your model, you can create a soft shadow to your image, or a hard light – the choice is yours. In this image an LED light was used to light paint the model

◀ Consider your location
Shooting in low light can be advantageous as your background may look industrial and ugly in the day, but at night, its lights can make for an attractive backdrop

This is even more true if you are familiar with editing software such as Photoshop, because any noise that does appear can easily be dispatched with using dedicated tools.

Essential equipment

To get the best results from low light shooting, you should always carry a tripod with you, and a sturdy one at that. Because you are taking from one to give to the other in exposure value terms, be prepared to sacrifice your shutter speed first. If you are shooting a landscape and the air is calm, then you can afford to drop your shutter speed so that you can let light into the sensor for longer, reducing the noise and keeping a narrower aperture. Opening up the shutter speed is a perfect reason for why you will need a tripod; you can keep the camera perfectly still and fire the shot either remotely or via the timer option.

As with all techniques, there is a caveat and that is the extra light being let in will have a warmer tone, setting the colour temperature to a warmer point on the Kelvin scale. The fix is to assess the lighting conditions and adjust your white balance accordingly.

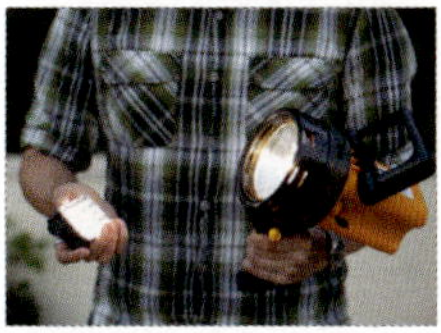

Carry a torch with you; not just to see where you are going, but so you can light paint your subject.

Always be prepared to shine

If you are travelling to a location, always make sure you have a torch at hand. Not just to see where you are going, but also so you can light paint. Light painting is a technique where you steady your camera on a tripod and by using either a shutter release cable or a long exposure time, you then expose your image to the available light and define your subject by washing over it with torch light. Cool LED lights are the best to use for this, as the cooler temperature of the LEDs cut through the natural warmth created by long exposure to light.

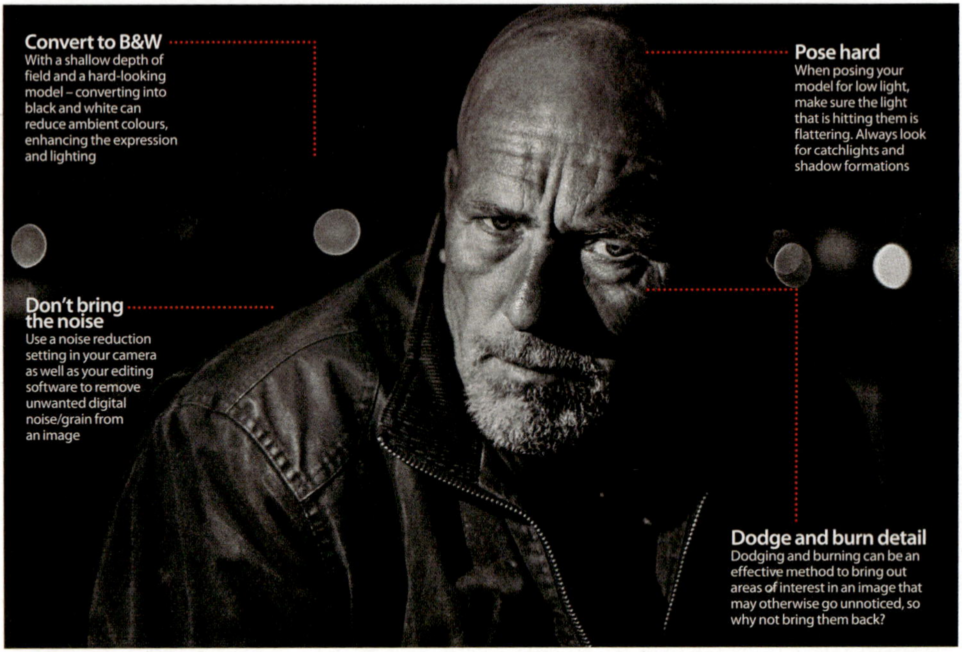

▲ **Create a sense of atmosphere**
By shooting in low light, already you add a sense of story telling to your imagery, but what about pushing that story further?

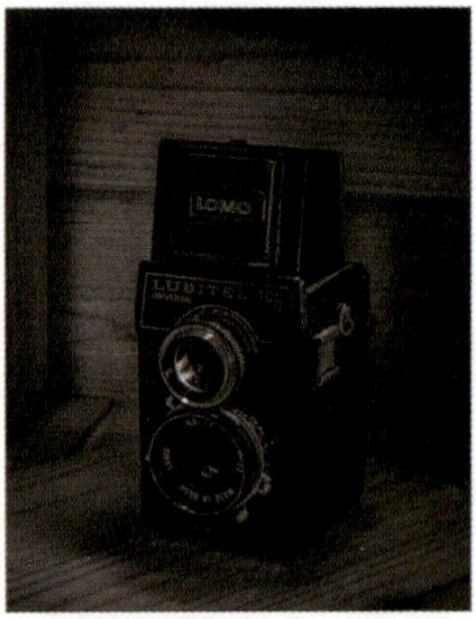

▲ **Bring your toys**
Bring a tripod with you if you are using off board flash, that way you can keep your camera still when taking the shot

When shooting portraits in low light you will need to see detail, so how do you get around that? Well the answer is simple; use light. Obviously the art to low light shooting is that you aim for a true rendition of what the eye sees at night by using only available light. You want to see the ambient lights and colours, so that rules out using a flash, right? Wrong. If you have a flash gun that can pivot at an angle, be powered down manually or that can be fired remotely, you can bounce the light back into the model's face. Of course firing directly at the model will bleach out detail and darken the background, so be cautious of your angle when using flash.

If you are at all unsure about using the flash, especially since sometimes the result can be quite harsh, why not invest in an LED light or even a torch? This way you can stage your model, set your camera up and light paint your model. Light painting is a technique where you use a constant light and aim it manually at your subject and shoot your image with a relatively high ISO and a relatively slow shutter speed.

For music photography there are a few deviations on the theme. Firstly, you can't use a tripod, secondly, you will likely find that at

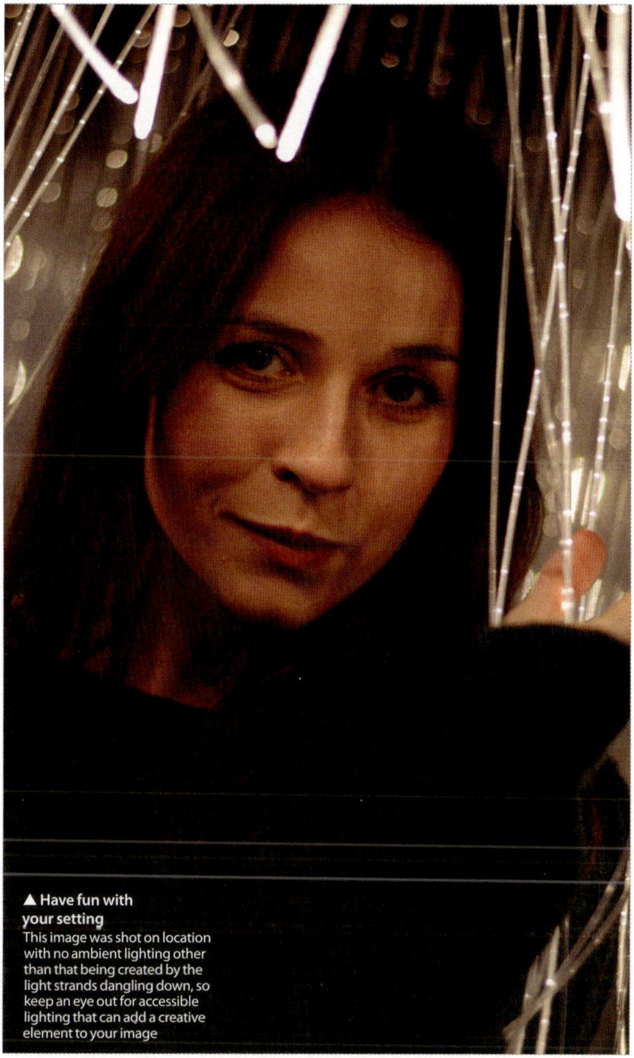

▲ **Have fun with your setting**
This image was shot on location with no ambient lighting other than that being created by the light strands dangling down, so keep an eye out for accessible lighting that can add a creative element to your image

shows you can only shoot the first three songs with no flash. The upshot to this is that most shows are now lit for film, meaning that at the brightest point, you will be looking at a great mid-range of exposure values, somewhere in the line of ISO 800, f5.6 and 1/60th sec. Obviously singers move around, so you will need to have a steady hand and watch out for the shot.

The effect of using different ISO settings

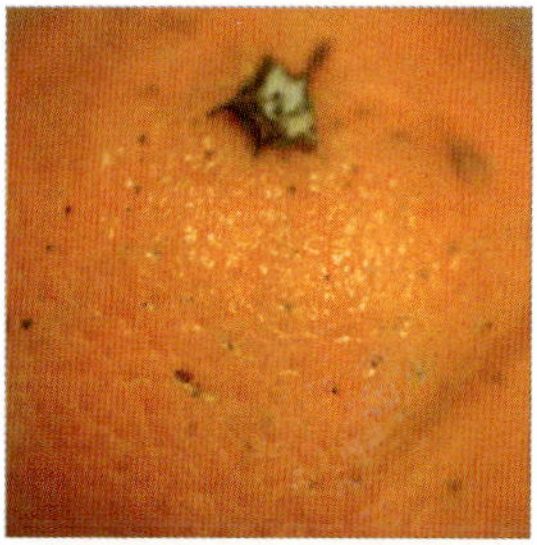

1 ISO 800 This image has been shot with the aid of a tripod in a low light environment using ISO 800 and a low aperture.

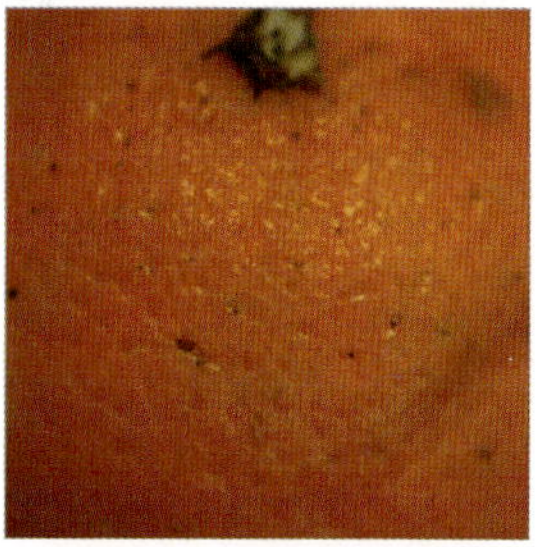

2 ISO 1600 This image has been shot with a higher ISO of 1600 and a low aperture, increasing the noise in the image.

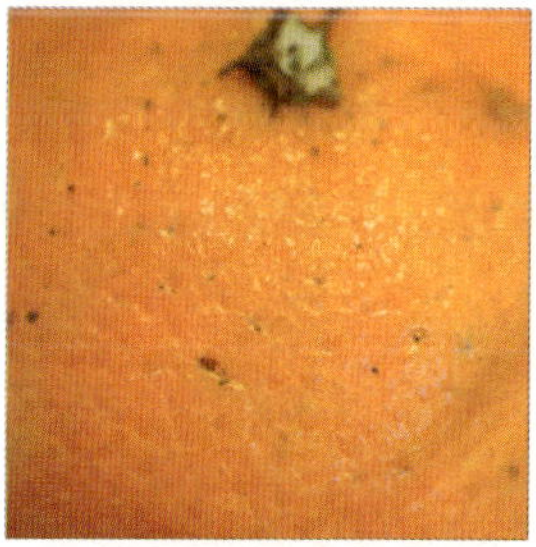

3 ISO 3200 This has been shot hand held, with an ISO of 3200, on a faster shutter speed and cooler white balance, again increasing the noise levels.

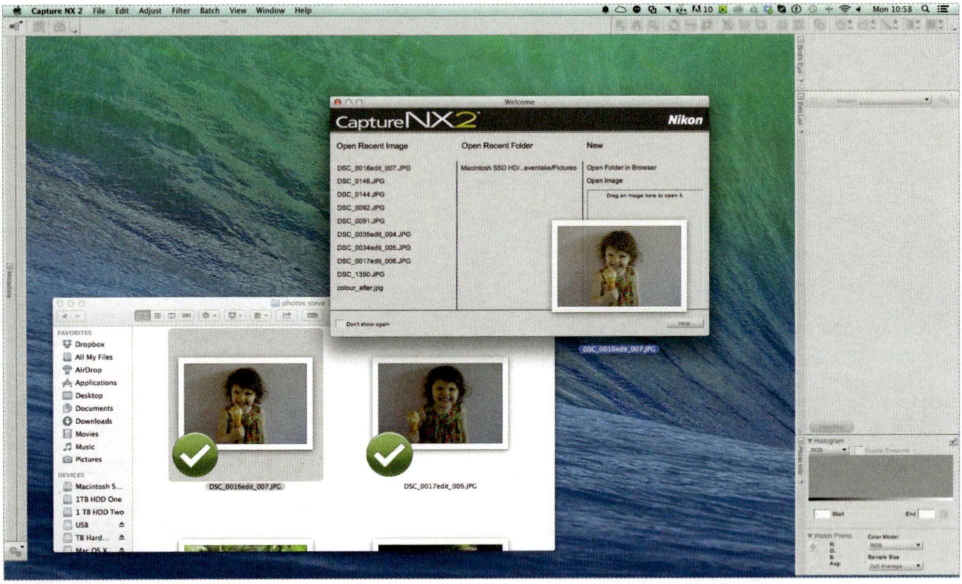

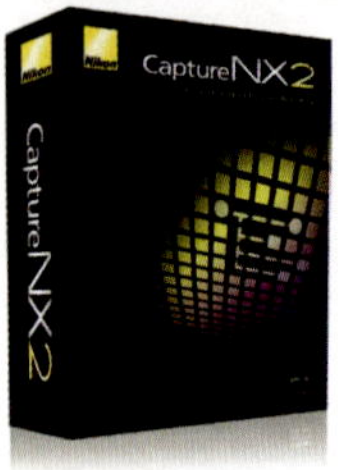

Use it to…

Batch edit images
Add effects to multiple images with the click of a button using the Batch Processing tool

Resize your images
Format your image size to make them easier to upload and share with other people

Change file formats
Re-export your images into a variety of different file formats

How to import and export your images

Import and export individual images for editing and discover how to batch edit entire folders of photos

When you open Capture NX 2 you'll be presented with the Import window. Here you can browse for a single image or multiple photos or simply drag and drop an image to open it. To export an edited image go to File>Save As. When saving you'll need to select a file format. Click on the Format dropdown menu to select one; JPEG is a popular choice. Click Save and select a quality type. The Good Compression Ratio option will give you the best quality combined with the lowest file size, making your photo easier to share online.

Batch edits
Steps can be selected, copied and pasted onto other images in Capture NX 2 from the Batch menu

Manual replication
Replicating effects applied in another image can take a long time compared to applying the effect through a batch process

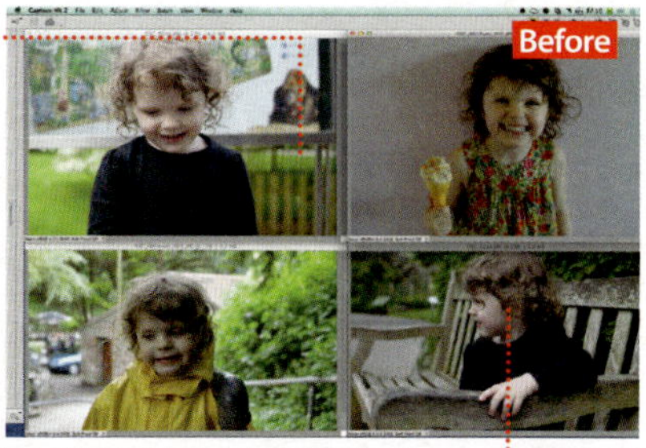

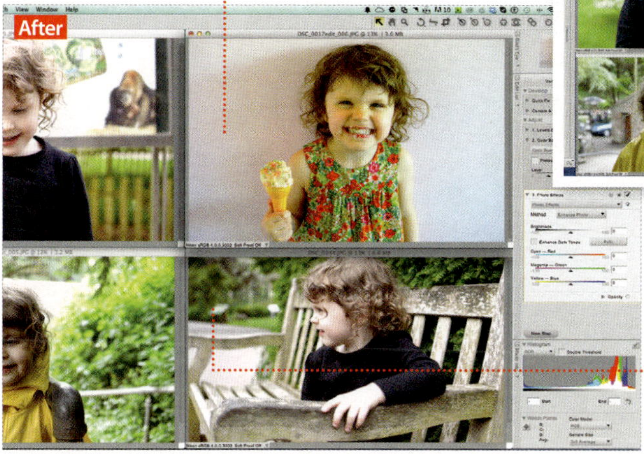

Individual edits
Without batch processing you'll have to edit each image individually by adding different effects manually

Adding steps
You can add as many steps as you like to an edit, choosing a different effect to apply each time

Save time with batch processing

If you have a folder of photographs that you want to edit in a similar way, a batch process can be used to apply an effect, or a series of effects to every single photo in that folder. Once you've batch-processed the folder you can then go back if need be to edit each individual image as you like. Batch processing is also useful for reducing the size of a collection of images, or to re-export images into a specific file format. Each effect you apply to an image counts as a step. You can then save these steps and apply them to other photographs. This tutorial will show you how to work with steps to create your own adjustments, to then apply to other photos.

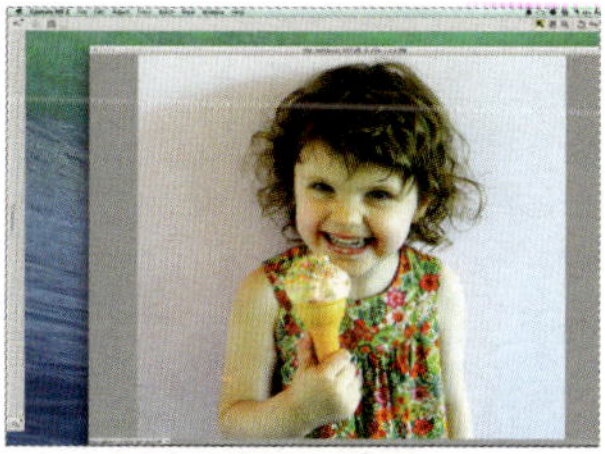

01 Add an effect Open an image in Capture NX 2. Click Window and make sure that Edit List is ticked. At the bottom of the Adjust subheading, click New Step. Click the Select Adjustment subheading. Go to Light>Auto Adjust. The effect will be applied

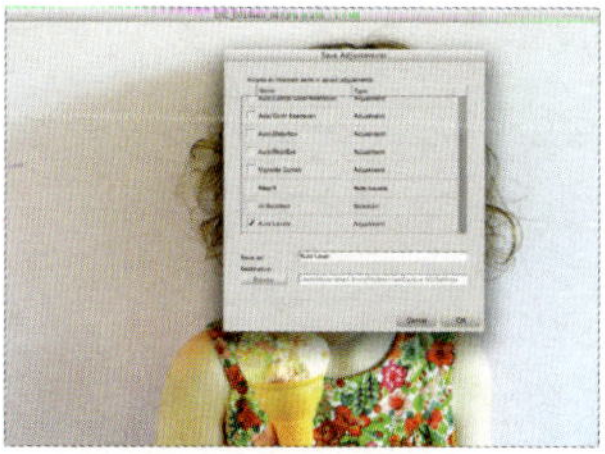

02 Save your adjustment Go to Batch>Save Adjustment. A tick list of effects will appear. The top effects are default adjustments. Scroll down to Step 1. You'll see the Auto Levels effect you applied. Make sure it's ticked and select any other default adjustments.

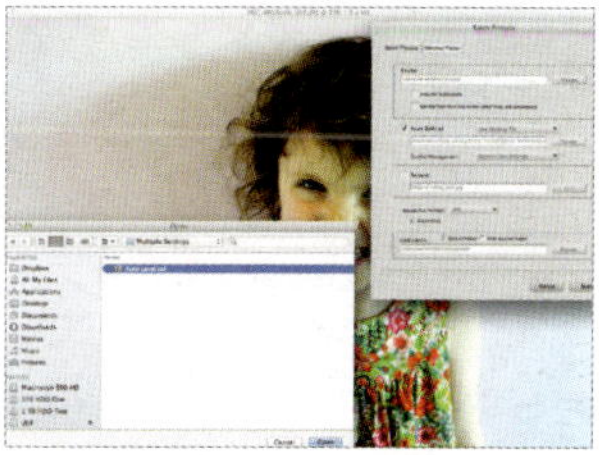

03 Batch process Click Batch>Run Batch Process. In the Source folder browse for the folder of images you want to apply the adjustment to. Under Apply Settings select the saved Adjustment effect, pick a file format and destination then click Start.

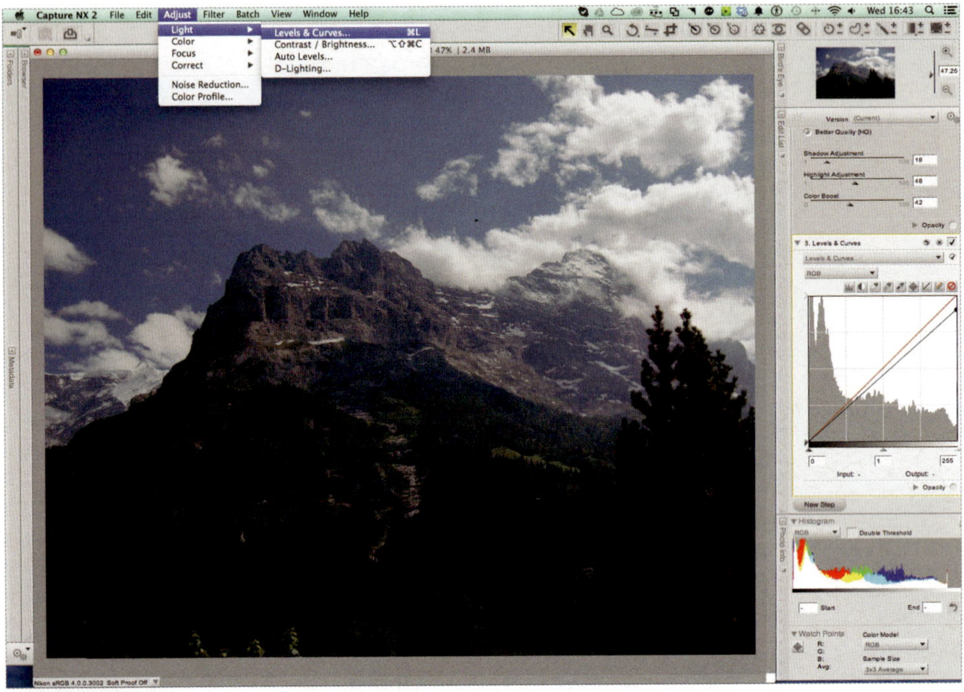

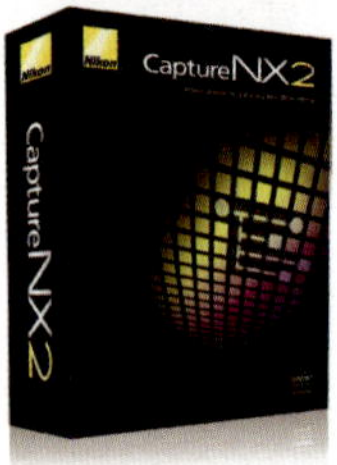

Fix exposure

Tackle uneven exposure in your images by learning to use the Levels & Curves command

By mastering the lighting tools available in Capture NX 2, you can quickly remedy any over- or underexposed images. This can be achieved with Curves and Levels. By adding a lighting curve to your photo, you can even out the exposure of the entire image. Use Curves combined with the Levels tool to work on the shadows, midtones and highlights of an image all individually. The most important thing to learn about affecting exposure levels is that you don't have to bump up the overall brightness of an image. When working with Levels you'll be presented with an adjustable histogram. The left side of the histogram represents the dark parts of the image; the right side represents the light parts.

Use it to…

Apply lighting effects
Highlight certain areas in an image whilst darkening other areas

Curves
Use Curves to add contrast and brightness manually, fully controlling the output

Histogram
Read the histogram to measure exposure levels of your image

Selections
Select specific parts of an image to be affected by light curves

Details There is a lot more detail in the clouds and the trees now that the shadows and highlights have been adjusted

Lost detail A lot of detail has been lost in the underexposed trees and the overexposed clouds

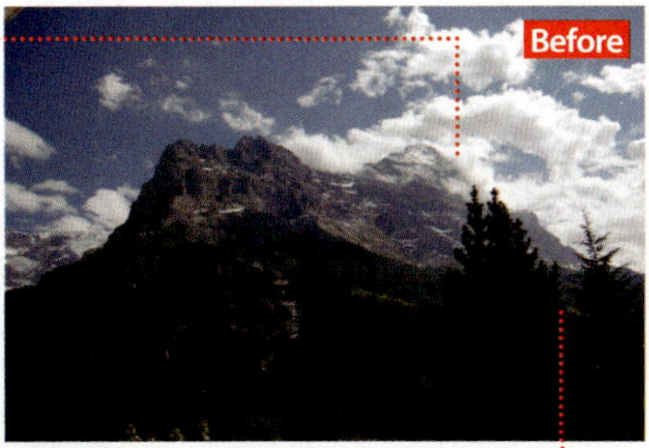

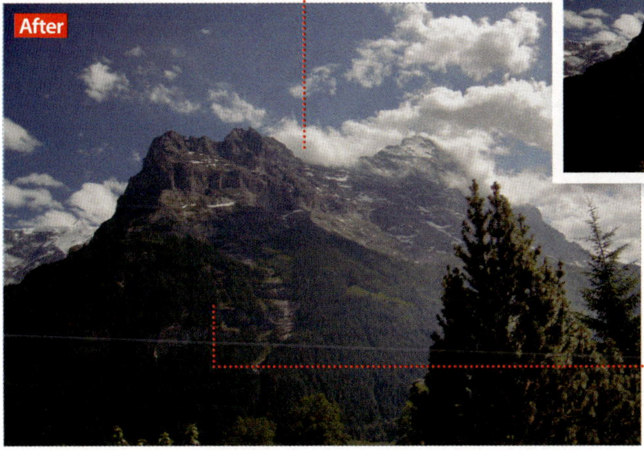

Uneven exposure Notice how the exposure of the sky is not even to that of the trees in the foreground

Even exposure The exposure levels between the dark parts of the image and the light parts are much more even now

Even exposure in images

The lighting tools in Capture NX 2 can be broken down into three commands; Levels & Curves, Auto Level and D Lighting. The Levels & Curves tool allows you to isolate specific parts of the image in terms of its light balance and adjust those areas. This is useful if you want to increase the brightness of the shadows in an image, without blowing out the exposure of the highlights. Auto Level will automatically boost or reduce the exposure levels of an image. The D Lighting option allows you to select a region of the image using the selection tool, so you can then adjust its exposure and Levels as you like without affecting the rest of the photo. In this tutorial you'll learn how to use Curves to brighten the shadows and darken the highlights.

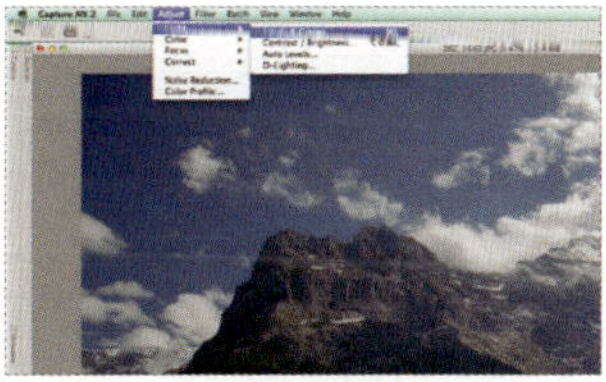

01 The Curves histogram Go to Adjust>Light>Levels & Curves. In the edit list window under the Adjust subheading you'll see a histogram. This has the adjustment line (black) and the base line (red), which shows where your adjustment line started.

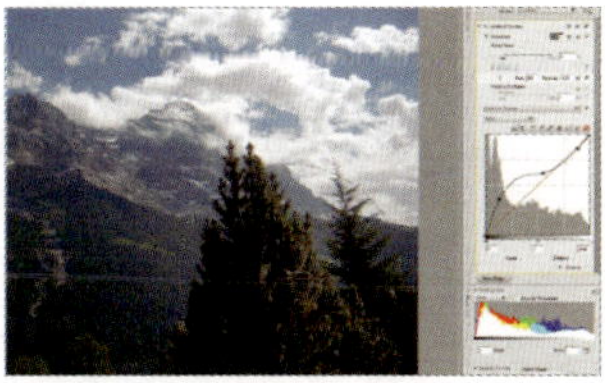

02 Make a selection Pick the Selection Control Point. Click where you want to adjust the exposure. A selection circle will appear; reposition it as need be. Click and drag on the upper bar to adjust the selection size, and the lower bar to adjust opacity.

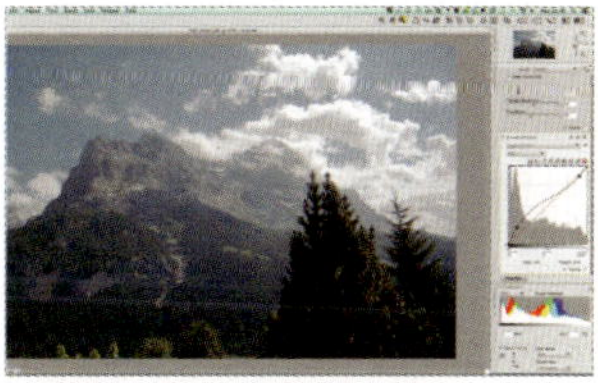

03 Make adjustments Drag the top-left of the adjustment bar in the Curves histogram to edit brightness and the bottom-right to affect the darkness. Repeat step one and two as much as you like to create different selection control points in an image.

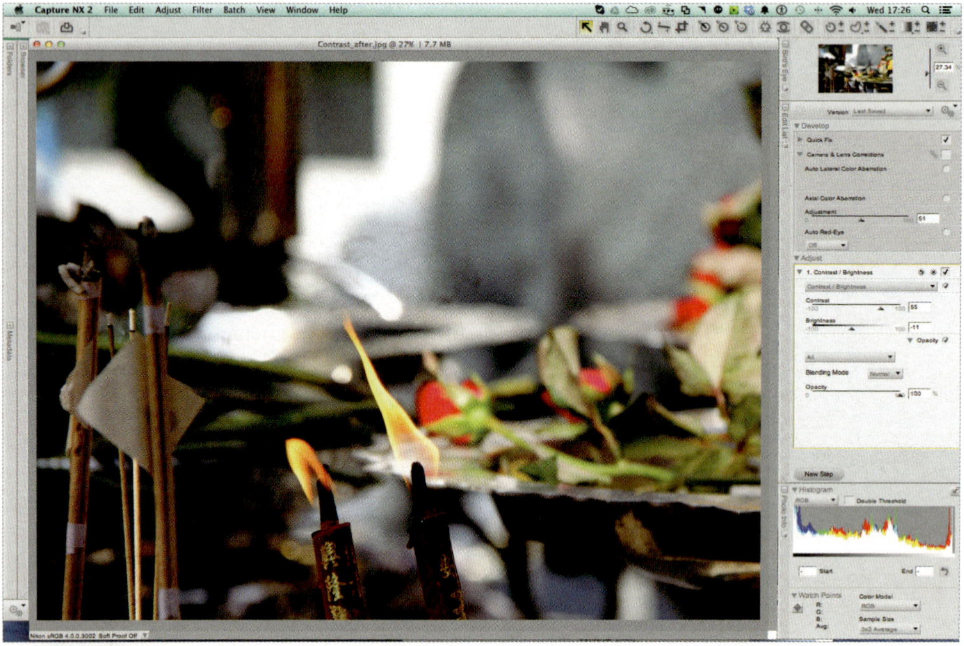

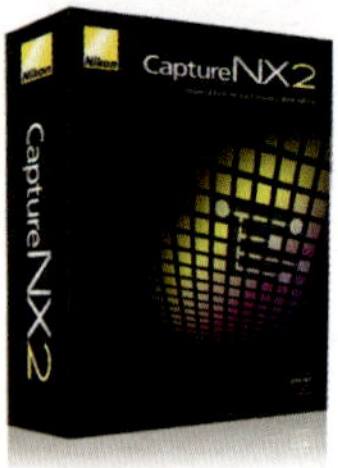

Use it to...

Enhance colours
Make the strongest colours in your image stand out

Add depth
Remove the flatness of an image by adding contrast to different areas

Create a mood
Images that have a lot of dark and light areas will be given a moody tone when contrast is added

Boost contrast

Don't suffer from feeble images; ensure that your photos are bold by adding contrast to them to strengthen your colours

In the previous tutorial you learnt about adjusting the exposure of an image so both the shadows and highlights are less juxtaposed. It is important, however, that there is some contrast between the light and dark areas in a photograph. Without contrast an image can start to feel flat and uninspiring. Use exposure adjustments to make your image feel as though it were evenly exposed, so that your highlights aren't blown out and your shadows aren't so dark that you can't see them, but then use contrast adjustments to bring a bit of depth and character to your image. Adding contrast is a great way to help to bring out strong colours and light sources from your images, which will improve the whole feel.

Greater depth
The foreground colours stand out from the grey background now that a bit of contrast is added

A lack of colour
There are some beautiful reds, greens and yellows in this shot that have potential to stand out

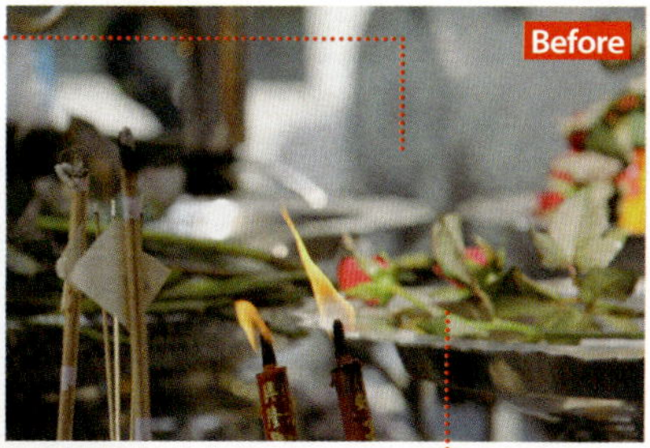

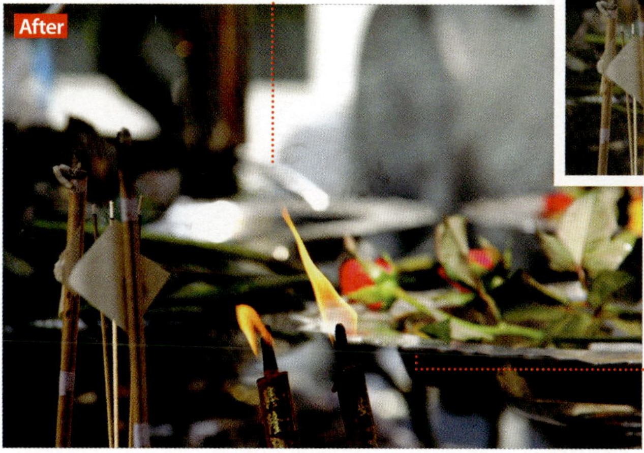

Flat image
There is plenty going on in this image, but the foreground and background feel too close, making the shot flat

Harsher blacks and whites
The two most contrasting tones in the image (black and white) stand out much more now

The Contrast/Brightness tool

Contrast can be applied in two ways using Capture NX 2. The simplest way is through the Contrast/Brightness tool. With this you can simply move the Contrast slider to increase or decrease the contrast between shadows and highlights in your image. If the contrast adjustment begins to blow out the highlights or underexpose the shadows, you can then adjust the Brightness bar to even out the shot. You can also adjust the contrast using the Curves tool. The best way to add contrast using Curves is to form an S shaped curve (know professionally as an S-Curve) with the adjustment line. This shape increases the brightness of the highlights whilst decreasing the brightness of the shadows, giving you much better control of your image's contrast.

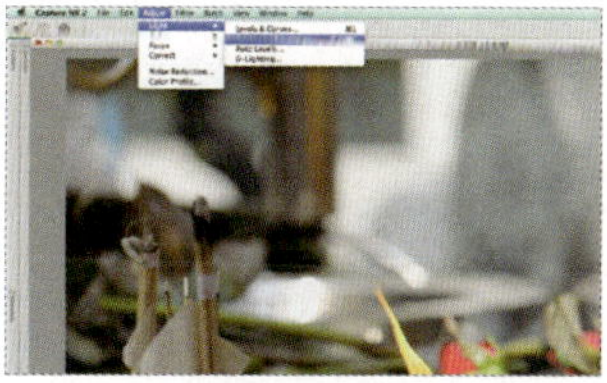

01 Make contrast adjustments Click Adjust>Light Contrast/Brightness. In the edit list window underneath the Adjust subheading you'll see the Contrast/Brightness tool. Click on the right-facing arrow next to the word Opacity to reveal more options.

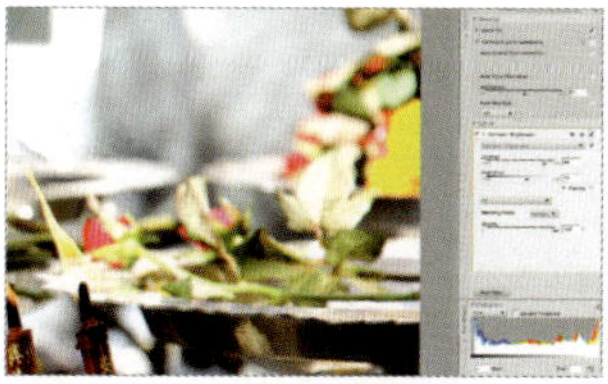

02 Apply contrast Click and drag the Contrast slider to increase the intensity. Notice how the colours begin to stand out. If the brightness of the image becomes too dark or too bright, adjust the Brightness slider below the Contrast slider to correct this.

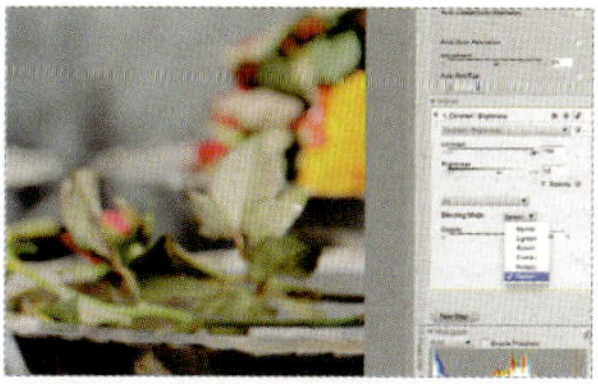

03 Selective contrast Click on the dropdown menu next to Blending Mode in the advanced options of the Contrast/Brightness tool. Select Darken to only adjust the dark parts of the image. Select Multiply to restrict changes to lighter parts of the image.

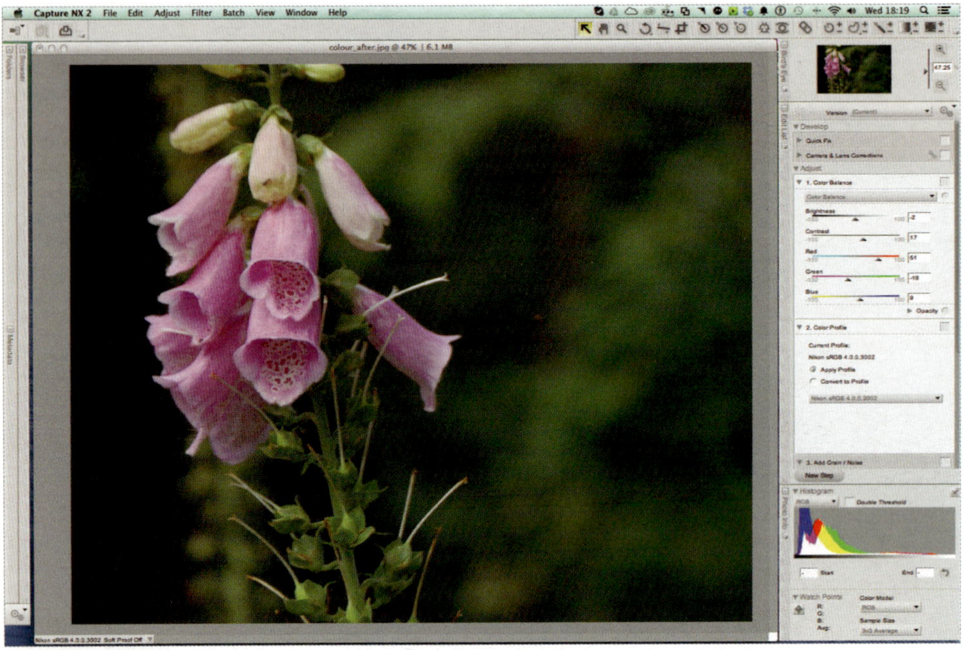

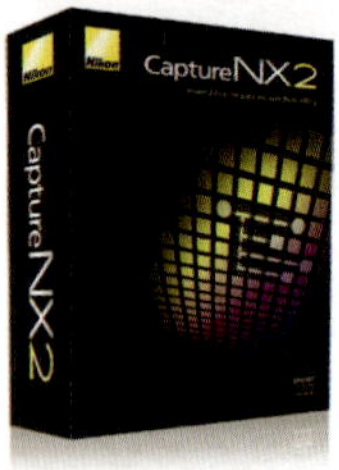

Use it to...

Boost your colours
Make your colours pop with vibrancy using the colour tools

Change colour temperatures
Add a warm tone to your photos, or add a tint of blue to cool the shot down

Make black and white photos
Remove all of the colour from your shot, or create a sepia tone

Colourize images
Add a dominant colour tint to photos to create interesting colourizing effects

Isolate and enhance colours
Be selective with what colours stand out, enhancing some while subduing others

Experiment with colour

Manipulate colours in Capture NX 2 to create different effects and change colour temperatures

Often when shooting photography you'll be dealing with a variety of light conditions. Light comes with its own colour temperature, which determines the colour temperature of your photo. If shooting in candlelight you'll get a warm shot, if shooting in natural daylight you'll get a cool shot. When editing your photographs you'll be able to readjust the temperature to your liking. You can also use Capture NX 2 to adjust the colour of different artefacts within an image, making certain colours stand out. You can even remove certain colours from a photo whilst retaining others.

Filmic effects
By adding high contrast and grain the image begins to get away from its original digital look

Uninspired colours
In this shot the purple of the flowers isn't standing out as strongly as it could be

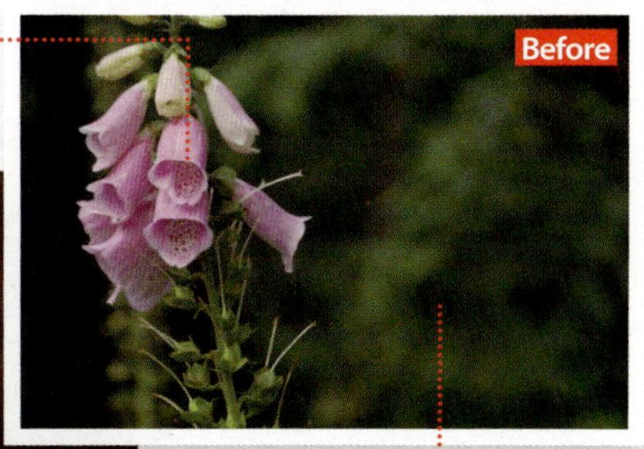

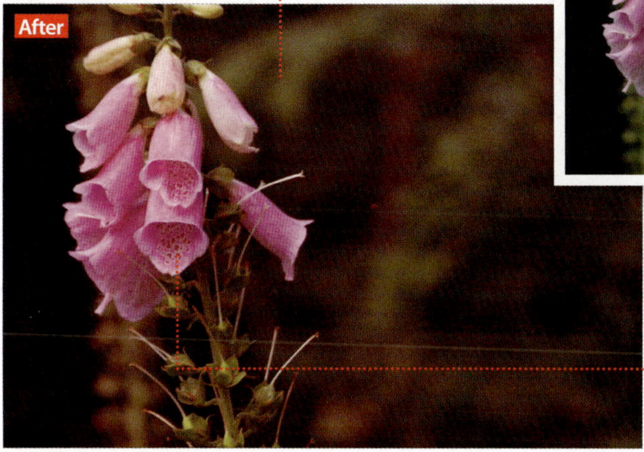

Natural tones
This photo has a well-balanced colour temperature making it easier to edit and manipulate

Harsher reds
By bumping up the reds in the shot the image begins to look more filmic

Add a film effect to photos

If you would like to correct or adjust the colour temperature of your shot, to either warm it up or cool it down, then you can use the Saturation/Warmth tool. In the top toolbar Go to Adjust>Color>Saturation/Warmth. Use the slider to adjust the colour temperature. With this tool you can also reduce the saturation of an image, making it completely black and white, or increase the saturation which will make all of the boldest colours stand out. If you have a specific colour, or set of colours that you want to stand out, then you can use the Color Balance tool to achieve this. In this tutorial you'll learn how use Color Balance to give your photographs a filmic look.

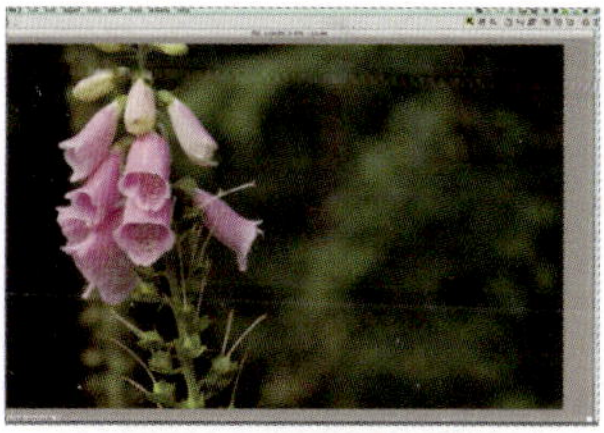

01 Color Balance tool Go to Adjust>Color>Color Balance. This tool has a Brightness and Contrast slider to adjust the overall exposure of the image before you begin working on the colours. Set the brightness and contrast before you continue.

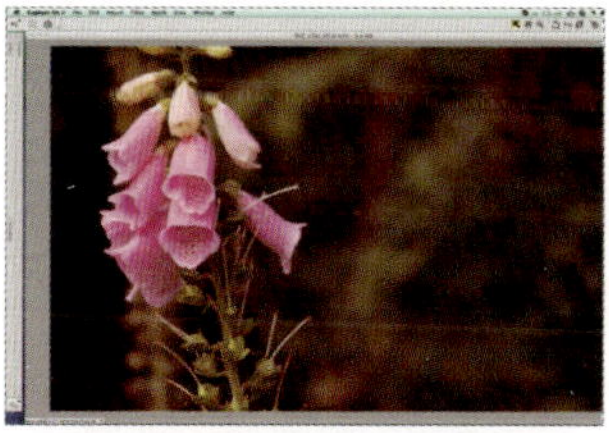

02 Adjusting colours You can't reduce a colour without increasing another, so think about the overall tone you want to go with. By increasing the reds, decreasing the greens and pushing the contrast up you'll achieve a more filmic look.

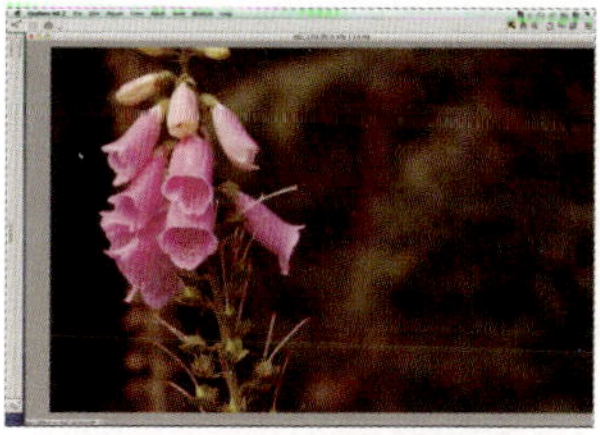

03 Add grain To add grain to your image, in the top toolbar go to Filter>Add Grain/Noise. Select Monochrome as your grain colour and Small Grain as your grain size. Now slide the Grain dial upwards to add a small amount of grain to your image.

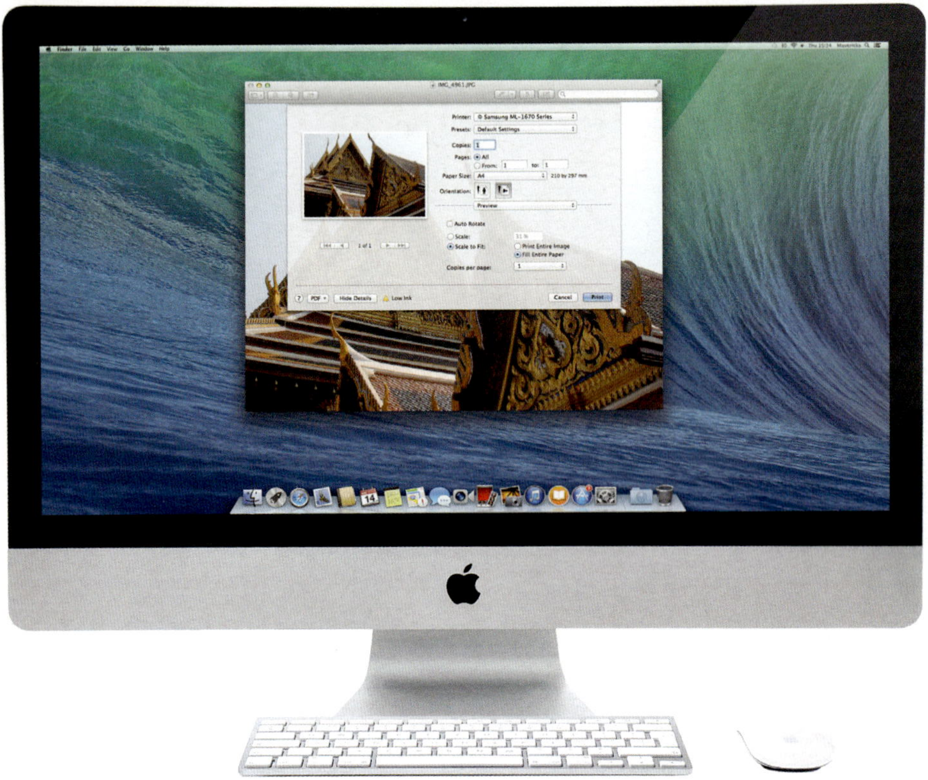

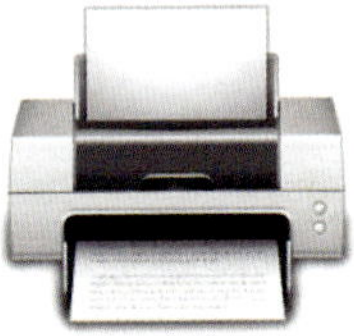

▲ **Preparation is key** Take the time to set up your photographic printout correctly to get the best possible results

Printing images

Print top-quality images from home or order prints of your best photography online

Sharing photographs online may be the easiest way to exhibit your work, but nothing beats a printed image that can be physically put on display. The act of printing photographs has diminished, but it doesn't take much work to create high-quality prints of your favourite image at home using a standard printer. When printing photographs at home it's advised that you print using photography paper, which is a little more expensive than normal paper but the jump in quality is massive. Purchase from a stationery store or online.

Size and orientation Swap between landscape and portrait with Orientation. Change the paper size depending on what paper type you are using

Presets Once you've managed your print settings you can save it as a preset to be used again

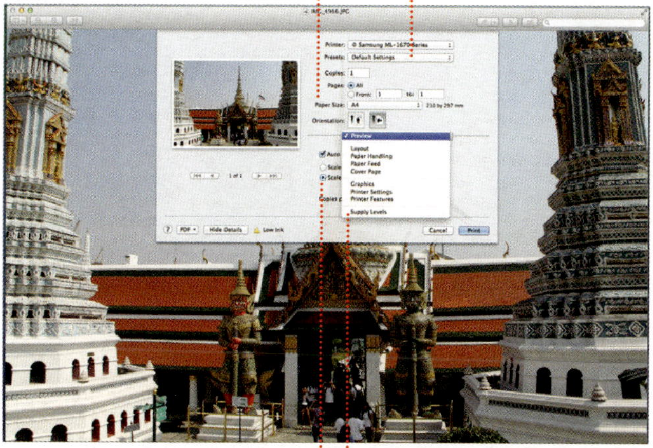

Scaling The way an image is scaled on the paper will affect how it prints and how much of the image is cropped

Advanced tools Most printing tools will offer different options for printing, including paper type

If you don't own a printer there is a variety of online printing services available, including Flickr's print ordering tool and sites such as **photobox.co.uk** which offers a variety of different print types to be ordered and delivered to your home. Ordering prints online is great for creating high-quality photo books, portfolios or large prints of your photography.

When printing from home, there is plenty of different software available that provide printing options. The anno above refers to printing using Apple's Preview software. Depending on what software you prefer, you'll find some of the settings may vary, but the general instructions for printing will be the same.

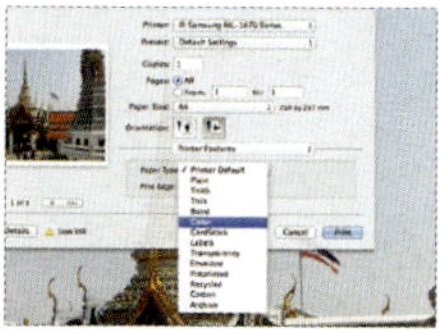

Paper type determines the quality of the print; ensure it matches the paper you're using.

Ordering online prints

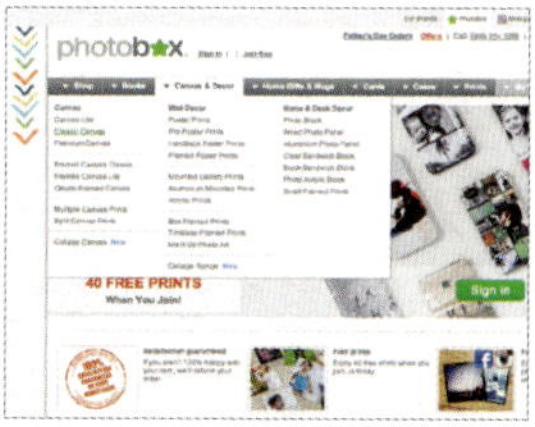

1 Select a product Once you've found a printing service, select a product such as a canvas print.

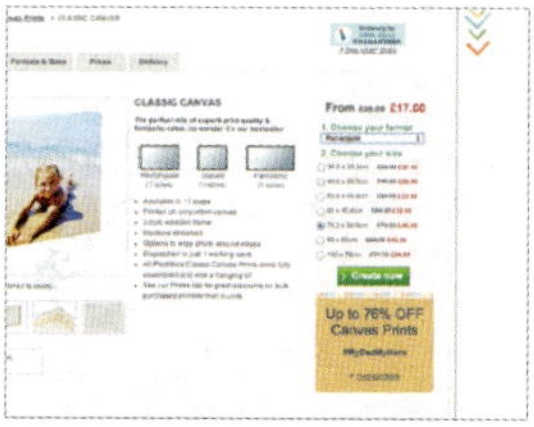

2 Preferences Select a size and format. Each product will have different options and prices.

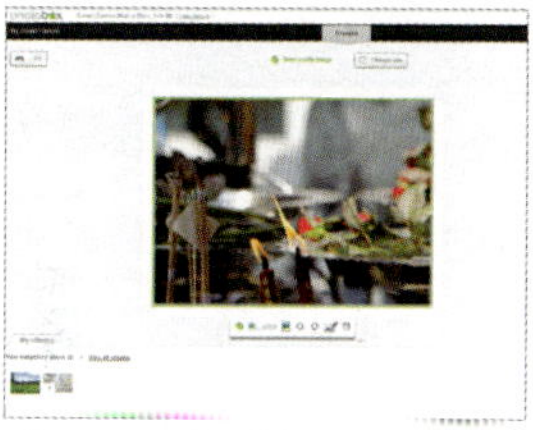

3 Image upload Import an image to preview, adjusting its size and formatting if needed.

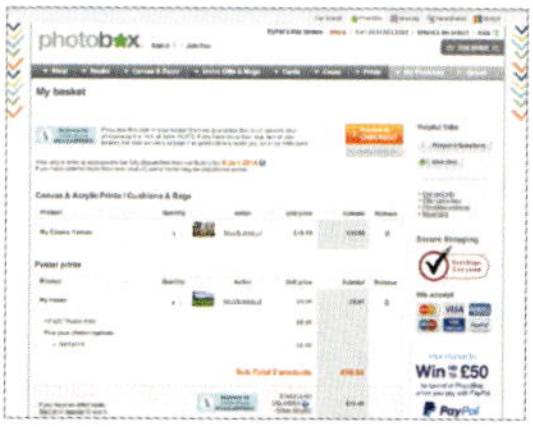

4 Purchase your print Add payment and delivery details then make your purchase.

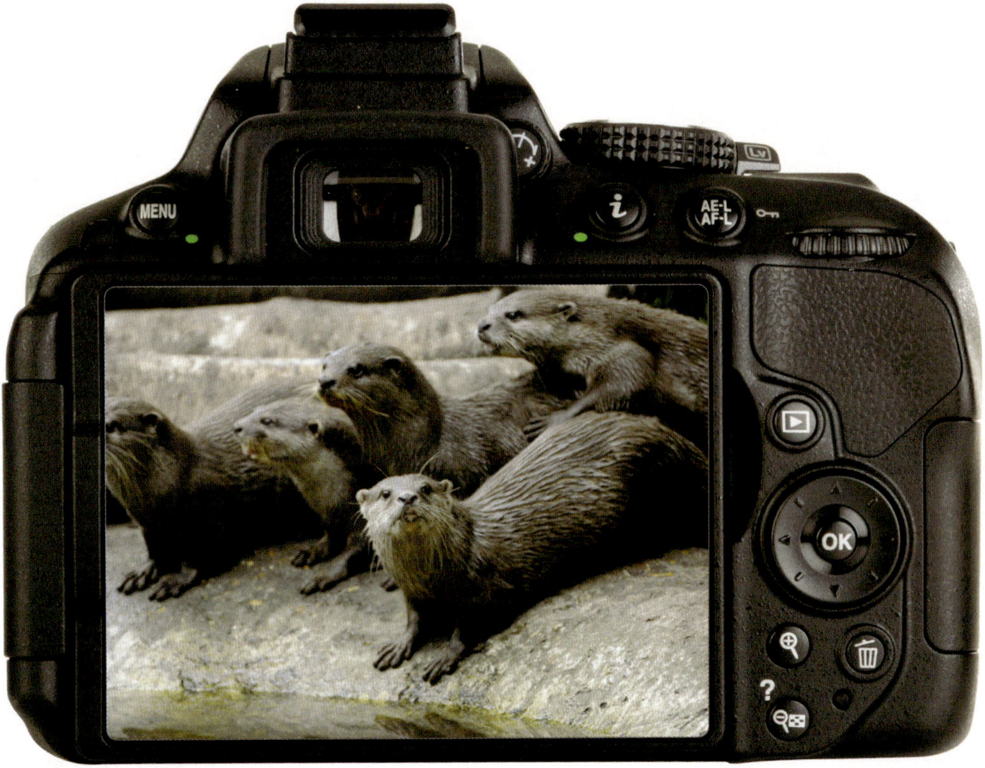

▲ **Mobile photo station** Use your Wi-Fi compatible Nikon camera to not only share your pictures remotely, but also shoot and download them, too

Wireless sharing

Discover how to transmit captures with Wi-Fi compatible Nikon cameras

A range of new Nikon cameras feature in-built Wi-Fi technology that allows users to take, share and download images instantaneously. This is a fantastic facility; particularly when you are away from home or your memory card has reached its capacity. And the beauty of it is that beginners right through to professional photographers can make use of the technology, so whether you're a proud parent wanting to share your recent pictures with family, or a professional on location who needs to beam sports, news, fashion or product

Remote control access
If you've installed the Wireless Mobile Utility App on your Android or iOS device you can now use this to shoot, share and download images remotely

Pop it in
You need to slot the wireless adapter into its port. Take it out when not in use to avoid it getting damaged or lost

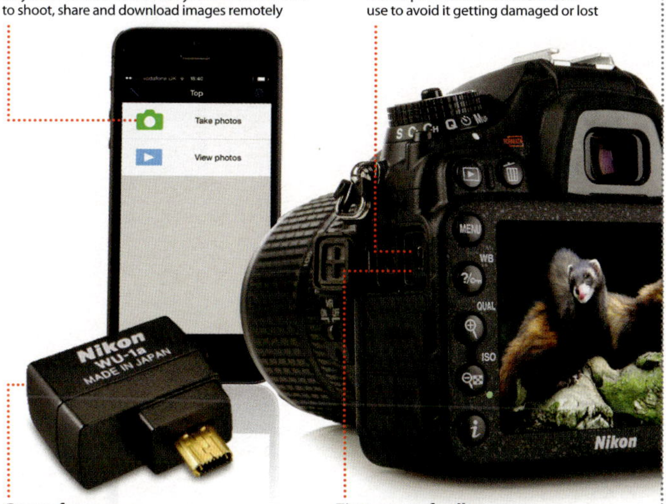

Green for go
After it's inserted, simply hold down its button until its little LED light turns green, then turn the camera on and you're ready to go

First port of call
The wireless adapter's port is located on the side of the camera with the other ports. Its sturdy door is designed to keep it safe from damage and debris

images straight to a client or agency, you can do so in a matter of a few seconds and clicks.

While not every Nikon sports this feature, most are at least compatible with Nikon's Wi-Fi adapters (WU-1a and WU-1b) and what's more, photographers don't even need to be near a Wi-Fi hotspot to get it to work; you can use your smart device to create your own connection. When using the adapter, Android and iOS powered phones and tablets can also be harnessed as a remote control using Nikon's dedicated app; perfect for triggering the shutter even at a considerable distance, as well as sharing and downloading remotely.

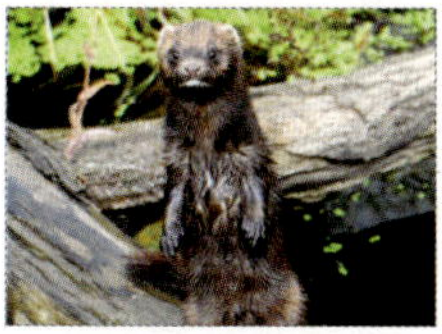

For wildlife photography, fire remotely using the app, which is less likely to scare skittish animals

Use the Wireless Remote Utility app

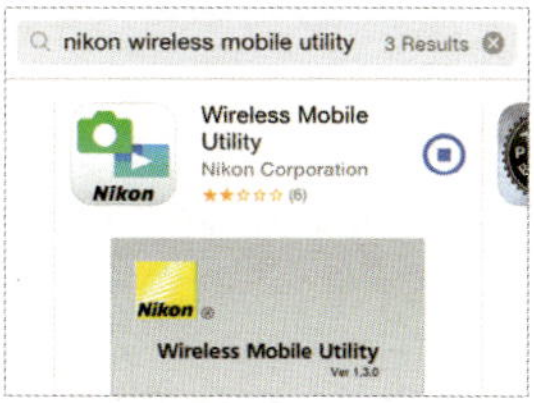

1 Install the app Head into the Play or iTunes App store, find the free app and download it.

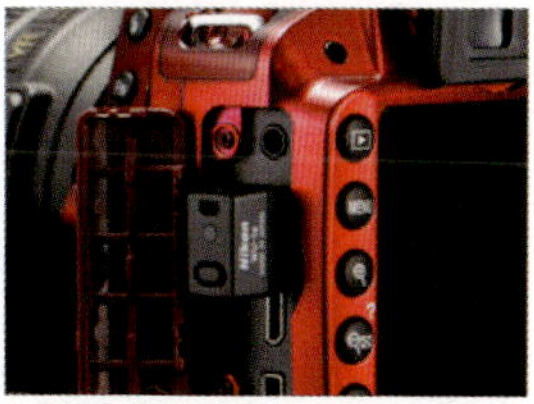

2 Plug in and play Push the adapter (if needed) into the designated port and turn it on.

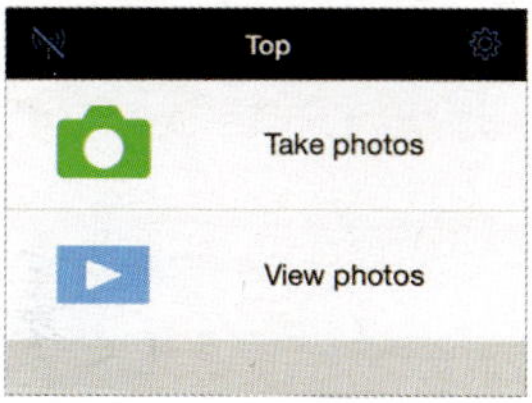

3 Make a connection Head into Settings to connect to the camera and then open the app.

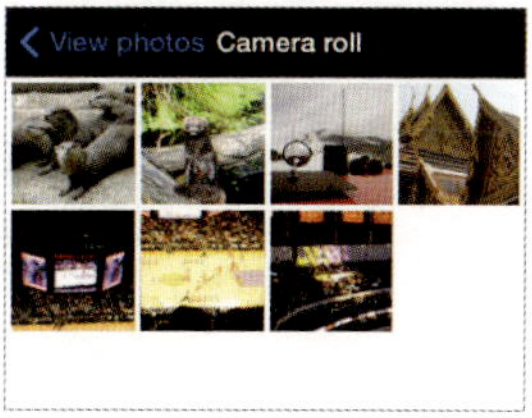

4 Shoot! Share! Download! The blue Wi-Fi icon should appear so you can now get started.

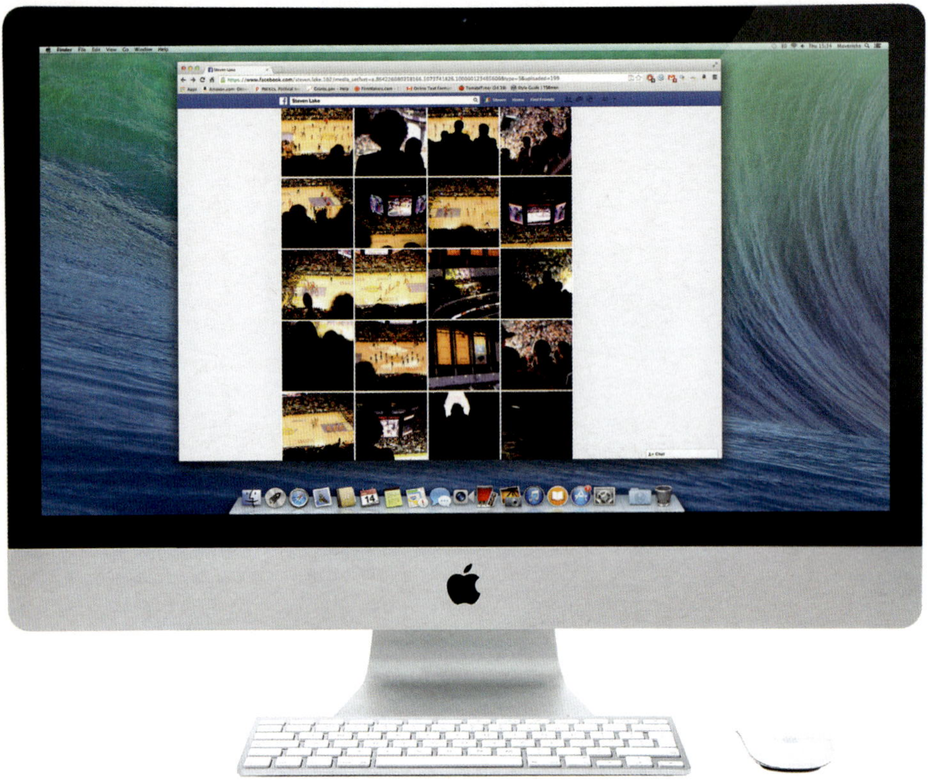

Share on Facebook

Share your best work with your friends by uploading images to a Facebook gallery

Facebook is perfect for sharing photos, since you've already got an audience to see them! Photos can be uploaded in a variety of ways; you can upload individual images to a Facebook post adding location information, other users and a status update, or you can add entire galleries of images in the form of a Facebook gallery.

▲ **Create a gallery** Exhibit your best photos online. Share, edit and tag photographs using Facebook's gallery creation tool

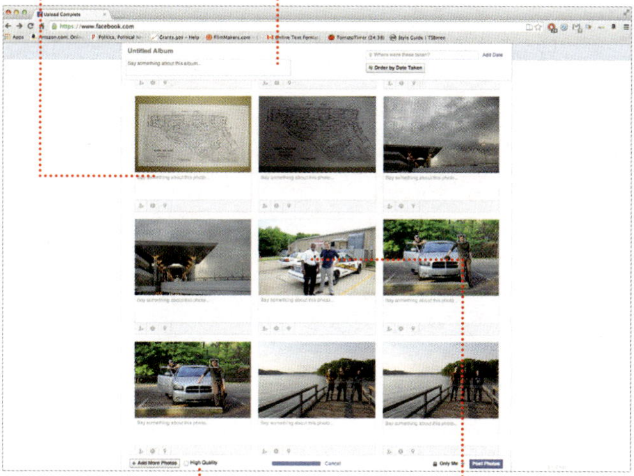

Galleries can also include videos. In the Status Update window click Add Photos/ Video. Here you'll be able to choose whether you want to upload individual photos or an entire album. Click Create Photo Album. Select the images from your computer that you want included and click Open.

You can edit and manage your photos in the Upload window while the selection is uploaded. Click the dropdown arrow in an image thumbnail to remove the image or make it your album cover. Click and drag a photo to change its order in the album. Once uploaded, select who you want to have access to the album then click Post Photos, posting the album in a status update.

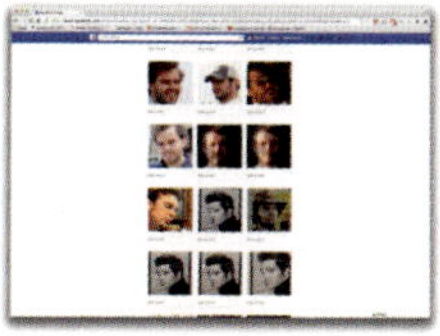

Identify all faces recognised in the images. This will increase your album's popularity

Facebook album tips

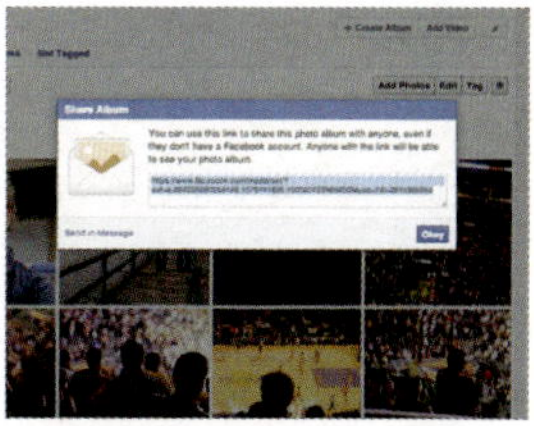

1 Share with anyone Click the settings icon, then Get Link to share your album with anyone.

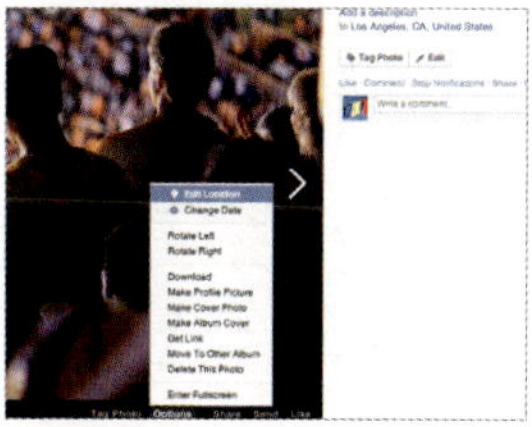

2 Image options Click an image then click Options to download, or re-organise an image.

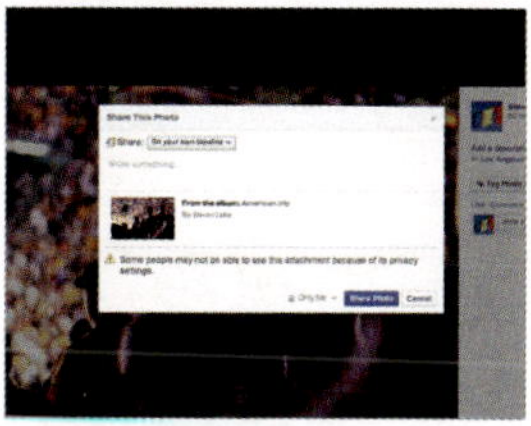

3 Share a photo When viewing an image, click Share to send it to another user's timeline.

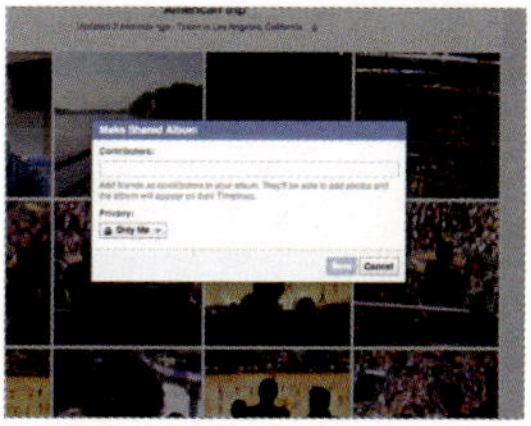

4 Shared Albums Click Make Shared Album so others can edit and upload images to it.

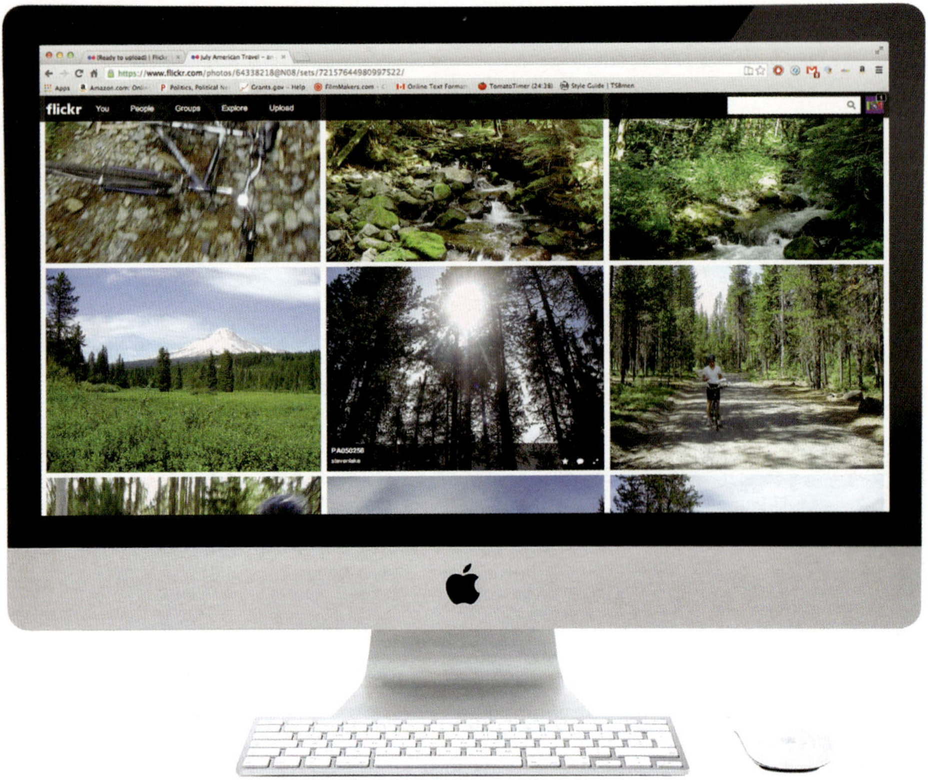

flickr

Share on Flickr

Discover how to upload entire image galleries to share publicly or privately at **flickr.com**

Flickr makes uploading and sharing photography easy, presenting your photographs in a professional interface. Flickr is widely accepted as one of the best ways to create a digital portfolio for your work. It functions like any other image upload service; simply select your favourite photos from your computer and before uploading them, review the image previews to weed out any photos you don't want included in your gallery. Once you're ready you can then upload your collection to a Flickr Photostream.

▲ **Enjoy the photographs** Flickr will display your images for you in a well-presented gallery format

Tags
The more relevant tags you add the easier people will be able to find your photos

Upload screen
Upload images here to be shown thumbnail previews of them to sort through

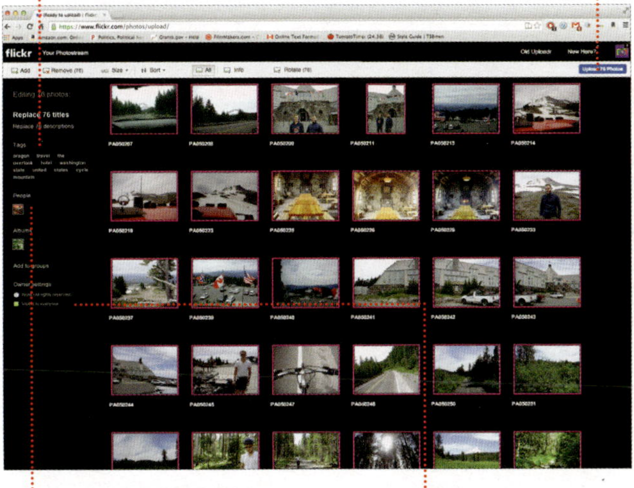

People, Albums and Groups
You can add other Flickr users who are included in your Photostream and categorise images by galleries and groups

Licencing
Add a licence to your images so users know if they are royalty-free or not

Flickr is all about categorisation of content. You can have the most breathtaking landscape photography in the world, but if people can't find it, nothing will be seen. You can make your work more noticeable by adding tags to your images. You can also join groups on Flickr, which are relevant to your style of photography.

Once you've joined a group you can link a newly uploaded Photostream to the group. You can also add a licence to your photos to restrict redistribution of your images by other users. You can then licence your photos for money to buyers via Getty Images. Go to Explore>Getty Collection to find out more about selling images with Flickr.

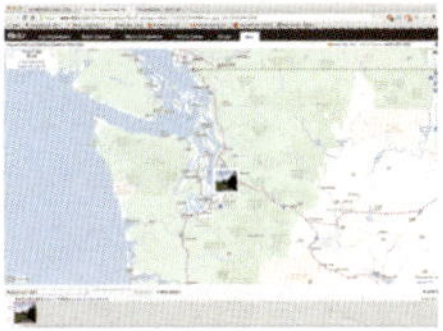

In the toolbar, click You> Organise to batch edit photos, including adding location information.

Edit your photos

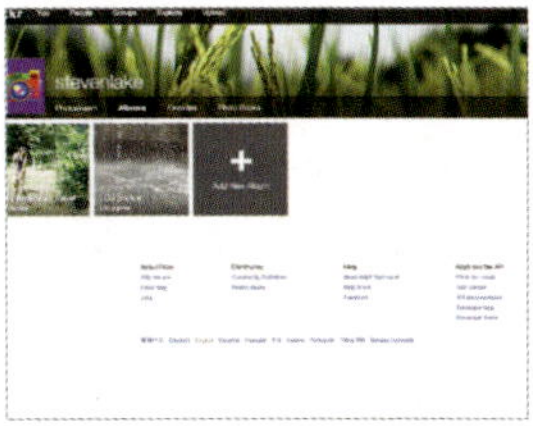

1 Open your album Once your photos are uploaded click You>Albums. Select an album.

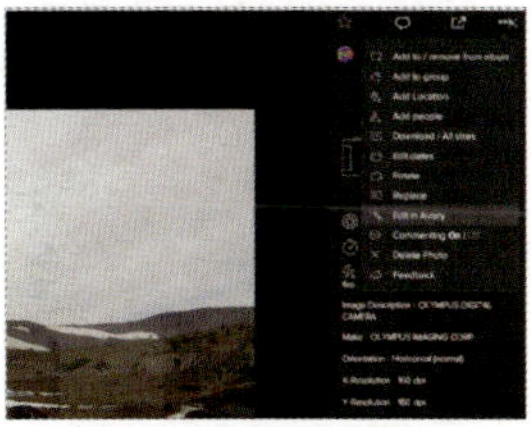

2 Edit in Aviary Click on an image, click on the Options button and click Edit in Aviary.

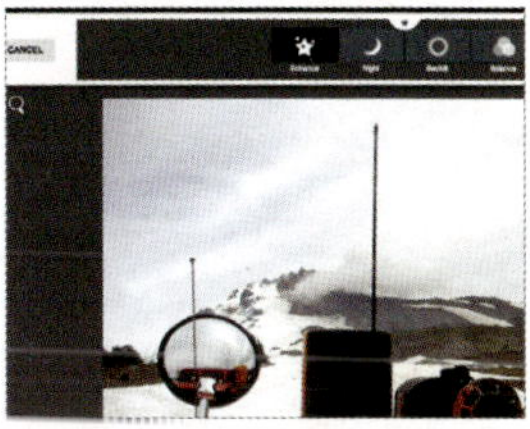

3 Enhance Click Enhance and select one that suits your photo. Click Apply to add the effect.

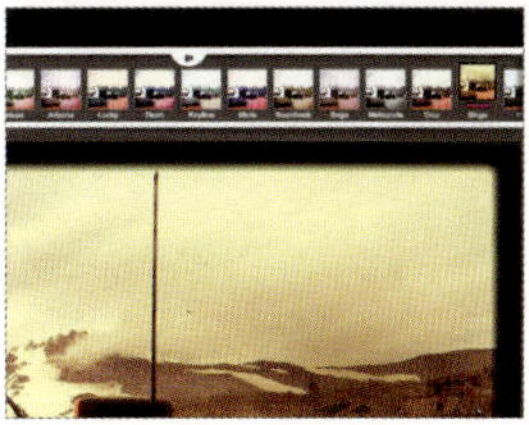

4 Add effects Browse the different editing tools. Click Effects to add a quick filter.

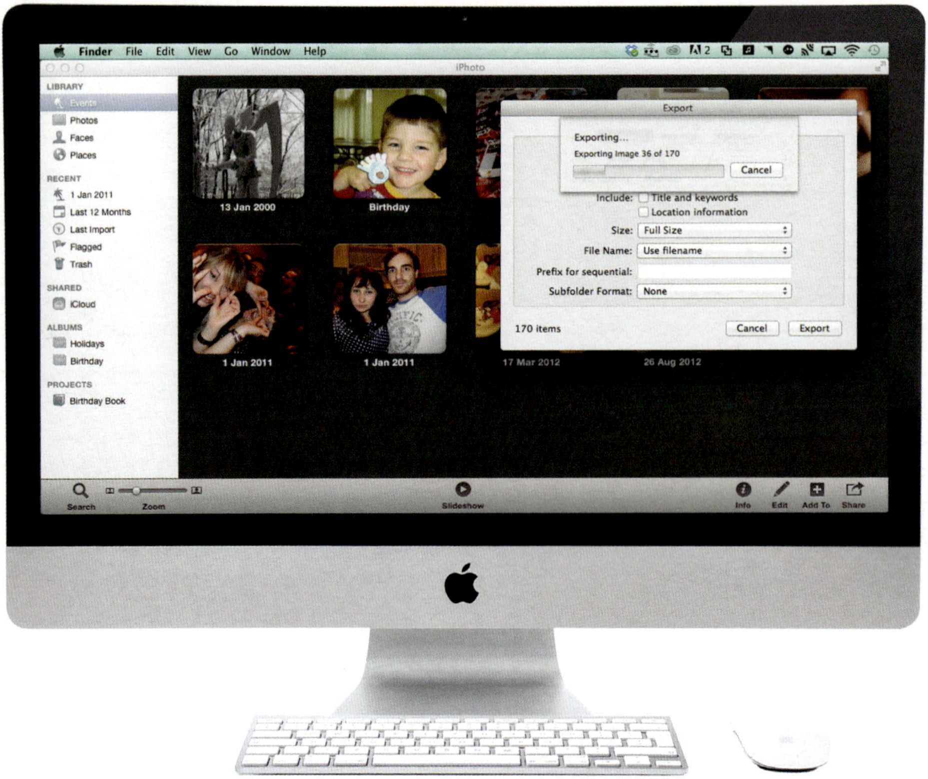

Back up your photographs

Ensure that your photos are always going to be safe and secure by setting up a backup system

Backing up your photographs is crucial in securing your images. There is always a risk that a hard drive could suddenly fail, so it's important that you have your photos stored on a backup hard drive. Purchase a hard drive online with the capacity to hold your images then drag and drop them into it.

▲ **Keep them safe** With a hard drive or cloud storage backup solution, you can secure your photos cost effectively

Backup tools
To export images in a gallery software, go to File>Export for the exporting options

Batch exporting
Exporting through a gallery software such as iPhoto allows you to batch export all your images at their full, or reduced quality

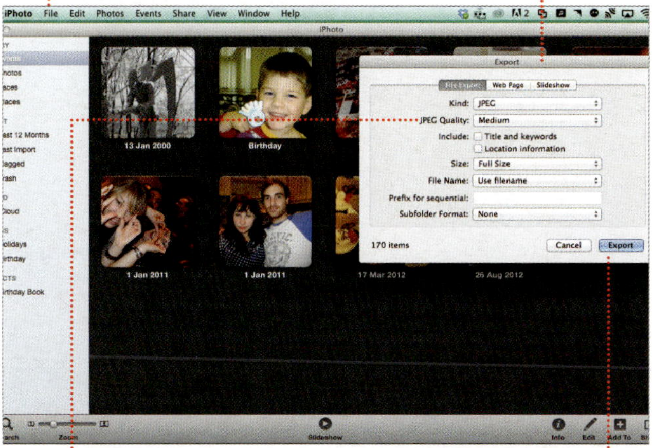

Image formatting
Select a file type and size. If you can spare the space, export at the highest quality available

Export to device
Click Export to pick a destination to export to, ideally an external hard drive which can be stored separately from your master copies

There are other cost-effective options for backing up your images. Free image library software is provided by both Windows (Photo Gallery) and Apple (iPhoto). These enable you to export your entire library to an external storage device.

Another option is to use a cloud service where you can access and download your photos at any time. Services such as Google Drive and Dropbox make this easy, providing you with desktop folders that you can simply drag and drop your files into. If you are concerned about how much space you will need, then consider batch exporting them at a compressed size. Obviously, the downside to this is that your backups will have a reduced quality.

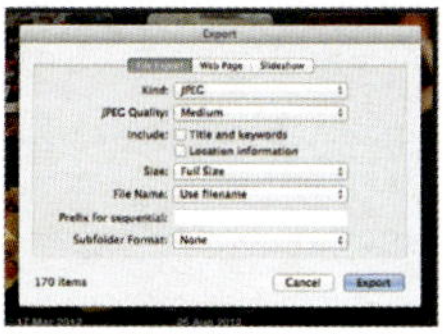

Most batch backup software has a renaming option. This prevents duplicate names clashing.

Work with Dropbox

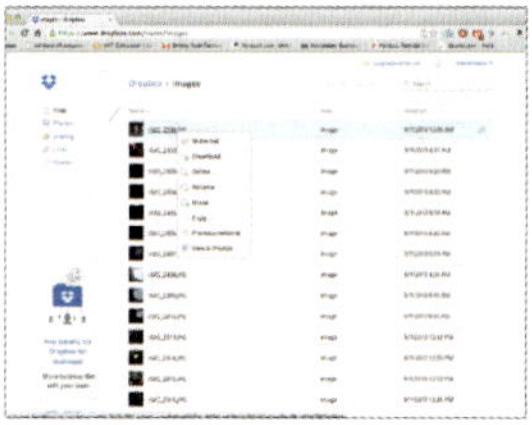

1 Dropbox.com Visit the site and sign up to get free storage space to upload images.

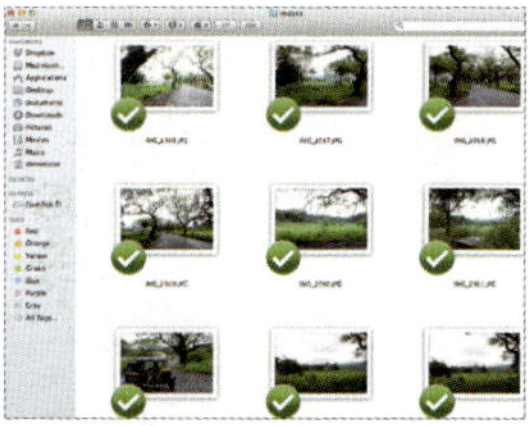

2 Dropbox software Add images to your desktop Dropbox folder to upload them.

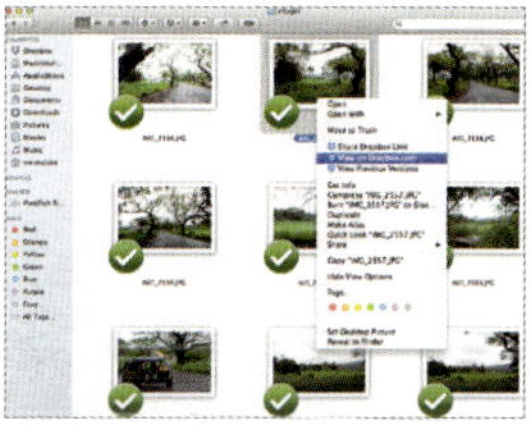

3 Manage and share Right-click a Dropbox-stored image to view it at **dropbox.com** or share it.

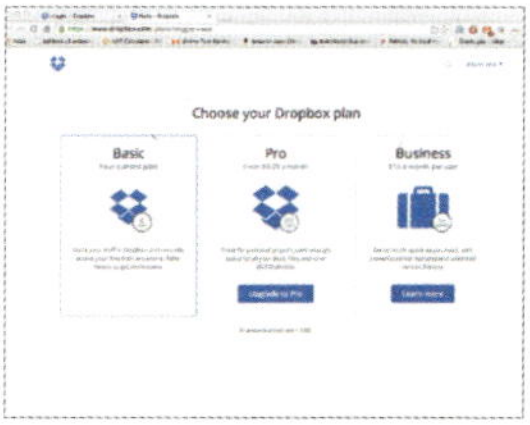

4 Upgrade Dropbox You can upgrade to back up more than 20,000 images.

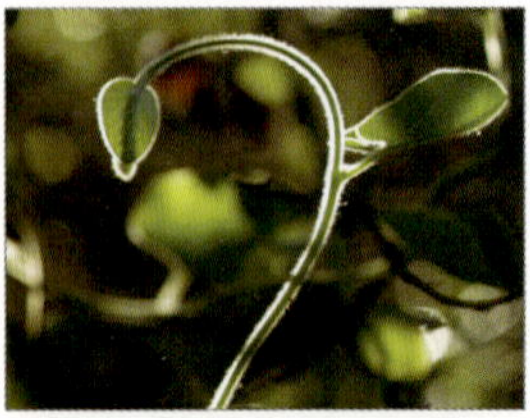

The wider the aperture, the shallower the focus of a shot becomes

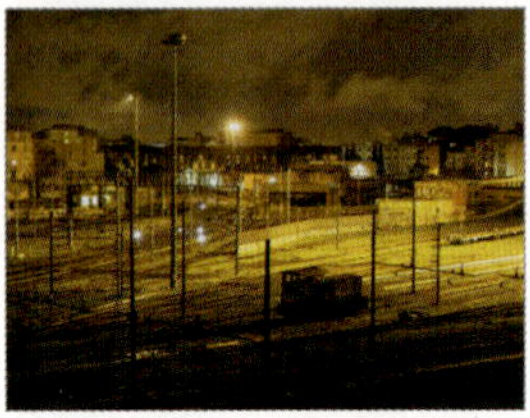

When increasing ISO, you'll notice more grain, brightening the shot but decreasing quality

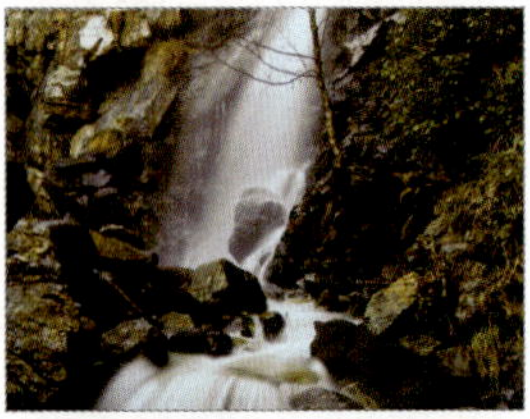

A slow shutter speed can be used to create interesting effects with motion

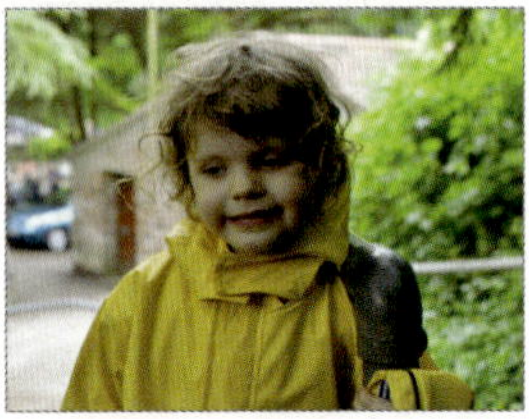

This photograph was taken with a wide aperture, narrowing the overall depth of field

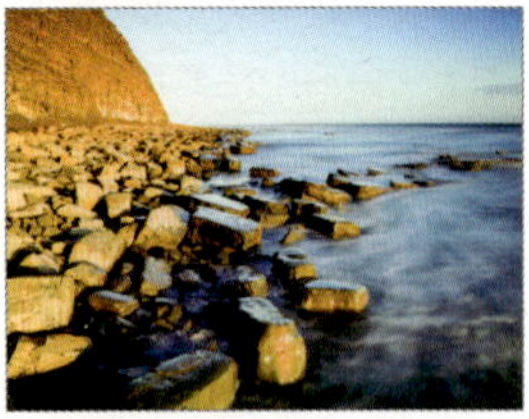

Gradient filters can be used to evenly expose the sky and land in landscape images

Glossary

Find out what the most relevant terms in photography mean, and why they're important

AF (auto focus) Most new lenses come with an auto focus function, making focusing on your subject easy. The faster a lens the quicker it will be able to focus, helping you capture that crucial shot.

AF-S Stands for Auto Focus Silent. This is a more advanced focusing function found on Nikon lenses that allows for faster and silent focusing. Lenses that boast AF-S are more expensive than those with standard AF.

Aperture/ F Stop Use aperture to control your camera's exposure. The wider the aperture of a lens, (a low f-stop) the more light will pass through it. The smaller the aperture, (a high f-stop) the less light.

Aperture Priority Setting your camera to Aperture Priority allows you to adjust the aperture to your liking, while the camera's Auto function will change the shutter speed and ISO to give you a constantly even exposure.

Bokeh A type of focusing effect that draws attention to areas of a shot that are out of focus, creating circles out of any highlighted area. The roundness of the circles relates to the roundness of the lens.

Depth of field Describes how much of the shot around your point of focus is out of focus. A wider aperture will narrow the depth of field, and a smaller one will widen it.

DX DX Lenses are optimised to work best with Nikon cameras that have a DX sensor. These lenses will typically start with a slightly wider focal length, to make up for the crop factor that occurs on a Nikon DX camera.

Exposure When shooting photography use your camera's light meter to determine the correct exposure of a shot. The exposure of a shot will depend on the ISO, aperture and shutter speed settings. All three of these tools can be used to create an even exposure.

FX If you own an Nikon camera with an FX sensor then you'll be best off buying FX lenses. The FX sensor is a full frame sensor, providing you with the true focal length of a lens, without any crop.

Grid The grid view can help you better compose you shot. The grid breaks up your shot into three vertical and three horizontal sections. This makes it easier for the shooter to apply the rule of thirds to their shot.

Histogram A histogram is a graph that can be viewed on your Nikon's LCD to display a shot's highlights, midtones and shadows, helping you to better manage its exposure levels. Histograms are a useful reference point when working with bright shots that are hard to expose by eye.

IS (Image stabiliser) Often a lens will come with an image stabilisation function. IS works best to reduce minor shake when taking a shot, and is especially useful for shooting video.

ISO If you're struggling for light, use ISO to bump up the brightness. Increasing a camera's ISO increases the sensitivity of its image sensor.

Noise The amount of noise found on a shot will depend on how high the ISO is that you are shooting with. Noise accounts for the graininess of a shot, which is more noticeable in night and low light images.

Post processing Refers to editing photographs in editing software such as Photoshop. It's important to try and get your photos as close to perfect as possible when taking them, but if need be you can fix exposure and other issues with post processing, as well as adding artistic effects.

Prime lens A prime lens is a lens that has a fixed focal length, such as 35mm. You can't zoom with a prime lens, however the quality of the lens is normally higher than a telephoto lens due to its simplicity.

RAW/ JPEG Most DSLRs offer two shooting formats; RAW and JPEG. JPEG is a lower file size image. RAW is a higher-quality file size containing much more data. RAW files are better for editing images.

Rule of thirds The rule of thirds is a composition term referring to the composition of a shot that places the main point of focus off centre, typically in the upper or lower corner of a shot.

Shutter Priority Shutter Priority mode works in the same way as Aperture Priority, but allows you to change the shutter speed to your liking whilst the aperture and ISO is set automatically.

Shutter speed The shutter speed determines how long your camera's image sensor is exposed to light. The more light the sensor is exposed to, the brighter the shot becomes. When shooting with a slow shutter speed any movement will blur, so when shooting action use a fast shutter speed.

Telephoto lens A telephoto lens can zoom between focal lengths, such as 24-70mm. Telephoto lenses let you capture a range of focal lengths without having to change your lens, saving you time when you're out shooting. A quality telephoto lens will be more costly than a prime lens.

Vignette A vignette effect is created in camera when a lens can't evenly distribute light across the camera's sensor, creating dark edges. Vignettes are also used as a way to purposely draw attention to a part of an image.

White balance Different lighting conditions have different white balances. When shooting indoors, the light is much warmer than when shooting outdoors. Digital cameras allow you to set the white balance to various scenarios, as well as setting a manual white balance.

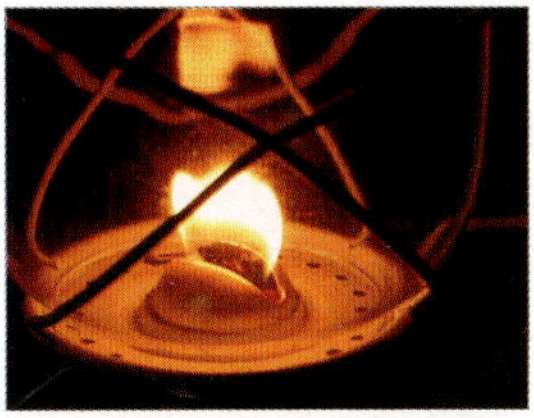

Candles and tungsten lights create warm shots, whereas natural lighting is much cooler

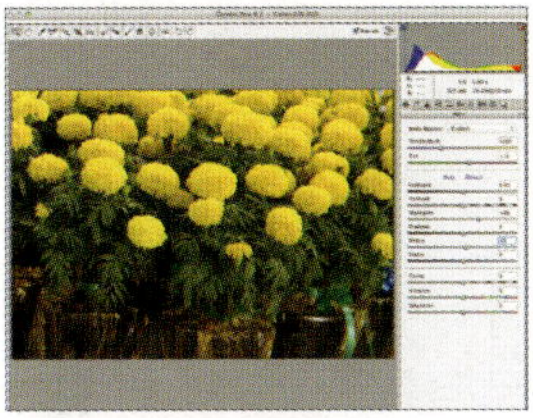

Raw files allow for much more control of exposure and colour balance

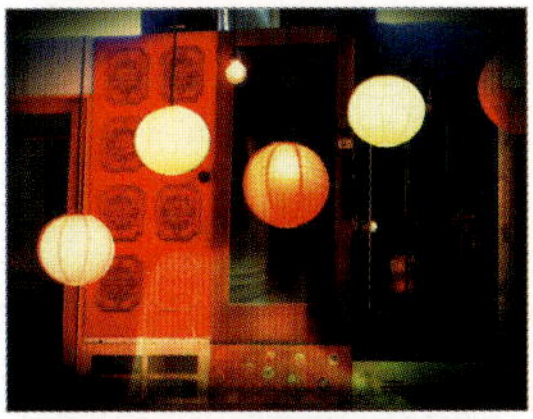

Adding a vignette can help draw focus to a specific part of an image

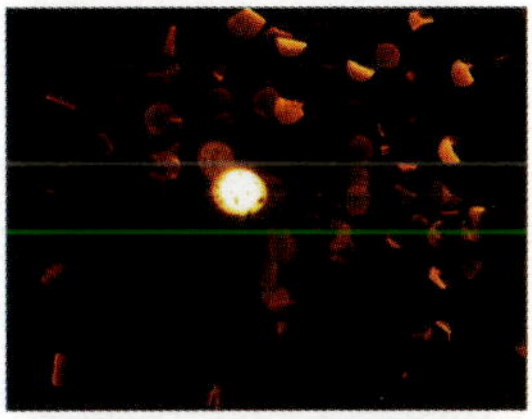

In this photo, fragmented light is pushed out of focus to create a Bokeh effect

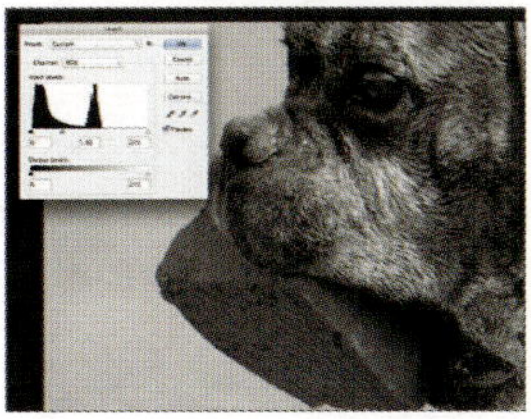

The midtones of this photo have been pushed up, emphasising the dark colour of the dog

Special trial offer

Enjoyed this book?

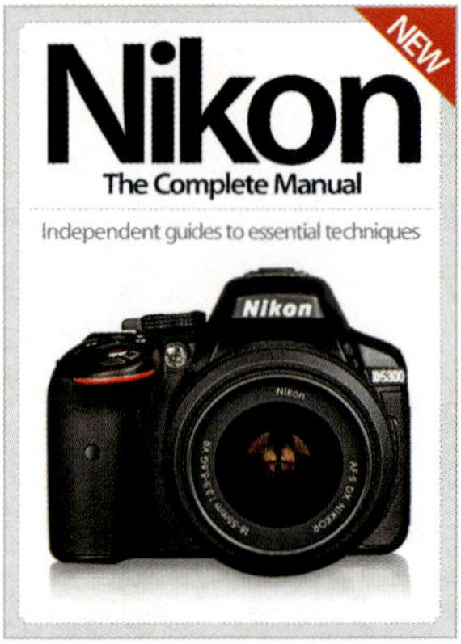

Exclusive offer for new

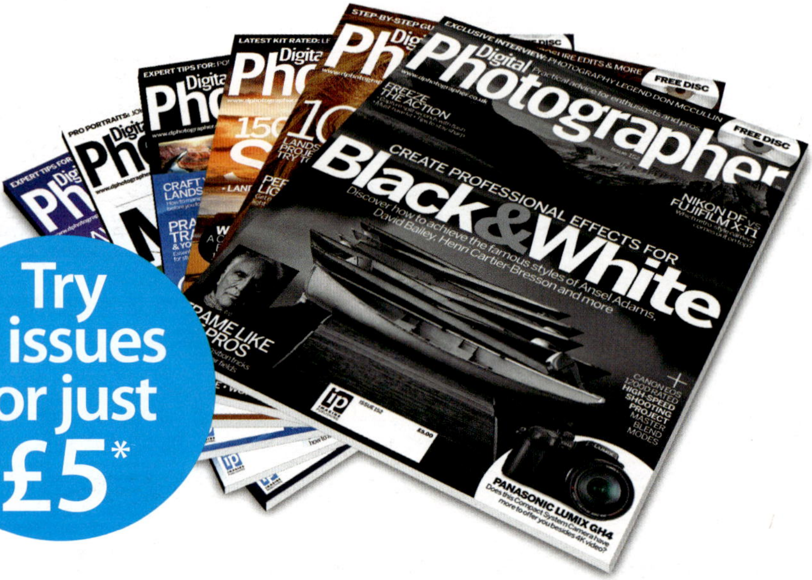

Try 3 issues for just £5*

* This offer entitles new UK direct debit subscribers to receive their first three issues for £5. After these issues, subscribers will then pay £21 every six issues. Subscribers can cancel this subscription at any time. New subscriptions will start from the next available issue. Offer code ZGGZINE must be quoted to receive this special subscriptions price. Direct debit guarantee available on request. This offer will expire 30th September 2015.

** This is a US subscription offer. The USA issue rate is based on an annual subscription price of £65 for 13 issues, which is equivalent to $102 at the time of writing compared with the newsstand price of $12.99 for 13 issues, being $168.87. Your subscription will start from the next available issue. This offer expires 30th September 2015.